FuelPHP Application Development Blueprints

Supercharge your projects by designing and implementing web applications with FuelPHP

Sébastien Drouyer

BIRMINGHAM - MUMBAI

FuelPHP Application Development Blueprints

First published: February 2015

Production reference: 1200215

Published by Packt Publishing Ltd.
Livery Place
35 Livery Street
Birmingham B3 2PB, UK.

ISBN 978-1-78398-540-1

www.packtpub.com

Credits

Author
Sébastien Drouyer

Reviewers
Ivan Đurđevac
Márk Sági-Kazár
Kenji Suzuki
Aravind Udayashankara

Commissioning Editor
Kartikey Pandey

Acquisition Editor
Nikhil Chinnari

Content Development Editor
Melita Lobo

Technical Editors
Sebastian Rodrigues
Mohita Vyas

Copy Editors
Pranjali Chury
Sameen Siddiqui
Ashwati Thampi

Project Coordinator
Kinjal Bari

Proofreaders
Simran Bhogal
Kevin McGowan
Linda Morris

Indexer
Tejal Soni

Graphics
Sheetal Aute
Disha Haria
Abhinash Sahu

Production Coordinator
Alwin Roy

Cover Work
Alwin Roy

About the Author

Sébastien Drouyer is a computer science research engineer from France. He has a master's degree in computer science from the National Institute of Applied Sciences of Lyon, one of the most prestigious engineering schools in France. He has been developing web applications since 2005 and has won various contests and awards from GitHub, NASA, and Intel. He has also been a member of the Novius OS core team (an open source content management system based on the FuelPHP framework) and published many additional open source projects. He has trained several teams on FuelPHP and is a conference speaker on the subject.

First of all, I would like to thank the FuelPHP core team and its community for improving this wonderful framework every day.

If there are only a countable number of errors in this book, then it is due to Aravind Udayashankara, Kenji Suzuki, Sági-Kazár Márk, Ivan Đurđevac, Craig Hooghiem, and John Alder who all did excellent reviews.

I would like to salute the amazing Novius OS core team and I wish them the best in their future endeavors.

I would also like to thank the Packt Publishing team, especially Melita Lobo, for their patience and professionalism.

Last, but not least, I would like to thank my very supportive family and friends. A special thanks to my mother and father for making me the person I am today; I wouldn't be here without you two.

About the Reviewers

Ivan Đurđevac is a PHP developer from Serbia, Pančevo. Long time ago, he found out the "development" word with Delphi. Prior to 2000, the Web was a huge deal, and he decided to pick PHP as his main tool. He started with CodeIgniter as his first framework. After a while, he realized that CodeIgniter did not allow him to write beautiful code to solve problems with design patterns, and he saw it would stay that way, trapped in PHP4. So, he switched to Kohana and Zend Framework and it was a big step forward. FuelPHP was a new kid on the block. It took all the best features from others and created a modern framework. He used FuelPHP to build large-scale applications. At the time this book was written, he used Laravel as his codebase. No matter which framework he uses, clean code is always a priority for him. He will never stop learning from better developers and modern practices.

He has worked for various companies on many projects, such as e-learning platforms, CMS-ES, social network sites, and business applications. Currently, he is working for a USA-based company that builds various internet marketing tools, which collaborate with AWeber, Infusionsoft, and other tools. He is also interested in DevOps and likes to play with Linux administration and set up server boxes and maintain them.

Márk Sági-Kazár was previously working with CodeIgniter, and picked up FuelPHP in 2011. Since 2014, he has been actively developing for FuelPHP, starting with the E-mail package. From the autumn of 2014, he has been an official member of the FuelPHP team.

Mark started playing with programming at the age of 6. While in high school, he worked with several Microsoft languages; Visual Basic is one of them. After finishing high school, he switched to PHP as his programming language of choice. Starting with CodeIgniter, he quickly switched to FuelPHP and delivered his first production application (an e-commerce site) in 2012, followed by IndigoPHP in 2013, which is an application framework and CMS built on top of FuelPHP. Besides his work on FuelPHP V2, he's currently working on some good quality packages such as a SupervisorPHP (`http://supervisorphp.com`) and shopping cart abstraction, to name some.

Kenji Suzuki is a programmer and web developer living in Japan. He is a contributor to FuelPHP, BEAR.Sunday, CodeIgniter, and many other open source projects. He is a PHP expert, Certified PHP 5 Engineer Expert by the Engineer Certification Corporation for PHP (`http://www.phpexam.jp/about/English/`), and coauthor of the Japanese best-seller and highly-praised PHP recipe book, *PHP gyakubiki reshipi, SHOEISHA.Co.,Ltd*. He has published several books about PHP with famous Japanese IT book publishers. His latest book is *Hajimeteno Framework toshiteno FuelPHP, Rutles, Inc*. You can find the repositories of his various projects on GitHub at `https://github.com/kenjis`.

Aravind Udayashankara is an autodidactist and software engineer. He has been working on several open source server-side technologies, such as NodeJS, PHP, and Ruby, and browser-side technologies such as AJAX, JavaScript, XML, HTML, and many more since 2008. He loves and enjoys to learn, understand, and express complex things, as well as blog on his own website, `http://aravindhu.com`. He is now eagerly eyeing the world of mobile application development and big data.

www.PacktPub.com

Support files, eBooks, discount offers, and more

For support files and downloads related to your book, please visit `www.PacktPub.com`.

Did you know that Packt offers eBook versions of every book published, with PDF and ePub files available? You can upgrade to the eBook version at `www.PacktPub.com` and as a print book customer, you are entitled to a discount on the eBook copy. Get in touch with us at `service@packtpub.com` for more details.

At `www.PacktPub.com`, you can also read a collection of free technical articles, sign up for a range of free newsletters and receive exclusive discounts and offers on Packt books and eBooks.

`https://www2.packtpub.com/books/subscription/packtlib`

Do you need instant solutions to your IT questions? PacktLib is Packt's online digital book library. Here, you can search, access, and read Packt's entire library of books.

Why subscribe?

- Fully searchable across every book published by Packt
- Copy and paste, print, and bookmark content
- On demand and accessible via a web browser

Free access for Packt account holders

If you have an account with Packt at `www.PacktPub.com`, you can use this to access PacktLib today and view 9 entirely free books. Simply use your login credentials for immediate access.

Table of Contents

Preface

The main idea behind *FuelPHP Application Development Blueprints* is to teach you FuelPHP's basic and advanced features by building various projects of increasing levels of complexity. It is very result-oriented; at the beginning of the chapters, we specify the application we want to build, and then we progressively implement it by learning how to use new FuelPHP features along the way. Our approach will therefore be very practical; a lot of concepts will be explained using code examples, or by integrating them directly into our projects. Thus, it is important to highlight that there will be a lot of code and you should be comfortable with reading and understanding PHP and HTML. As we will use them from time to time, having some knowledge about server/system administration and some foundation in JavaScript, jQuery, and CSS will be an added advantage.

Though this book is for intermediary to advanced web developers, any prior knowledge of the FuelPHP framework, or any other PHP framework, is not required. In order to understand this book, you don't have to know common concepts such as MVC, HMVC, or ORM. We take into account this shortcoming some of you might have, and important notions will be explained. We won't explain all of those in the first chapter though, as we want this to be as painless as possible; we will instead approach them when they become necessary for the project completion.

The ultimate purpose of *FuelPHP Application Development Blueprints* is to give you the ability to build any project using FuelPHP. By the end of this book, you certainly won't know every little detail of the framework, but you will hopefully have the necessary toolbox required to implement complex and maintainable projects.

What this book covers

Chapter 1, Building Your First FuelPHP Application, covers the very basics of the FuelPHP framework; how to install it, how to configure it, how it is organized, and its main components. Along the way, we will generate our first FuelPHP application using the oil utility and tweak some files, in order to illustrate how things work.

Chapter 2, Building a To-do List Application, focuses on FuelPHP's ORM and debugging features. We will illustrate these features using a lot of examples, and then implement a small to-do list application. We will also use some JavaScript and jQuery to send AJAX requests.

Chapter 3, Building a Blog Application, will teach you how to generate and tweak an administration interface easily, how to create your own modules and tasks, how to manage paginations easily, and how to use the Auth and Email packages. We will create a blog application implementing all these features.

Chapter 4, Creating and Using Packages, will approach the FuelPHP package system. This is a rather short chapter; we will first try to protect our website from spam bots by installing an existing package, and then create our own original solution by creating a new package.

Chapter 5, Building Your Own RESTful API, covers more advanced subjects such as building a JSON API, using language agnostic template engines, allowing user subscriptions, and implementing unit tests. To illustrate this, we will create a responsive micro blogging application featuring a public API.

Chapter 6, Building a Website Using Novius OS, will quickly introduce you to Novius OS, a FuelPHP-based Content Management System. Using such a system can greatly speed up the implementation of complex projects.

What you need for this book

The applications in this book are based on FuelPHP 1.7.2, which requires:

- A web server: The most common solution is Apache
- A PHP interpreter: The 5.3.3 version or greater
- A database: we will use MySQL

FuelPHP works on Unix-like and Windows operating systems. The mod_rewrite Apache module and some additional PHP extensions are recommended; the complete list is available at `http://fuelphp.com/docs/requirements.html`.

Who this book is for

This book is for intermediary to seasoned web developers who want to learn how to use the FuelPHP framework and to build complex projects using it. You should be familiar with PHP, HTML, CSS, and JavaScript, but no prior knowledge about MVC frameworks is required.

Conventions

In this book, you will find a number of text styles that distinguish between different kinds of information. Here are some examples of these styles and an explanation of their meaning.

- Code words in text, database table names, folder names, filenames, file extensions, pathnames, dummy URLs, user input, and Twitter handles are shown as follows: "Remove `APPPATH/classes/controller/welcome.php` as we don't need this controller anymore."

A block of code is set as follows:

```
<?php
echo Form::checkbox(
    'still_here',
    1,
    Input::post(
        'still_here',
        isset($monkey) ? $monkey->still_here : true
    )
);
?>
```

New terms and **important words** are shown in bold. Words that you see on the screen, for example, in menus or dialog boxes, appear in the text like this: " Click on the **Generate** button."

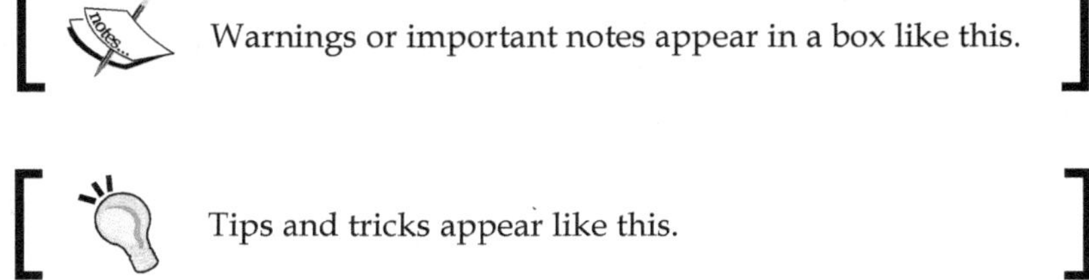

Warnings or important notes appear in a box like this.

Tips and tricks appear like this.

Reader feedback

Feedback from our readers is always welcome. Let us know what you think about this book—what you liked or disliked. Reader feedback is important for us as it helps us develop titles that you will really get the most out of.

To send us general feedback, simply e-mail `feedback@packtpub.com`, and mention the book's title in the subject of your message.

If there is a topic that you have expertise in and you are interested in either writing or contributing to a book, see our author guide at `www.packtpub.com/authors`.

Customer support

Now that you are the proud owner of a Packt book, we have a number of things to help you to get the most from your purchase.

Downloading the example code

You can download the example code files from your account at `http://www.packtpub.com` for all the Packt Publishing books you have purchased. If you purchased this book elsewhere, you can visit `http://www.packtpub.com/support` and register to have the files e-mailed directly to you.

Downloading the color images of this book

We also provide you with a PDF file that has color images of the screenshots/diagrams used in this book. The color images will help you better understand the changes in the output. You can download this file from: `https://www.packtpub.com/sites/default/files/downloads/5401OS.pdf`.

Errata

Although we have taken every care to ensure the accuracy of our content, mistakes do happen. If you find a mistake in one of our books—maybe a mistake in the text or the code—we would be grateful if you could report this to us. By doing so, you can save other readers from frustration and help us improve subsequent versions of this book. If you find any errata, please report them by visiting `http://www.packtpub.com/submit-errata`, selecting your book, clicking on the **Errata Submission Form** link, and entering the details of your errata. Once your errata are verified, your submission will be accepted and the errata will be uploaded to our website or added to any list of existing errata under the Errata section of that title.

To view the previously submitted errata, go to `https://www.packtpub.com/books/content/support` and enter the name of the book in the search field. The required information will appear under the **Errata** section.

Piracy

Piracy of copyrighted material on the Internet is an ongoing problem across all media. At Packt, we take the protection of our copyright and licenses very seriously. If you come across any illegal copies of our works in any form on the Internet, please provide us with the location address or website name immediately so that we can pursue a remedy.

Please contact us at `copyright@packtpub.com` with a link to the suspected pirated material.

We appreciate your help in protecting our authors and our ability to bring you valuable content.

Questions

If you have a problem with any aspect of this book, you can contact us at `questions@packtpub.com`, and we will do our best to address the problem.

1
Building Your First FuelPHP Application

Throughout the book, we will use the **FuelPHP** framework to build different types of projects. The objective of this chapter is to make you familiar with the basics of the framework and create your first project as quickly as possible. We won't create anything exceptional in this chapter and there will be very little coding, but we will go through the whole process from installing FuelPHP to publishing your project on a production server. You will learn the necessary basics for the other projects as well.

By the end of the chapter, you should know the following:

- A common development process of a FuelPHP application
- How to install FuelPHP (the latest or a specific version)
- The FuelPHP file system hierarchy
- Two different ways to configure Apache to access your application
- How to configure FuelPHP to connect to a database
- The oil command line and how to use it for scaffolding your application
- How does an application respond to a URL requested by a visitor
- What are the FuelPHP templates
- How to publish your project to a host

Since this book is intended for intermediate developers, we will assume that you have already installed Apache and MySQL on your system. Some prior knowledge of Git and Composer is an added advantage as you might need it, but you should be fine in this book if you are not familiar with these tools. However, for advanced applications that need collaboration between several developers mastering them is highly recommended.

In this chapter, we will go from installing the FuelPHP framework to having a functional - though limited - web application. As our objective here is to introduce the framework and create a sample application as quickly as possible, we won't address important topics such as the ORM, which will be addressed in *Chapter 2, Building a To-do List Application*.

About FuelPHP

Dan Horrigan started the FuelPHP framework in late 2010, and was later joined by Phil Sturgeon, Jelmer Schreuder, Harro Verton, Frank de Jonge, Steve West and Márk Sági-Kazár. The first stable version was released on July 31st, 2011 and this book is based on FuelPHP 1.7.2, the latest stable version available as of writing this book. With over 300 contributors, its community is large and active.

The core team is currently working on the second version of FuelPHP; several alpha versions of it have already been released.

If you want to know more about the FuelPHP team and the framework philosophy, I recommend you to read the **About FuelPHP** section of the official website at:

`http://fuelphp.com/about`

You can read the latest news about the framework on its official blog at:

`http://fuelphp.com/blogs`

The official documentation can be found at: `http://fuelphp.com/docs/`

If you have any questions about FuelPHP or encounter any issues, you can search the official forum (`http://fuelphp.com/forums/`) and start a new discussion if you don't find any answer. In a general manner, the official website (`http://fuelphp.com`) is an excellent resource.

Development process of a FuelPHP application

The development process of a FuelPHP application generally contains the steps shown in the following image:

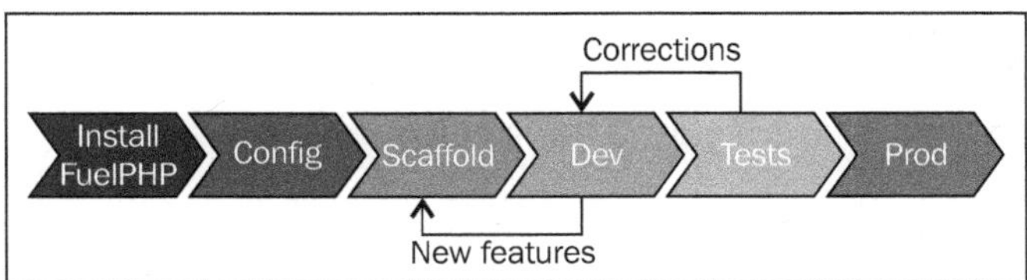

- **Install FuelPHP**: Since we are using this framework, this first step is quite obvious.
- **Config (configuration)**: At the beginning, you will generally need to specify how to connect to the database and which package you will use. Later on, you might also need to create and use your own configuration files to improve the maintainability of your application.
- **Scaffold**: The oil command line of FuelPHP allows you to easily generate code files ready to be used. This step is not necessary, but we will often use this functionality in this book because it really speeds up the implementation of your application.
- **Dev (development)**: This is where you, as a developer, step in. You customize the generated code to get exactly what you want. When you want to add new features (for instance a new model), you go back to the scaffolding step.
- **Tests**: Functional and unit testing are important if you want large applications to stay maintainable. When bugs are discovered, you go back to the development step in order to fix them. Unlike the other steps, we won't approach this subject in this chapter for the sake of its conciseness. It will be addressed in *Chapter 5, Building Your Own RESTful API*.
- **Prod (production)**: Having a project working locally is nice, but the final objective is generally to publish it online. We will give you some directions about this step at the end of this chapter, but we won't get too much into the details, given the diversity of available hosting services.

Just to be clear, this is a very general guideline, and of course the order of the steps is not rigid. For instance, developers using the test-driven development process could merge the fourth and fifth steps, or a preproduction step could be added. The development process should only depend on each developer and institution's standards.

Installing the environment

The FuelPHP framework needs the following three components:

- **Web server**: The most common solution is Apache
- **PHP interpreter**: The 5.3.3 version or greater
- **Database**: We will use MySQL

FuelPHP works on **Unix-like** and **Windows** operating systems, but the installation and configuration procedures of these components will depend on the operating system used. In the following sections we will provide some directions to get you started in case you are not used to installing your development environment. Please note that these are very generic guidelines, so you might need to search the web for complimentary information. There are countless resources on the topic.

Windows

A complete and very popular solution is to install **WAMP**. This will install Apache, MySQL, and PHP, in other words everything you need to get started. It can be accessed at `http://www.wampserver.com/en/`.

Mac

PHP and Apache are generally installed on the latest version of the OS, so you just have to install MySQL. To do this, you are recommended to read the official documentation at `http://dev.mysql.com/doc/refman/5.1/en/macosx-installation.html`.

A very convenient solution for those who have the least system administration skills is to install **MAMP**, the equivalent of WAMP, but for the Mac operating system. It can be downloaded from `http://www.mamp.info/en/downloads/`.

Ubuntu

As this is the most popular Linux distribution, we will limit our instructions to Ubuntu.

You can install a complete environment by executing the following command lines:

```
# Apache, MySQL, PHP
sudo apt-get install lamp-server^

# PHPMyAdmin allows you to handle the administration of MySQL DB
sudo apt-get install phpmyadmin

# Curl is useful for doing web requests
sudo apt-get install curl libcurl3 libcurl3-dev php5-curl

# Enabling the rewrite module as it is needed by FuelPHP
sudo a2enmod rewrite

# Restarting Apache to apply the new configuration
sudo service apache2 restart
```

Recommended modules and extensions

The Apache **mod_rewrite** module and some additional PHP extensions are also recommended, but not required:

`http://fuelphp.com/docs/requirements.html` (can be accessed through the FuelPHP website by navigating to **DOCS** | **TABLE OF CONTENTS** | **FuelPHP** | **Basic** | **Requirements**)

Getting the FuelPHP framework

As this book is being written, there are four common ways to download FuelPHP:

- Downloading and unzipping the compressed package which can be found on the FuelPHP website.
- Executing the FuelPHP quick command-line installer.

- Downloading and installing FuelPHP using Composer.
- Cloning the FuelPHP GitHub repository, it is a little bit more complicated but allows you to select exactly the version (or even the commit) you want to install.

These approaches are very well-documented on the website installation instructions page at `http://fuelphp.com/docs/installation/instructions.html` (It can be accessed through the FuelPHP website by navigating to **DOCS** | **TABLE OF CONTENTS** | **FuelPHP** | **Installation** | **Instructions**)

Installing FuelPHP 1.7.2

FuelPHP is always evolving and will continue to evolve even after this book is published. As we used FuelPHP 1.7.2 in this book, you might want to install the same version in order to prevent any conflict. You can do this by either downloading the appropriate ZIP file, cloning the 1.7/master branch of the GitHub repository, or using Composer.

Downloading the appropriate ZIP file

This is the simplest solution. You should be able to download it by requesting the URL `http://fuelphp.com/files/download/28`.

Alternatively, you can access all the compressed packages of important FuelPHP releases at `http://fuelphp.com/docs/installation/download.html` (It can be accessed through the FuelPHP website by navigating to **DOCS** | **TABLE OF CONTENTS** | **FuelPHP** | **Installation** | **Download**)

Using Composer

First, if you didn't do it yet, you need to install **Composer**. You can find out how by reading the official website at `https://getcomposer.org/`.

The installation instructions for major operating systems are given in the **Getting Started** guide. Please note that you can install Composer either globally or locally.

From now on, we will generally assume that you have installed Composer globally. If Composer is installed locally into your working directory, our instructions will work if you replace `composer` by `php composer.phar`.

In order to specifically install FuelPHP 1.7, you can simply execute the following command line (replace `TARGET` by the directory in which you want to download FuelPHP):

```
composer create-project fuel/fuel:dev-1.7/master TARGET
```

Updating FuelPHP

If you have downloaded FuelPHP by cloning the GitHub repository, or if you simply want to update FuelPHP and its dependencies, you have to enter the following command line at the location you installed your instance of FuelPHP:

```
php composer.phar update
```

As you can see, Composer is locally installed in the FuelPHP root directory.

Installation directory and apache configuration

Now that you know how to install FuelPHP in a given directory, we will give you the two main ways you can integrate the framework in your environment.

The simplest way

Assuming you have activated the **mod_rewrite** Apache module, the simplest way is to install FuelPHP in the root folder of your web server (generally the `/var/www directory` on Linux systems). If you install FuelPHP in the `DIR` directory of the root folder (`/var/www/DIR`), you will be able to access your project at the following URL:

```
http://localhost/DIR/public/
```

However, be warned that FuelPHP has not been implemented to support this, and if you publish your project this way in the production server, it will introduce security issues you will have to handle. In such cases, you are recommended to use the second way we will explain in the upcoming section, although, for instance if you plan to use a shared host to publish your project, you might not have the choice. A complete and up-to-date documentation about this issue can be found in the FuelPHP installation instruction page at `http://fuelphp.com/docs/installation/instructions.html` (It can be accessed through the FuelPHP website by navigating to **DOCS** | **TABLE OF CONTENTS** | **FuelPHP** | **Installation** | **Instructions**)

By setting up a virtual host

Another way is to create a virtual host to access your application. You will need a little bit more Apache and system administration skills, but the benefit is that it is more secure and you will be able to choose your working directory. You will need to change two files:

- Your Apache virtual host file(s) in order to link a virtual host to your application
- Your system host file in order to redirect the wanted URL to your virtual host

In both cases, the files' location will be dependent on your operating system and the server environment you are using; therefore, you will have to figure out their location yourself (if you are using a common configuration, you won't have any problem to finding instructions on your preferred search engine).

In the following example, we will set up your system to call your application when requesting the `my.app` URL on your local environment (*nix system recommended).

Let's first edit the virtual host file(s). Add the following code at the end:

```
<VirtualHost *:80>
    ServerName my.app
    DocumentRoot YOUR_APP_PATH/public
    SetEnv FUEL_ENV "development"
    <Directory YOUR_APP_PATH/public>
        DirectoryIndex index.php
        AllowOverride All
        Order allow,deny
        Allow from all
    </Directory>
</VirtualHost>
```

Then, open your system host file and add the following line at the end:

```
127.0.0.1 my.app
```

Depending on your environment, you might need to restart Apache after this. You can now access your website at: `http://my.app/`.

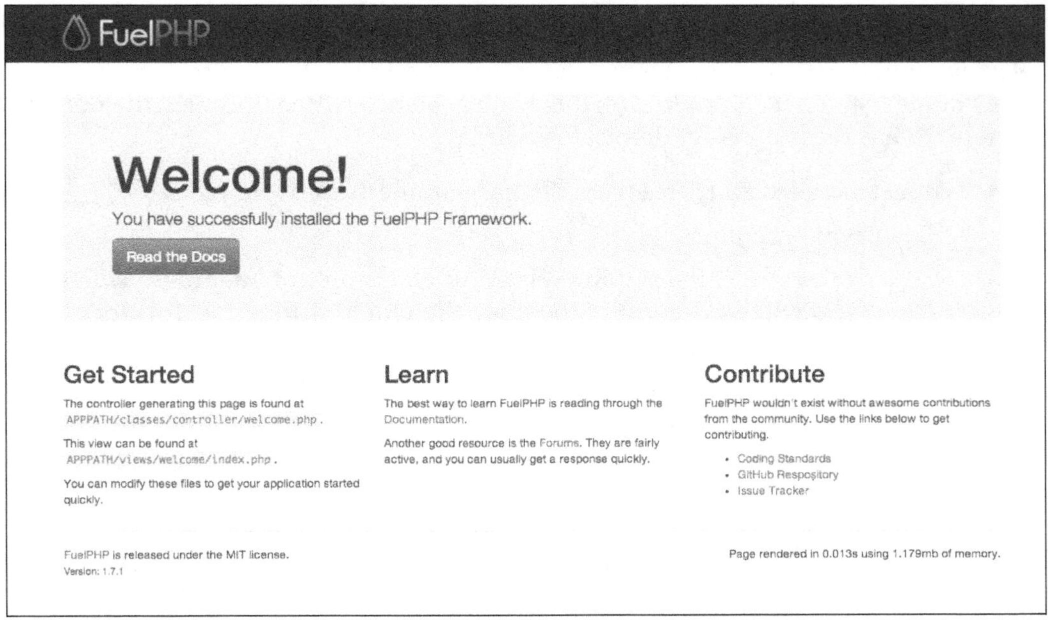

Congratulations! You just have successfully installed the FuelPHP framework. The welcome page shows some recommended directions to continue your project.

FuelPHP basics

Now that we have installed a working version of FuelPHP, let's analyze, on a very basic level, how the framework works. We won't go into the details here; the idea is to only understand the necessary information to use the framework. In this section, you are recommended to follow and check our explanations on your installed instance; don't hesitate to explore files and folders, this will make you more comfortable when we will begin our project's implementation. In this section, we will approach the following:

- The FuelPHP file system hierarchy
- MVC, HMVC, and how it works on FuelPHP
- The oil utility

The FuelPHP file system hierarchy

Let's dive into the directory where we have installed FuelPHP. You might want to follow along using a file browser. As this book is being written, the current version of FuelPHP has the following directory hierarchy:

- `/docs`: contains an HTML version of the framework documentation
- `/fuel`, which contains:
    - `/fuel/app`: Everything related to your application. This is where you will work most of the time. We will look into this directory in the upcoming *The app directory* section.
    - `/fuel/core`: The core classes and configuration. You should not change anything inside it, unless of course you want to contribute to the FuelPHP core.
    - `/fuel/packages`: Packages are core extensions, they are bundles containing reusable classes and configuration files. Using the FuelPHP default configuration, this is the only directory where you can install packages (your own as well as from external sources). Notice that there are already five installed packages. We will use each of them in this book.
    - `/vendor`: This directory contains third-party packages and libraries that are generally not FuelPHP-specific.
- `/public`: This directory is accessible by external visitors. You want to put here files publicly available, as CSS or JS files for instance.

The app directory

As written earlier, the app directory is where you will work most of the time. Thus, you should be familiar with its hierarchy, which is given as follows:

- `/cache`: This directory is used to store cache files that improve your application's performance.
- `/classes`: Classes used by your application:
    - `/classes/controller`: Where you have to implement your controllers (see the *MVC, HMVC, and how it works on FuelPHP* section)
    - `/classes/model`: Where you have to implement your models (see the *MVC, HMVC, and how it works on FuelPHP* section)
    - `/classes/presenter`: Where you have to implement your presenters (see the *MVC, HMVC, and how it works on FuelPHP* section).

- `/config`: Every configuration file. Since some files are important, we will list them as well:
    - `/config/config.php`: Defines important FuelPHP configuration items such as activated packages or security settings.
    - `/config/db.php`: Defines database connection information.
    - `/config/routes.php`: Defines the application's routes (we will approach them later in this chapter).
    - `/config/development`, `config/production`, `config/staging`, `config/test`: All configuration files in the `config/ENV` directory, `ENV` being the current environment, are merged with the ones in the `config` folder. For instance, if the FuelPHP environment is set to `development` (as it is by default), the `config/development/db.php` file will be recursively merged with the `config/db.php` file. In concrete terms, this means that configuration items defined in the `config/ENV/db.php` file overwrite those in the `config/db.php` file. We will illustrate this through an example in *The oil utility and the oil console* section.
- `/lang`: Contains the translation files.
- `/logs`: Contains the log files. The log file path depends on the day it is written. For instance, if you log a message on July 1, 2015, it will be saved in the file located in `logs/2015/07/01.php`.
- `/migrations`: Contains the migration files, which allow you to easily alter your database in a structured manner. For instance, if many people are working on the same project, or if there are many instances of the same project (development/production), they make the database change easier. We will often use them in the book.
- `/modules`: Contains your application's modules. Each module can be described as a bundle of code that can respond to requests and be easily reused on other projects. We will create a module for the blog project in *Chapter 3, Building a Blog Application*.
- `/tasks`: Contains task files, which are classes that can be executed from the command line (for cron jobs for instance).
- `/tests`: Contains test files, which can be used to automatically test your application. We will approach them in *Chapter 5, Building Your Own RESTful API*, to test our application.

- `/tmp`: Contains temporary files.
- `/vendor`: This directory contains third-party libraries and packages only used by your application.
- `/views`: Contains the view files used by your application (see the *MVC, HMVC, and how it works on FuelPHP* section).

The packages

The `fuel/packages` directory contains five default packages that, when activated, can add interesting features to FuelPHP:

- The `auth` package provides a standardized interface for user authentication. We will use this package in *Chapter 5, Building Your Own RESTful API.*
- The `email` package provides an interface to send e-mails using different drivers. We will use this package in *Chapter 3, Building a Blog Application.*
- The `oil` package allows you to speed up your application's implementation by generating code files, launching tests and tasks, or providing a CLI PHP console. We will use this package in all chapters and we will explore its features in *The oil utility and the oil console* section.
- The `orm`: This package is an improvement of the FuelPHP's core models; it allows them to fetch complex queries and to define the relations between them. We will use this package in *Chapter 2, Building a To-do List Application.*
- The `parser`: This package allows your application to render view files in common template systems such as Twig or Smarty. We will use this package in *Chapter 5, Building Your Own RESTful API.*

We will also create our own package in *Chapter 4, Creating and Using Packages.*

Class name, paths, and coding standard

In FuelPHP, there are five constants that define the location of the most important directories as follows:

- **`APPPATH`**: The application directory (`fuel/app`)
- **`COREPATH`**: The core directory (`fuel/core`)
- **`PKGPATH`**: The packages directory (`fuel/packages`)
- **`DOCROOT`**: The public directory (`public`)
- **`VENDORPATH`**: The vendor directory (`fuel/vendor`)

You are recommended to read the official documentation about these constants at `http://fuelphp.com/docs/general/constants.html` (It can be accessed through the FuelPHP website by navigating to **DOCS** | **TABLE OF CONTENTS** | **FuelPHP** | **General** | **Constants**)

Please keep in mind, that we will often use these constants in the book to shorten file paths.

An interesting point is that FuelPHP allows you to change quite easily the folder structure: for instance, you can change in the `public/index.php` file the value of the constants that we just introduced, or you can change the directory where FuelPHP will load modules by changing the `module_paths` key in the `APPPATH/config/config.php` configuration file.

You might also have noticed that class names are related to their own path, as given in the following:

- In the app directory, the `classes/controller/welcome.php` class is named `Controller_Welcome`
- The `classes/model/welcome.php` class is named `Model_Welcome`
- You can notice that classes are named the same way in the `fuel/core` directory

This result was not achieved by accident; FuelPHP follows by default the PSR-0 standard. You are recommended to read the official documentation about this standard at `http://www.php-fig.org/psr/psr-0/`.

MVC, HMVC, and how it works on FuelPHP

We will now look into one major aspect of the FuelPHP framework - the MVC and HMVC software architecture patterns.

What is MVC?

Model-view-controller (**MVC**) is a software architecture pattern that states that the code should be separated in three categories: models, views, and controllers.

For those who are not familiar with it, let's illustrate this through an example:

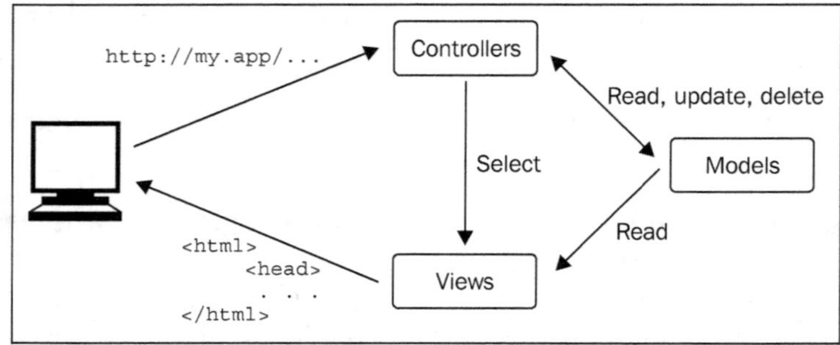

Suppose a user tries to access your website. The following are some URLs he/she might request:

```
http://my.app/
```

```
http://my.app/welcome/
```

```
http://my.app/welcome/hello
```

Depending on the requested URL, your website is generally expected to return some HTML code and it also sometimes needs to update the database, for instance when you want to save the users' comments.

The returned HTML code is generated by the views, because this is what is received by the browser and indirectly seen by the user.

The database is generally updated through models. In concrete terms, instead of executing raw SQL code to access and update the database, the best practice is to use classes and instances to do so. Each class represents a model that is related to a specific table: for example, the `car` model would access the `cars` table. Each class' instance is a model instance linked to a specific row in a table: for example, your car's information can be saved as a `car` instance that will be linked to a specific row in the `cars` table. As we use classes instead of raw SQL code, the framework has already implemented frequently needed features such as reading, creating, saving, or deleting model's instances. A further advantage is that, as we used packaged and well-implemented methods to access our database, it can prevent most unintended security breaches that we can create when requesting the database using raw SQL.

The controllers allow the website to handle the user's request by selecting the correct view to send back (the response) and updating the database (through models) if necessary. Controllers handle a specific section of the website: for instance, the `car` controller will handle everything that is related to cars. Controllers are subdivided by actions that will handle specific features: for instance, the `list` action of the `car` controller will return a list of cars in HTML code. In practice, controllers are classes and actions are methods.

When the user requests a URL, the framework will select an action inside a controller to handle it. Those are generally chosen by convention; for instance, when requesting `http://my.app/welcome/hello`, the framework will choose the `hello` action inside the `welcome` controller. Sometimes, they can also be chosen using a routes configuration file that matches URLs to actions and controllers.

The views sometimes need to access models; for example, we need to access the `car` model's instances when we want to display a list of cars. However, views should never update models or the database; only the controllers and preferably models should do that.

Please note that additional code components as helpers or presenters can be added to ease the development process, but if you understood this section, you got the most important points.

How it works on FuelPHP

Let's illustrate how it works by testing our newly created website. We suppose that your application is available at the following URL:

```
http://my.app/
```

Actions and controllers

If you request a random URL, you will probably get a 404 exception. For instance:

```
http://my.app/should_display_404
```

But, if you request the following URL, you will display the same page as the home page:

```
http://my.app/welcome/index
```

If you request the following URL, you will display a different page:

```
http://my.app/welcome/hello
```

Let's first explain how the last two requests worked. You can notice that both URLs contain the *welcome* word just after the base URL. You can also find this word in the file name `fuel/app/classes/controller/welcome.php`; it turns out that *welcome* is a controller. Now, open this file using your preferred text editor. You will then read the following:

```
//...
class Controller_Welcome extends Controller
{
    //...
    public function action_index()
    {
        //...
    }

    //...
    public function action_hello()
    {
        //...
    }
    //...
}
```

You can notice the `action_index` and `action_hello` methods. These functions are called actions. Now, as you have probably guessed, when you request `http://my.app/welcome/index`, the `action_index` method will be called. In a more general manner, if you request `http://my.app/CONTROLLER/ACTION`, the `action_ACTION` method of the `CONTROLLER` controller will be called. Let's test that. Edit the `action_index` function to add a simple echo at the beginning:

```
public function action_index()
{
  echo 'Test 1 - Please never print anything inside an action';
  //...
}
```

Now, if you request `http://my.app/welcome/index`, you will read the printed content at the beginning of the web page. Though this is an easy way to test how things work, never print anything in your action or controller. When you print a message, you are already implementing the view entity; thus, printing something in the controller breaks the MVC pattern.

Views

But then how are the pages rendered? Let's analyze the only line of code in our `index` action:

```
public function action_index()
{
  return Response::forge(View::forge('welcome/index'));
}
```

`View::forge('welcome/index')` returns a `View` object generated from the `fuel/app/views/welcome/index.php` view file. We will use this function a lot in this chapter and this book, and will cover all its parameters, but you can read its official documentation in the FuelPHP website:

`http://fuelphp.com/docs/classes/view.html#/method_forge`. (It can be accessed through the FuelPHP website by navigating to **DOCS** | **TABLE OF CONTENTS** | **Core** | **View**)

`Response::forge(View::forge('welcome/index'));` returns a response object created from the `View` object. Additional parameters allow us to change headers or the page status. A response object contains all the necessary information that will be sent to the browser: the headers and the body (generally the HTML code). You are recommended to read the official documentation on the FuelPHP website at `http://fuelphp.com/docs/classes/response.html#method_forge` (It can be accessed through the FuelPHP website navigating to **DOCS** | **TABLE OF CONTENTS** | **Core** | **Response**)

Since the view is generated from the `fuel/app/views/welcome/index.php` file, open it to discover its content. You can notice that this is the same HTML code as the one displayed when requesting the URL. Just after `<h1>Welcome!</h1>`, add `<p>This is my first view change.</p>`. Now, if you refresh your browser, you will see this message appear under the **Welcome!** title.

Parameters

It is possible to indicate parameters, both to the actions and to the views. For instance, replace your `index` action by the following code:

```
public function action_index($name = 'user', $id = 0)
{
    return Response::forge(
        View::forge(
            'welcome/index',
            array(
```

```
                    'name' => $name,
                    'id' => $id,
                )
            )
        );
    }
```

And in the `fuel/app/views/welcome/index.php` view file, replace

```
<h1>Welcome!</h1>
```

by

```
<h1>Welcome <?php echo ($name.' (id: '.$id.')'); ?>!</h1>
```

Now, if you request the following URL:

`http://my.app/welcome/index`

the title will display **Welcome user (id: 0)!**

If you request the following URL:

`http://my.app/welcome/index/Jane`

the title will display **Welcome Jane (id: 0)!**

And if you request the following URL:

`http://my.app/welcome/index/Jane/34`

the title will display **Welcome Jane (id: 34)!**

You might have understood that if you request the following URL:

`http://my.app/CONTROLLER/ACTION/PARAM_1/PARAM_2/PARAM3`

The `action_ACTION` method of `CONTROLLER` will be called with the `PARAM_1`, `PARAM_2`, and `PARAM_3` parameters. If there are less parameters defined in the URL than required in the method, either, if defined, the parameters take their default values (as illustrated previously), or, if no default value is defined, it will trigger a 404 error.

You can notice that we replaced

```
View::forge('welcome/index')
```

By

```
View::forge('welcome/index', array(
        'name' => $name,
        'id' => $id,
    )
)
```

View parameters are sent by the second parameter of `\View::forge` in an associative array. Here, the associative array has two keys, `name` and `id`, and their values are available inside the view file through the `$name` and `$id` variables.

In a more general manner, if you call the following:

```
View::forge('YOUR_VIEW', array(
        'param_1' => 1,
        'param_2' => 2,
    )
)
```

When the view file will be executed, parameters will be available through the `$param_1` and `$param_2` variables.

Routes

Though what we previously observed explains how the standard cases operate

`http://my.app/CONTROLLER/ACTION`

we haven't explained why the two following URLs return content though no associated controller and action can be found:

`http://my.app/`

`http://my.app/should_display_404`

For understanding why we have to open the `fuel/app/config/routes.php` configuration file:

```
<?php
return array(
  '_root_'  => 'welcome/index',  // The default route
  '_404_'   => 'welcome/404',    // The main 404 route

  'hello(/:name)?' => array('welcome/hello', 'name' => 'hello'),
);
```

You can first notice the following two special keys:

- `_root_`: This defines which controller and action should be called when requesting the website root URL. Note that the value is `welcome/index`, you can now understand why `http://my.app` and `http://my.app/welcome/index` are returning the same content.
- `_404_`: This defines which controller and action should be called when throwing a 404 error.

Beside specials keys, you can define the custom URLs you want to handle. Let's add a simple example at the end of the array:

```
'my/welcome/page'  => 'welcome/index',
```

Now, if you request the following URL:

`http://my.app/my/welcome/page`

it will display the same content as in the following URL:

`http://my.app/welcome/index`

You have probably noticed that there is also another key already defined: `hello(/:name)?`. The routing system is quite advanced, and to fully understand it you are recommended to take a look at the official documentation:

`http://fuelphp.com/docs/general/routing.html` (It can be accessed through the FuelPHP website by navigating to **DOCS** | **TABLE OF CONTENTS** | **FuelPHP** | **Routing**)

Presenters

You might have seen that the `hello` action doesn't use the `View` class to display its content, but instead it uses the `Presenter` class:

```
public function action_hello()
{
    return Response::forge(Presenter::forge('welcome/hello'));
}
```

Let's analyze what is happening in this case. First, you can notice that, as for the views, a view file exists at the following path: `fuel/app/views/welcome/hello.php`. If you open this file, you will see that the code is the same as the one displayed when requesting the URL `http://my.app/welcome/hello`, except for one tiny difference. You can find the following code:

```
<h1>Hello, <?php echo $name; ?>!
```

In a normal view, we would have to define the `name` parameter, except here we didn't. Though, when displaying the web page, this parameter seems to have a defined value (it displays **Hello, World!**). Where could it be defined then?

Probing a little further, you can find another file located at `fuel/app/classes/presenter/welcome/hello.php`. It contains the following:

```
class Presenter_Welcome_Hello extends Presenter
{
    //...
    public function view()
    {
        $this->name = $this->request()->param('name', 'World');
    }
}
```

This file contains a `Presenter` class. The `view` function is called before rendering the view and it is here that the `name` parameter is set. It tries to get the name from the request parameter, `name`, but if it is not defined, the default value is `World`.

If you wonder how to change this parameter, refer to the routes. For instance, request the URL `http://my.app/hello/Jane`.

One could then wonder the use of `Presenter` classes, since we could change the previous code into a more classic view and controller approach.

Let's show its usefulness by an illustration. Suppose you have created an internal website managing the clients of your corporation. Each client is associated to a client category. In your creation, edition, and other forms, you thus display a selectable list of client categories. Each time you display the exact same selectable list, though you access it by using different controllers and actions. You can come up with three solutions:

- You can create a classic view for your selectable list, load the list of client categories inside each of your actions, and pass this list to each view until you reach the location where you want to display your list. The problem is that it would induce a lot of code repetition.

- You can create a classic view and load the list of clients inside this view. This way, you wouldn't have to pass along the necessary parameter. The problem is that you would break the MVC pattern by mixing models and views.
- You can create a `Presenter` class, load the list inside the `Presenter` class, use it inside the view file, and display the view file using `Presenter::forge`. This solution is the best because it doesn't mix views and models but still limits the code duplication.

What is HMVC?

FuelPHP is a **Hierarchical Model-View-Controller** (**HMVC**) framework, meaning that it allows you to request internal controllers from your application. In concrete terms, the following code:

```
echo Request::forge('welcome/index')->execute();
```

will print exactly what the following URL would return:

`http://my.app/welcome/index`

Though we suggest you to use this feature in moderation, it can come handy when you want to implement and display widgets on several web pages.

You are recommended to read the following resources if you want to learn more about this pattern:

`http://en.wikipedia.org/wiki/Hierarchical_model-view-controller`

`http://stackoverflow.com/questions/2263416/what-is-the-hmvc-pattern`

The oil utility and the oil console

The `oil` utility is a very handy command-line tool. As the `rails` utility of Ruby on Rails, oil allows you to do the following:

- Easily generate code files: models, controllers, migrations, and entire scaffoldings
- Run tasks and migrations
- Easily install, update, or remove packages
- Test your code using PHPUnit test or a real-time console
- Even run a PHP-built-in web server hosting your FuelPHP application (for PHP >= 5.4)

Though we will use all these features, except the last one in this book, we recommend that you take a look at the official documentation at:

`http://fuelphp.com/docs/packages/oil/intro.html` (It can be accessed through the FuelPHP website by navigating to **DOCS** | **TABLE OF CONTENTS** | **Oil** | **Introduction**)

In this section, we are going to use the oil console, which is an important tool if you want to test your website, or, as in this case, a FuelPHP feature.

First, open your command-line utility and go to the root of your website directory. Then, enter the following line:

```
php oil console
```

If you use a web development platform such as WAMP or MAMP, you are recommended to use the PHP executable inside the platform directory for launching the oil utility (it might not work otherwise). As I wrote this book, this executable is located at `WAMP_DIRECTORY\bin\php\phpVERSION\php.exe` for WAMP, and at `MAMP_DIRECTORY/bin/php/phpVERSION/bin/php` for MAMP (VERSION depends on the version of PHP you installed, the best is to check this directory by yourself using a file explorer).

This will open the command-line interface oil provides. When you press *Enter*, something similar to the following should appear:

```
Fuel 1.7.2 - PHP 5.4.24 (cli) (Jan 19 2014 21:18:21) [Darwin]

>>>
```

You can now type any PHP code and it will be executed. Let's start with something simple:

```
>>> $a = 2
```

If you press *Enter*, nothing will be printed, but the `$a` variable will be set to `2`. Now, if you want to check a variable value, simply enter its name and then press *Enter*:

```
>>> $a
2
```

It also works for more complex variables:

```
>>> $a = array('a' => 'b', 'c' => 'd')
>>> $a
array (
  'a' => 'b',
  'c' => 'd',
)
```

But be aware, that you might have trouble displaying complex objects.

Let's now test a FuelPHP feature. Earlier, when discussing the `app` directory structure, we explained that the configuration files in the `fuel/app/config` directory were merged with the ones with the same filenames in the `fuel/app/config/ENV` directory, `ENV` being FuelPHP's current environment. We will now test this behavior.

First, let's check FuelPHP's current environment:

```
>>> Fuel::$env
development
```

The environment should be set to `development`.

Now, create a PHP file located at `fuel/app/config/test.php` where you will write:

```
<?php
return array(
    'this_is_the_root_config_file' => true,
);
```

Then create another PHP file located at `fuel/app/config/development/test.php` and write the following:

```
<?php
return array(
    'this_is_the_dev_config_file' => true,
);
```

and an additional one located at `fuel/app/config/production/test.php`, where you will write the following:

```
<?php
return array(
    'this_is_the_prod_config_file' => true,
);
```

Now, if you return to the command-line interface, you can load the `test` configuration file by writing the following:

```
>>> $conf = Config::load('test', true)
```

You are recommended to read the `Config::load` official documentation for more information at:

`http://fuelphp.com/docs/classes/config.html#/method_load`. (It can be accessed through the FuelPHP website by navigating to **DOCS** | **TABLE OF CONTENTS** | **Core** | **Config**)

As explained before, the value returned will be a mix of the `fuel/app/config/test.php` and the `fuel/app/config/development/test.php` configuration files:

```
>>> $conf
array (
  'this_is_the_root_config_file' => true,
  'this_is_the_dev_config_file' => true,
)
```

If we change the FuelPHP environment to `production`:

```
Fuel::$env = 'production'; // only do that for testing purposes
```

And load again the `test` configuration file:

```
>>> Config::load('test', true, true)
array (
  'this_is_the_root_config_file' => true,
  'this_is_the_prod_config_file' => true,
)
```

The merging will be done with the configuration file in the `production` folder.

> You have probably noticed that we added a third parameter for `Config::load`. This parameter allows you to clear the configuration cache. If we didn't set it to `true`, the method would have returned the old configuration we loaded when we were in the `development` environment.

But what happens when the `fuel/app/config/production/test.php` and `fuel/app/config/test.php` configuration files contain the same key? The console can find the answer for us.

Change the content of the `fuel/app/config/test.php` configuration file to the following:

```
<?php
return array(
    'complex_value' => array(
        'root' => true,
    ),
    'this_is_the_root_config_file' => true,
);
```

and change the content of the `fuel/app/config/production/test.php` configuration file to the following:

```
<?php
return array(
    'complex_value' => array(
        'prod' => true,
    ),
    'this_is_the_root_config_file' => false,
    'this_is_the_prod_config_file' => true,
);
```

Let's now reload the `test` configuration files as follows:

```
>>> Config::load('test', true, true)
array (
  'complex_value' =>
  array (
    'root' => true,
    'prod' => true,
  ),
  'this_is_the_root_config_file' => false,
  'this_is_the_prod_config_file' => true,
)
```

It is interesting to analyze how the preceding two configuration files have been merged:

- The `this_is_the_root_config_file` key shared by the two configuration files is associated in both cases to a simple value. In the resulting configuration, it is the value from the production file that prevails.
- The `complex_value` key is associated in both cases to an array. The two arrays seem to have been merged in the resulting configuration.

This is because the configuration files are not merged by the `array_merge` native PHP function, but instead by the `Arr::merge` FuelPHP function, which merges arrays recursively. You are recommended to take a look at its official documentation at `http://fuelphp.com/docs/classes/arr.html#/method_merge` (It can be accessed through the FuelPHP website by navigating to **DOCS** | **TABLE OF CONTENTS** | **Core** | **Arr**)

It should be clear now that the console is a great tool that allows you to test your application. It can also be used as a great complement to the documentation, as you can try FuelPHP methods and their parameters without changing any files in your application.

Building your first application

Now that we had a quick overview of the FuelPHP framework, let's build our first tiny application.

Suppose that you are a zoo manager and you want to keep track of the monkeys you are looking after. For each monkey, you want to save the following:

- Its name
- If it is still in the zoo
- Its height
- A description input where you can enter custom information

You want a very simple interface with the following five major features:

- You want to create a new monkey
- You want to edit existing ones
- You want to list all monkeys
- You want to view a detailed file for each monkey
- You want to delete monkeys from the system

The preceding five major features, very common in computer applications, are part of the **Create, Read, Update and Delete** (**CRUD**) basic operations. This is a perfect example to use the oil utility to generate a scaffold. Oil will quickly generate for us the controllers, models, views, and migrations to handle our monkeys. All we will have to do, then, is to refine the generated code and adapt it to our needs.

Database configuration

As we will store our monkeys into a MySQL database, it is time to configure FuelPHP to use our local database. If you open `fuel/app/config/db.php`, all you will see is an empty array, but, as we demonstrated it in the *FuelPHP basics* section, this configuration file is merged to `fuel/app/config/ENV/db.php`, `ENV` being the current FuelPHP's environment, which in that case is `development`.

You should, therefore, open `fuel/app/config/development/db.php`:

```
<?php
//...
return array(
  'default' => array(
    'connection'  => array(
      'dsn'        => 'mysql:host=localhost;dbname=fuel_dev',
      'username'   => 'root',
      'password'   => 'root',
    ),
  ),
);
```

This is the generated default configuration, which you should adapt to your local configuration, particularly the database name (currently set to `fuel_dev`), the username, and password. You must create the database of your project manually.

Scaffolding

Now that the database configuration is set, we will be able to generate a scaffold. We will use the `generate` feature of the oil utility.

Open the command-line utility and go to your website root directory. To generate a scaffold for a new model, you will need to enter the following line:

```
php oil generate scaffold/crud MODEL ATTR_1:TYPE_1 ATTR_2:TYPE_2 ...
```

where:

- `MODEL` is the model name
- `ATTR_1`, `ATTR_2...` are the model's attribute names
- `TYPE_1`, `TYPE_2...` are attribute types

In our case, it should be as follows:

```
php oil generate scaffold/crud monkey name:string still_here:bool
height:float description:text
```

Here we are telling oil to generate a scaffold for the `monkey` model with the following attributes:

- `name`: The name of the monkey. Its type is string and the associated MySQL column type will be VARCHAR(255).
- `still_here`: Whether or not the monkey is still in the facility. Its type is boolean and the associated MySQL column type will be TINYINT(1).
- `height`: Height of the monkey. Its type is float and the associated MySQL column type will be FLOAT.
- `description`: Description of the monkey. Its type is text and the associated MySQL column type will be TEXT.

You can do much more using the oil generate feature, such as generating models, controllers, migrations, tasks, packages, and so on. We will see some of these later in the book, but you are recommended to take a look at the official documentation at `http://fuelphp.com/docs/packages/oil/generate.html` (It can be accessed through the FuelPHP website by navigating to **DOCS** | **TABLE OF CONTENTS** | **Oil** | **Generate**)

When you press *Enter*, you will see the following lines appear:

```
Creating migration: APPPATH/migrations/001_create_monkeys.php
Creating model: APPPATH/classes/model/monkey.php
Creating controller: APPPATH/classes/controller/monkey.php
Creating view: APPPATH/views/monkey/index.php
Creating view: APPPATH/views/monkey/view.php
Creating view: APPPATH/views/monkey/create.php
Creating view: APPPATH/views/monkey/edit.php
Creating view: APPPATH/views/monkey/_form.php
Creating view: APPPATH/views/template.php
```

Oil has generated for us nine files, which are as follows:

- A migration file, containing all the necessary information to create the model's associated table
- The model

- A controller
- Five view files and a template file

We will take a closer look at these files in the next sections.

> You might have noticed that we used the `scaffold/crud` command, and, if you read the official documentation, we could have typed only `scaffold`. This is because two types of scaffold can be generated: `scaffold/crud`, which uses simple models, and `scaffold/orm` alias `scaffold`, which uses the `orm` models. Since using FuelPHP's native ORM was out of the scope of this chapter, and we didn't have to use complex model features such as relations, we chose to use `scaffold/crud`.

Migrating

One of the generated files was `APPPATH/migrations/001_create_monkeys.php`. It is a migration file and contains the required information to create our monkey table. Notice that the name is structured as `VER_NAME`, where `VER` is the version number and `NAME` is the name of the migration.

If you execute the following command line:

```
php oil refine migrate
```

All migration files that have not yet been executed will be executed from the oldest version to the latest version (001, 002, 003, and so on). Once all migration files are executed, oil will display the latest version number.

Once executed, if you take a look at your database, you will observe that not one but two tables have been created:

- `monkeys`: As expected, a table has been created to handle your monkeys. Notice that the table name is the plural version of the word we typed for generating the scaffold; such a transformation was internally done using the `Inflector::pluralize` method. The table will contain the specified columns (`name`, `still_here`), the `id` column, and also `created_at` and `updated_at`. These columns store the time an object was created and updated, and are added by default each time you generate your models. It is possible to not generate them with the `--no-timestamp` argument.

- `migration`: This table is automatically created the first time you execute migrations. It keeps track of the migrations that were executed. If you look into its content, you will see that it already contains one row; this is the migration you just executed. You can notice that the row does not only indicate the name of the migration, but also a type and a name. This is because migration files can be placed at many places such as modules or packages (see *Chapter 3, Building a Blog Application*).

> It is important to note that the `migration` table is not the only location where FuelPHP keeps track of the already executed migrations. This information is also stored in `fuel/app/config/ENV/migrations.php`, `ENV` being FuelPHP's environment. If you decide to edit the `migration` table, you might want to also edit or delete this file, as it might prevent the execution of your migrations.

The `refine migrate` feature of oil allows you to have much more control on migrations than simply executing all the new ones. For instance, you can also revert to a previous version using the following command line:

```
php oil refine migrate:down
```

Or revert to a specified version using the following command line:

```
php oil refine migrate --version=3
```

Or even choose which modules or packages you want to update using the `--modules` or `--package` arguments. To have a complete overview, you are recommended to take a look at the official documentation at `http://fuelphp.com/docs/general/migrations.html` (It can be accessed through the FuelPHP website by navigating to **DOCS** | **TABLE OF CONTENTS** | **FuelPHP** | **Migrations**)

But how do migration files allow such complex manipulations? Let's open our migration file located at `APPPATH/migrations/001_create_monkeys.php` to find out. You should see the following:

```
<?php

namespace Fuel\Migrations;

class Create_monkeys
{
    public function up()
    {
```

```
            \DBUtil::create_table('monkeys', array(
                'id' => array(
                    'constraint' => 11,
                    'type' => 'int',
                    'auto_increment' => true,
                    'unsigned' => true
                ),
                'name' => array(
                    'constraint' => 255,
                    'type' => 'varchar'
                ),
                'still_here' => array(
                    'type' => 'bool'
                ),
                'height' => array(
                    'type' => 'float'
                ),
                'description' => array(
                    'type' => 'text'
                ),
                'created_at' => array(
                    'constraint' => 11,
                    'type' => 'int',
                    'null' => true
                ),
                'updated_at' => array(
                    'constraint' => 11,
                    'type' => 'int',
                    'null' => true
                ),
            ), array('id'));
        }

        public function down()
        {
            \DBUtil::drop_table('monkeys');
        }
    }
```

The file contains a class named `Create_monkeys` that has the following two methods:

- `up`: This method defines how to update your data structure. Note that this migration file creates the monkey table using the `DBUtil::create_table` method, but you could perfectly execute a handmade SQL request to do that. Though migrations are generally used to update your database, you can also use them to update custom data files or old configuration files.

In some cases, if you want to implement your own migrations, you might find the idea of using your application's methods (in models or helpers) attractive. Though it can allow you to limit your code duplication, it is not recommended. This is because, for compatibility reasons, the migration files are intended to stay in your application indefinitely, whereas your application's code can evolve a lot. Therefore, by changing or deleting a method in your application, you might unexpectedly break some migration files (that use this method) without even noticing it, making the future installation of your application complicated.

- `down`: This method defines how to cancel all changes that were made by the `up` method. Suppose you realize that the feature was a mistake and you want to revert to an older version: this is when this method will be executed. In our case, the method simply deletes the monkey table.

If the information contained in the table is important, it might be a good idea to instead move the table, for instance, to an archive database. A human mistake could have disastrous consequences otherwise.

The migration files are a powerful tool and their usefulness increase tenfold as the number of instances and the number of developers working on the same project rise. Using them from scratch is always a good decision.

Using your application

Now that we have generated the code and migrated the database, our application is ready to be used. You might have noticed during the generation that a controller was created at `APPPATH/classes/controller/monkey.php` and that the route configuration file was not changed, meaning that the controller must be accessible through the default URL.

Let's request, then, the URL `http://my.app/monkey`.

As you can notice, this web page is intended to display the list of all monkeys, but since none have been added, the list is empty:

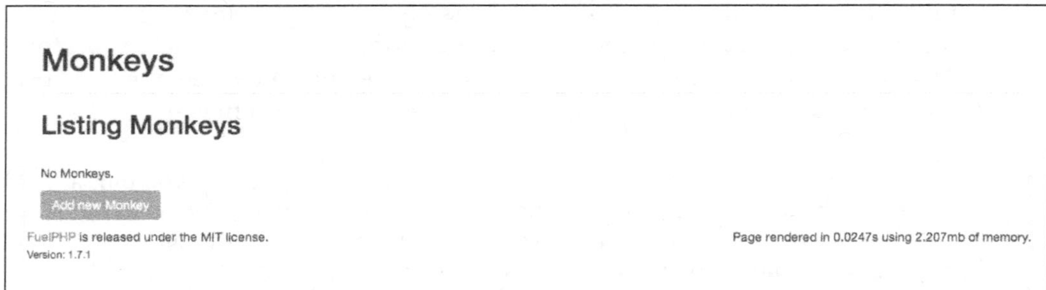

Then, let's add a new monkey by clicking on the **Add new Monkey** button. The following web page should appear:

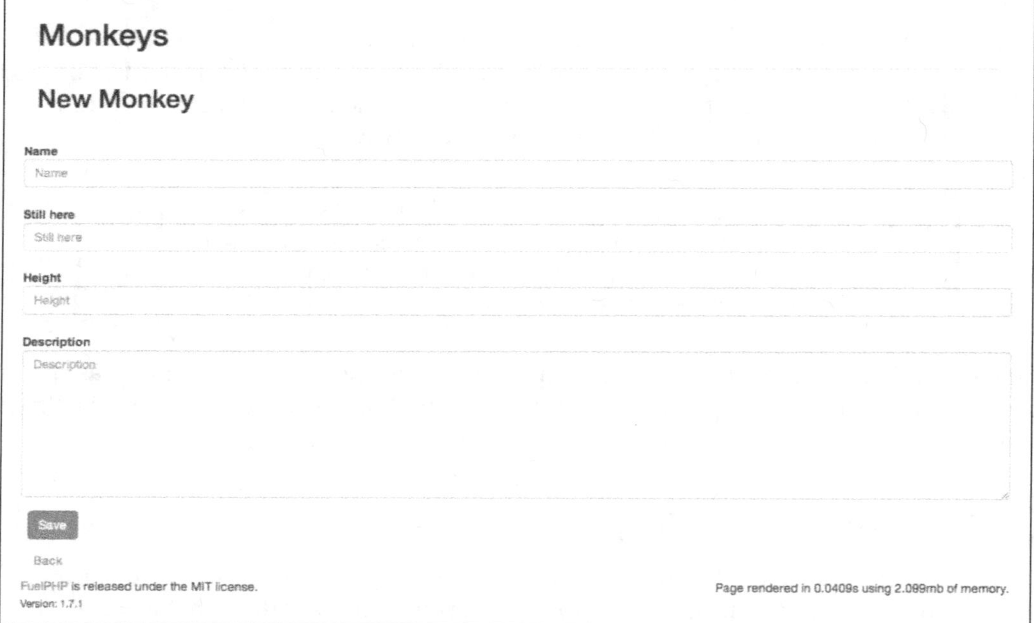

You can enter your monkey's information here. There are, however, several inconsistencies:

- All fields are required, meaning that you can't leave any field empty, otherwise errors will be triggered preventing you from adding the monkey. This is not what we might want for the description field.
- Though you can enter anything you want in the **Height** field without triggering any error, if you enter anything other than a float, it will be replaced by 0. We might want to trigger an error in such a case.
- **Still here** can only have two values: 0 or 1 (false or true). Though the type of the associated database column is correct, the generated form uses a standard input where we might want a checkbox.

The form is certainly not perfect, but it is a great start. All we will have to do is refine the code a little bit.

Once you have added several monkeys, you can again take a look at the listing page as follows:

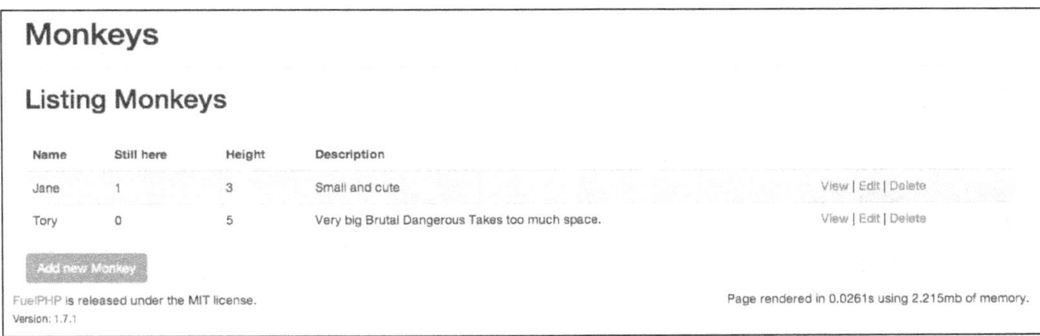

Again, this is a great start, though we might want to refine it a little bit: display **Yes** and **No** instead of **1** and **0**, respectively, for the **Still here** column, and remove the **Description** column because there might be too much text to display.

Each item on the list has three associated actions: **View**, **Edit**, and **Delete**.

Let's first click on **View**:

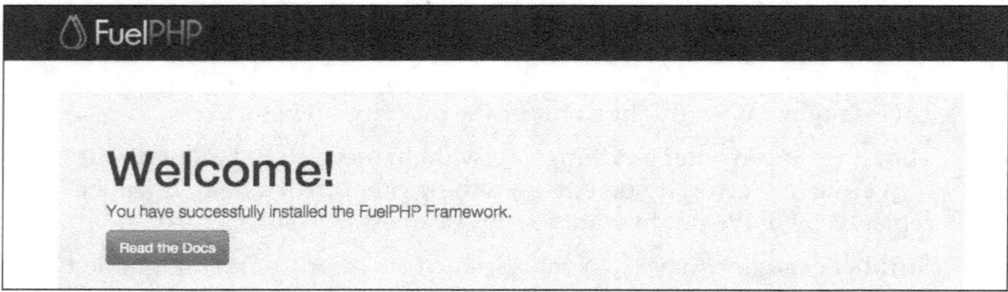

Again this is a great start, though we will also refine this web page.

You can return back to the listing by clicking on **Back** or edit the monkey by clicking on **Edit**. Accessed from either the listing page or the view page, it will display the same form as when creating a new monkey, except that the form will be prefilled of course.

Finally, if you click on **Delete**, a confirmation box will appear to prevent any miss clicking:

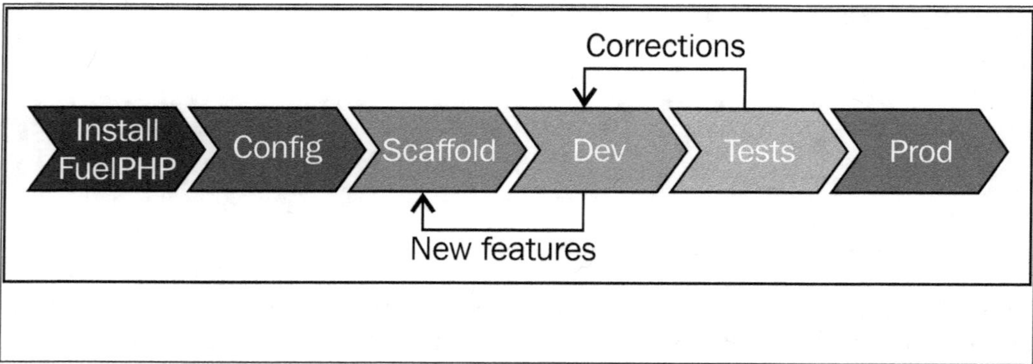

Refining the application

Now that we took a look at our interface, let's refine our application so that it becomes more user-friendly. In this section, we will explore the files that have been generated by oil and try to adapt them to our needs.

Refining the monkey listing

During the previous section, two small issues bothered us for the monkey's listing:

- We wanted more explicit values than 0 and 1 for the `Still here` column
- We wanted to remove the `Description` column

We know that the list appears when requesting the following URL:

```
http://my.app/monkey
```

You have probably noticed that in this URL we indicated a controller, but no action. It is important to know that, by default and without any routing configuration involved, this URL is equivalent to `http://my.app/monkey/index`

So, in fact, we are calling the `index` action of the `monkey` controller. If we open the generated controller at `APPPATH/classes/controller/monkey.php`, we will read the following:

```
<?php
class Controller_Monkey extends Controller_Template{
    //...
}
```

First, you can notice that `Controller_Monkey` extends `Controller_Template` instead of `Controller`, as we saw before in `Controller_Welcome`. `Controller_Template` is an extension of `Controller` that adds template support. The idea is that most of the time your web pages will have the same layout: the headers, footers, and menus generally stay the same, regardless of the web pages you are in. Templates allow you to achieve this by limiting the code duplication.

By default, `Controller_Template` is associated with the `APPPATH/views/template.php` template that was generated by oil. If you open this file, you will see that it generates the HTML code around the page content. You will also probably notice that it prints the `$title` and `$content` variables. We will find out how to set their values by exploring the `index` action. If you go back to the **Monkey** controller, the `action_index` method should contain the following:

```
public function action_index()
{
    $data['monkeys'] = Model_Monkey::find_all();
    $this->template->title = "Monkeys";
    $this->template->content = View::forge('monkey/index', $data);
}
```

The first line stores all the monkeys' instances into the `$data['monkeys']` variable. In a general manner, `MODEL::find_all()` returns all a model's instances, but it is definitely not the only method that retrieve instances. These methods will be discussed more thoroughly in *Chapter 2, Building a To-do List Application*.

The second and third lines set the `$title` and `$content` variables displayed in the template file. If you change the second line by `$this->template->title = "My monkeys";` and then refresh the web page, you will see that its title has changed accordingly.

The third line sets the `$content` variable to a view instance that, from what we have observed in the previous sections, executes the view file located at `APPPATH/views/monkey/index.php` with the `$monkey` variable set to all monkeys' instances. Let's open this view file. You should see the following:

```
<h2>Listing Monkeys</h2>
<br>
<?php if ($monkeys): ?>
<table class="table table-striped">
  <thead>
    <tr>
      <th>Name</th>
      <th>Still here</th>
      <th>Height</th>
      <th>Description</th>

  <th></th>
    </tr>
  </thead>
  <tbody>
<?php foreach ($monkeys as $item): ?>    <tr>

      <td><?php echo $item->name; ?></td>
      <td><?php echo $item->still_here; ?></td>
      <td><?php echo $item->height; ?></td>
      <td><?php echo $item->description; ?></td>
      <td>
        <?php /* Action buttons */ ?>

      </td>
    </tr>
<?php endforeach; ?>  </tbody>
</table>

<?php else: ?>
```

```
<p>No Monkeys.</p>

<?php endif; ?><p>
  <?php /* Add new Monkey button */ ?>

</p>
```

We have found where the table is displayed, so it is time to make our changes.

First, remove the `Description` column by removing the following:

```
<th>Description</th>
```

and

```
<td><?php echo $item->description; ?></td>
```

Then, let's refine how the `Still here` attribute is displayed by replacing the following:

```
<td><?php echo $item->still_here; ?></td>
```

by

```
<td><?php echo $item->still_here ? 'Yes' : 'No'; ?></td>
```

The **Still here** column should now display **Yes** and **No** instead of **1** and **0**, respectively.

Refining the monkey detailed view

On the list, when clicking on an item's **View** link, a detailed view of the monkey appears. We would like to change two details here:

- As in the previous section, display more explicit values for the **Still here** attribute
- Currently, if you save a monkey with a multiline description, it is displayed on one line only

First, if you are on a detailed view page, you can notice that the URL is similar to `http://my.app/monkey/view/1`

This means we are calling the `view` action of the `monkey` controller with the first and only parameter set to `1`. The `view` action is quite similar to the `index` action, as you can see in the following snippet:

```
public function action_view($id = null)
{
    is_null($id) and Response::redirect('monkey');

    $data['monkey'] = Model_Monkey::find_by_pk($id);

    $this->template->title = "Monkey";
    $this->template->content = View::forge('monkey/view', $data);
}
```

The first line simply checks if the parameter of the action (associated to the `$id` variable) is actually set, and otherwise redirects the user (using the `Response::redirect` method) to the listing page.

The second line stores the monkey with ID `$id` into the `$data['monkey']` variable. The `find_by_pk` (`pk` for primary key) method of a model finds one of its instances by its primary key. As we explained earlier, models' methods will be discussed more thoroughly in *Chapter 2, Building a To-do List Application*.

Just to be perfectly clear, requesting the URL `http://my.app/monkey/view/ID` will load the monkey instance with `id = ID`.

The third and fourth lines, as in the previous section, set the template variables. The template content is set to the view located at `APPPATH/views/monkey/view.php`.

```
<h2>Viewing #<?php echo $monkey->id; ?></h2>

<p>
  <strong>Name:</strong>
  <?php echo $monkey->name; ?></p>
<p>
  <strong>Still here:</strong>
  <?php echo $monkey->still_here; ?></p>
<p>
  <strong>Height:</strong>
  <?php echo $monkey->height; ?></p>
<p>
  <strong>Description:</strong>
```

```
    <?php echo $monkey->description; ?></p>

  <?php /* Edit button */ ?> |
  <?php /* Back button */ ?>
```

It is time to do some changes.

Replace:

```
<?php echo $monkey->still_here; ?>
```

By:

```
<?php echo $monkey->still_here ? 'Yes' : 'No'; ?>
```

And replace:

```
<?php echo $monkey->description; ?>
```

By:

```
<div><?php echo nl2br($monkey->description); ?></div>
```

Allowing an empty description

One of the issues we pointed out previously, is that the description field is required, though we want to be able to enter an empty value.

First, open your browser and request the following URL:

`http://my.app/monkey`

Click on the **Add a new Monkey** button, and you can see you are redirected to `http://my.app/monkey/create`

If you take a look at the page source, you will find that the form's `action` attribute is actually the same URL:

```
<form class="form-horizontal" action="http://my.app/monkey/create"
accept-charset="utf-8" method="post">
```

It means that whether we are opening the monkey's creation form or submitting it, we will always call the `create` action of the `monkey` controller. We should then read how this action is implemented:

```
public function action_create()
{
    if (Input::method() == 'POST')
    {
```

```
            $val = Model_Monkey::validate('create');

            if ($val->run())
            {
                // Saves the model (out of this chapter scope)
            }
            else
            {
                Session::set_flash('error', $val->error());
            }
        }

        $this->template->title = "Monkeys";
        $this->template->content = View::forge('monkey/create');

    }
```

As you can notice, the action is able to know whether or not it is accessed through a POST request by using `Input::method()`. You are recommended to take a look at the official documentation of the `Input` class at `http://fuelphp.com/docs/classes/input.html` (It can be accessed through the FuelPHP website by navigating to **DOCS** | **TABLE OF CONTENTS** | **Core** | **Input**)

`Model_Monkey::validate('create')` returns an object that seems to define whether or not the object can be saved (depending on what `$val->run()` returns). This is a method from the **Monkey** model, so we should look into it. Open `APPPATH/classes/model/monkey.php`:

```
<?php
class Model_Monkey extends Model_Crud
{
    protected static $_table_name = 'monkeys';

    public static function validate($factory)
    {
        $val = Validation::forge($factory);
        $val->add_field('name', 'Name', 'required|max_length[255]');
        $val->add_field('still_here', 'Still Here', 'required');
        $val->add_field('height', 'Height', 'required');
        $val->add_field('description', 'Description', 'required');

        return $val;
    }

}
```

The file contains the `Model_Monkey` class that extends `Model_Crud` and allows us to handle the monkey instances.

First, you can notice the `$_table_name` static attribute that defines the table name where the objects are saved (here, all our monkeys are saved into the `monkeys` table).

And then there is the `validate` static method we are looking for. It returns a `Validation` object, that in our case will check that:

- The `name` attribute is not empty and its length is less than 255 characters
- `still_here`, `height`, and `description` are not empty

For more detail about this class, you are recommended to read the official documentation at `http://fuelphp.com/docs/classes/validation/validation.html` (It can be accessed through the FuelPHP website by navigating to **DOCS** | **TABLE OF CONTENTS** | **Core** | **Validation** | **Introduction**)

In our case, simply comment or remove the following line:

```
$val->add_field('description', 'Description', 'required');
```

You might have read `Session::set_flash` several times in the `Controller_Monkey` controller and `Session::get_flash` several times in the template. Session flash variables have a very limited life span and are generally used to store temporary information, such as notices or errors displayed to the user.

Checking whether the height is a float

It is now easy to check if the height is a float. As we know that monkeys are generally not taller than 4 feet, we can even add a numerical constraint. In the `validate` method of `Model_Monkey`, replace the following line:

```
$val->add_field('height', 'Height', 'required');
```

by

```
$val->add_field(
    'height',
    'Height',
    'required|numeric_between[0,6]'
);
```

Using a checkbox instead of an input for the still_here attribute

This change will be a bit more complex. First, still in the `validate` method of `Model_Monkey`, remove the following line as we won't need this validation:

```
$val->add_field('still_here', 'Still Here', 'required');
```

Now, if you go back to our `create` action in `Controller_Monkey` (located at `APPPATH/classes/controller/monkey.php`), you will see that the template content is set to the view located at `APPPATH/views/monkey/create.php`. If you look at the file content, it is pretty simple:

```
<h2>New Monkey</h2>
<br>

<?php echo render('monkey/_form'); ?>

<p><?php echo Html::anchor('monkey', 'Back'); ?></p>
```

For your information, the `render` method is an alias of `View::render`, and in this case equivalent to `View::forge`. This illustrates that it is possible to render views inside other views. It can be convenient to prevent code repetition; the view located at `APPPATH/views/monkey/edit.php` also renders the same view (`monkey/_form`), and this makes sense since the forms displayed are exactly the same, whether you create a new monkey or edit an existing one.

Since we want to edit the form to replace the `still_here` input by a checkbox, open the view located at `APPPATH/views/monkey/_form.php` and replace the following lines:

```
<?php
echo Form::input(
    'still_here',
    Input::post(
        'still_here',
        isset($monkey) ? $monkey->still_here : ''
    ),
    array(
        'class' => 'col-md-4 form-control',
        'placeholder' => 'Still here'
    )
);
?>
```

By

```
<?php
echo Form::checkbox(
    'still_here',
    1,
    Input::post(
        'still_here',
        isset($monkey) ? $monkey->still_here : true
    )
);
?>
```

In the code above, the first parameter is the name attribute of the checkbox. The second parameter is the value attribute of the checkbox. The third parameter determines whether the checkbox is checked or not. You can notice that, when we create a new monkey (and therefore no monkey is set), the checkbox will be checked by default. You are recommended to read the official documentation for more information about the `Form` class at `http://fuelphp.com/docs/classes/form.html` (It can be accessed through the FuelPHP website by navigating to **DOCS** | **TABLE OF CONTENTS** | **Core** | **Form**)

Finally, you are probably aware that the `still_here` POST attribute won't be defined if the checkbox is unchecked when submitting the form. Thus, we need to define a default value when retrieving the `still_here` POST attribute, not only in the `create` action but also in the `edit` action. In both the methods, replace the following:

```
Input::post('still_here')
```

by

```
Input::post('still_here', 0)
```

Our solution works, but, in most cases, hard-coding a default value is not a good idea. When indicating a default value, for a request parameter or a configuration item, the best is to define this value inside a centralized configuration file and load it from there. Always avoid hard-coding constants, even for default values.

Setting custom routes

Last but not least, we don't want to display FuelPHP's welcome screen when requesting the root URL, but instead the monkeys' listing. For doing that we will have to change the routes' configuration file located at `APPPATH/config/routes.php`.

Replace:

```
'_root_'  => 'welcome/index',
```

By:

```
'_root_'  => 'monkey/index',
```

When requesting:

```
http://my.app/
```

You should now see your monkey listing.

Removing useless routes and files

Now that our project is working as intended, it might be a good idea to clean it:

- Remove `APPPATH/classes/controller/welcome.php` as we don't need this controller anymore
- Remove the `APPPATH/classes/presenter` folder
- Remove the `APPPATH/views/welcome` folder
- And remove the `_404_`, `hello(/:name)?`, `my/welcome/page` keys from the routes' configuration file located at `APPPATH/config/routes.php`.

A few notes about deploying your application

Now that you have a working application, you might want to publish it on hosts. Handling this is quite easy, the longer part being sending the project's files (using FTP, Git, or any other tool depending on your hosting service), but there are a couple of things you should know.

First, you have to set your apache `FUEL_ENV` environment to `production`. An easy way to do that is to edit `public/.htaccess` and uncomment the second line:

```
SetEnv FUEL_ENV production
```

Keep in mind, that in this case you will have two different files between your local environment and your production environment, so it will be prone to human error. You are recommended to read the official documentation at `http://fuelphp.com/docs/general/environments.html` (It can be accessed through the FuelPHP website by navigating to **DOCS** | **TABLE OF CONTENTS** | **FuelPHP** | **Environments**)

If you are using a shared hosting solution, keep in mind that, as explained in *The simplest way* section, you should take additional security precautions

Summary

In this chapter, we have seen the very basics of the FuelPHP framework and we have built our first project. We have learnt how to install FuelPHP, used the oil command line to generate code files and migrate our application, understood how routes work, and seen how models, views, presenters, and controllers interact with each other.

Though you are now able to create an application and implement basic features, you might not be yet ready for more complex projects. In the next chapter, we will improve your skills by using FuelPHP's Object Relational Mapper (ORM).

2

Building a To-do List Application

We saw in the last chapter a few basics of the FuelPHP framework, but there is still a lot to learn to be comfortable with it. We will create here our first real-world application to dive a little bit deeper into the main FuelPHP features. We will create a to-do list application, a common training example when introducing frameworks. Again, it won't be a very complicated application, but this project will be used as a basis to introduce essential FuelPHP components.

By the end of this chapter, you should know the following:

- What is a **Entity Relationship** (**ER**) diagram
- What is an profiler and how to use it
- How to use the `Debug` class
- What is an **Object Relational Mapper** (**ORM**) and how to use it in your project
- How to use the basic operations of `Model_Crud` and `Model_Orm`
- The ORM relations
- What are observers and how to use them
- How to handle Ajax requests

We will assume here, that you have read *Chapter 1, Building Your First FuelPHP Application*, as the very basics of the framework have been explained there. We will also use JavaScript and jQuery for improving the to-do list user interface. Since this book is intended for intermediary web developers, we will assume you have some knowledge about these technologies. If this is not the case, don't worry, we will use them very lightly and you can find a lot of resources about these tools on the web.

Specifications

First of all, let's define what should be expected in our final application as follows:

- A to-do list is created to monitor the progress of a project. A project is described by a name and has many tasks (the to-do list). We will assume here that a user could have many simultaneous projects and, therefore, can create and manage as many projects as he/she wants. Each project can also be deleted.
- A task is described by a name and has a Boolean status ("done" or "not done").
- Tasks are ordered in the project and the user should be able to easily move items in the list using drag and drop.

This is still a simple application, and we won't support any privacy feature such as authentication (this will be addressed in *Chapters 3, Building a Blog Application* and *Chapter 5, Building Your Own Restful API*).

Conception

This step should be pretty straightforward from the specification phase. We will generate the following two models:

- **Project**: This model will only have a name property.
- **Task**: This model will have a name, a status, and a rank property. A project contains many tasks, and each task is related to a project, so we will add an additional column here, named `project_id`. This column will contain the ID of the project each task is associated with.

We can represent our models by the following **ER** diagram:

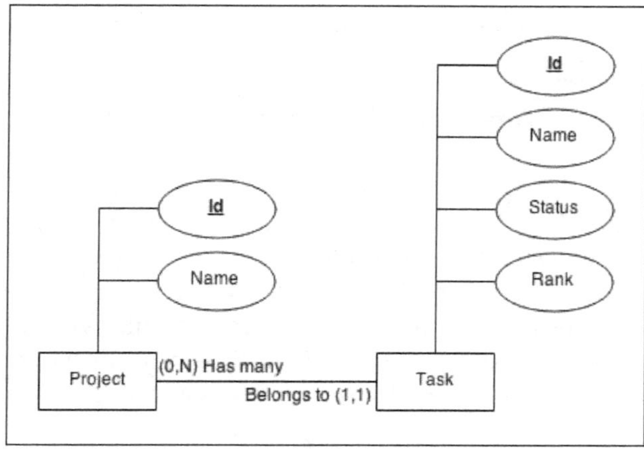

Entity Relationship diagram (Min-Max notation)

An **ER** diagram allows you to describe the data structure of your application. As you noticed, almost everything we wrote earlier can be found in the diagram:

- The models (called entities in ER diagrams), represented by rectangles
- The model's properties (called attributes), represented by ellipses (primary keys are underlined) and linked to models using lines
- The relationships between models, represented by a line from a model to another

We used the Min-Max notation for relations. Here is how to understand it:

On the line joining the **Project** model to the **Task** model, you can read **(0, N) Has many** next to the **Project** rectangle and **Belongs to (1, 1)** next to the **Task** rectangle. The **(0, N)** and **(1, 1)** you can read on the diagram represent the minimum and maximum number of elements an instance can be linked to: in our case, a project can be linked to any number of tasks (between *0* and *N*) and a task can be linked to only one project (between *1* and *1*). The text next to **(0, N)** and **(1, 1)** is the relation's name. Here, we simply used the FuelPHP relation's type we will use (we will explain those relations later in the *ORM relations* section). Even a non-programmer can understand it by reading it as follows: "Each project has many tasks", "Each task belongs to one project".

It can be convenient to draw an ER diagram if you struggle to understand how you can organize your data. We will use this diagram in the upcoming chapters, and it is especially recommended if you want to understand a complex data structure with many models and relations between them. You are recommended to read more on the subject at `http://en.wikipedia.org/wiki/Entity-relationship_model`.

FuelPHP installation and configuration

You first need to:

- Install a new FuelPHP instance
- Configure Apache and your host file to handle it: in this chapter, we will access our application by requesting the URL `http://mytodolists.app`
- Update Composer if necessary
- Create a new database for your application
- And configure FuelPHP in order to allow your application to access this database

These steps have been covered in *Chapter 1, Building Your First FuelPHP Application*, so you might want to take a look at it.

This project will also need the ORM package, and since it is already installed, we just need to enable it. For doing this, simply open the `APPPATH/config/config.php` file and insert the following at the end of the returned array:

```
'always_load'  => array(
  'packages'  => array(
    'orm',
  ),
),
```

Or you can uncomment the appropriate lines. This will load the ORM package every time the FuelPHP instance is loaded.

> You can also load a package in an ad hoc manner, using the `Package::load` method. This will be addressed in *Chapter 3, Building a Blog Application*.

Scaffolding

We will now generate, as in *Chapter 1, Building Your First FuelPHP Application*, the necessary code to handle our objects.

Let's first generate the scaffold of the project model:

```
php oil generate scaffold/orm project name:string
```

The command should print the following output:

```
Creating migration: APPPATH/migrations/001_create_projects.php
Creating model: APPPATH/classes/model/project.php
Creating controller: APPPATH/classes/controller/project.php
Creating view: APPPATH/views/project/index.php
Creating view: APPPATH/views/project/view.php
Creating view: APPPATH/views/project/create.php
Creating view: APPPATH/views/project/edit.php
Creating view: APPPATH/views/project/_form.php
Creating view: APPPATH/views/template.php
```

Note that we used `scaffold/orm` instead of `scaffold/crud` in *Chapter 1, Building Your First FuelPHP Application*: this way, oil will generate code files that use the ORM package. For instance, we will see later that the generated model will extend `Orm\Model` instead of `Model_Crud`.

We now need to generate the model for managing our tasks. We won't use scaffold here because we plan to manage tasks on the project's visualization page, so we only need the model.

```
php oil generate model/orm task name:string status:boolean rank:int
project_id:int
```

This command should print the following output:

```
Creating model: APPPATH/classes/model/task.php
Creating migration: APPPATH/migrations/002_create_tasks.php
```

As you can notice, we generated here only the model and the migration file. All you have to do now is to execute the migration files:

```
php oil refine migrate
```

Routes configuration

You can now manage your project by requesting the URL `http://mytodolists.app/project`.

Since this is our point of entry, we would like to access this page when requesting the root URL `http://mytodolists.app/`.

As we saw in *Chapter 1, Building Your First FuelPHP Application*, you just need to edit the `APPPATH/config/routes.php` configuration file. Replace `'_root_' => 'welcome/index'` with `'_root_' => 'project/index'`.

The profiler

Since we will need the profiler for the next section, we will introduce it here. FuelPHP supplies a profiler that enables you to get a sense of what is going on when you request a web page. It can indeed show many performance metrics, executed SQL requests, current logs, session, and POST / GET variables.

You will need to activate it though. It is wise to only use this tool in development mode, since otherwise you can have serious security issues. For doing that, you first need to create the `APPPATH/config/development/config.php` configuration file and write the following content:

```
<?php

return array(
    'profiling'  => true,
);
```

You also need to edit the `APPPATH/config/development/db.php` configuration file in order to see database queries (the profiler won't show them otherwise): at the end of the `default` array, add `'profiling' => true,`.

If you now request your root URL `http://mytodolists.app/`, you will see a black rectangle labeled **Code Profiler** at the bottom right of the screen. If you click on it, you should see the following:

The following describes the several tabs you can access:

- **NB Console** (**NB** being the number of logs): This tab displays all logs. For instance, if you add `Log::info('Index Action', 'This is a test');` at the beginning of the index action of the Project controller and then refresh the web page, you should see a new item appear in this tab .

- **TIME Load Time** (**TIME** being the web page total load time): This tab displays logs associated with time markers. Note that these logs also appear in the first tab. For instance, if you add `Profiler::mark('Index Action');` at the beginning of the index action of the Project controller, you should see a new item appear in this tab.
- **NB Queries Database** (**NB** being the number of queries): This tab displays database queries that have been executed when loading the web page. For each query, its analysis and its call trace are displayed. The number of duplicates is also displayed, and you can spot queries that appear to duplicate a previous one by seeing the word **DUPLICATE** next to **Speed**.
- **SIZE Memory Used** (**SIZE** being the amount of used memory): This tab displays logs associated with memory markers. Note that these logs also appear in the first tab. For instance, if you add `Profiler::mark_memory($this, 'Controller_Project object');` at the beginning of the index action of the Project controller, you should see a new item appear in this tab.
- **NB Files Included** (**NB** being the number of files): This tab displays all files (code or configuration) that have been loaded for displaying the web page.
- **NB Config items loaded** (**NB** being the number of items): This tab displays the configuration items (not the files) that have been loaded. For instance, if you load a configuration file that contains an associated array with 5 keys, 5 new items will appear in this tab.
- **NB Session vars loaded**, **NB GET vars loaded**, **NB POST vars loaded**: These tabs display request and session variables. For instance, a new item should appear in the **NB GET vars loaded** tab if you request the URL `http://mytodolists.app/?param=test`.

Models, relations, and the ORM

We have now done the preliminary steps: we installed FuelPHP, configured it, generated the scaffold for managing the projects, and created the task model. We didn't connect the two models though, and we haven't yet displayed tasks anywhere. More importantly, we haven't explained how to load objects until now. This is the aim of this section.

Differences between CRUD and ORM

As we explained earlier, we used oil to generate code, but instead of using `scaffold/crud` as in *Chapter 1, Building Your First FuelPHP Application*, we used `scaffold/orm` and `model/orm`. If you take a look at the files (controllers, views, and models), you will only see minor changes, except for the model files:

- The `$_table_name` attribute is no longer declared. It is still used by `Orm\Model` though, but it takes a default value that depends on the model name, so you can still define it if you want to use a custom table name.
- The `$_properties` attribute has been added. This attribute contains all the properties (linked to table columns) the model has to manage. Defining this attribute is not compulsory, but not doing so might reduce your website performance, as FuelPHP will need to synchronize the model with the table structure. Note that `Model_Crud` also uses this attribute, but the code generated by oil simply doesn't define it.
- The `$_observers` attribute has also been added. This attribute defines used observers and their parameters. We will explain what observers are and how to use them in the next section.

The FuelPHP ORM

ORM stands for Object Relational Mapper. It allows developers to do the following two things:

- It maps table rows to objects. For doing that, the ORM provides several functions to extract specific table rows and transform them to PHP objects. Other methods also exist that allow developers to save objects to table rows. The `find` and the `save` methods are both examples.
- It allows you to establish relations between models. In this chapter's project, we have created two models, **Project** and **Task**, and there exists a relationship between them: a project can have many tasks, and each task is associated to a project. When defining these relations to the ORM, it will enable methods allowing developers to access a project's tasks more easily for instance.

In short, the purpose of the ORM is to simplify the job of the developer. Beyond the preceding two main points, the ORM will also handle some security issues (as SQL injection) and handle observers that can affect how some properties are saved for instance. In a general manner, FuelPHP's ORM follows the active record pattern closely.

DB and ORM basics

Note that most methods we are going to use here are working on `Orm/Model`, as well as `Model_Crud`.

First, we need to create a PHP file that will test our code. We could have used the oil console here, and in most cases you should, but in this instance we won't because we want to see the executed SQL requests (we plan to use the profiler for doing so). Please note that this file should not be pushed into production. Create a file located at `public/test.php` with the following content:

```
<?php

// Fuel initialization (inspired from index.php)
define('DOCROOT', __DIR__.DIRECTORY_SEPARATOR);
define('APPPATH', realpath(__DIR__.'/../fuel/app/')
                    .DIRECTORY_SEPARATOR);
define('PKGPATH', realpath(__DIR__.'/../fuel/packages/')
                    .DIRECTORY_SEPARATOR);
define('COREPATH', realpath(__DIR__.'/../fuel/core/')
                    .DIRECTORY_SEPARATOR);
defined('FUEL_START_TIME') or define('FUEL_START_TIME',
                                    microtime(true));
defined('FUEL_START_MEM') or define('FUEL_START_MEM',
                                    memory_get_usage());
require COREPATH.'classes'.DIRECTORY_SEPARATOR.'autoloader.php';
class_alias('Fuel\\Core\\Autoloader', 'Autoloader');
require APPPATH.'bootstrap.php';

echo 'FuelPHP is initialized...';
```

The preceding code initializes FuelPHP (it is necessary when you have a PHP script in the public folder and you want to use FuelPHP features). This script should be accessible when requesting the following URL and should display **FuelPHP is initialized...**: `http://mytodolists.app/test.php`.

All the examples that follow must be progressively appended to the file. For those of you who didn't use any ORM yet, it is recommended you append the code inside each section, refresh, and take a deep look at the web page output and the executed queries in the profiler. Please note that this is just an introduction; to learn more about the ORM, you are recommended to read the official documentation at `http://fuelphp.com/docs/packages/orm/intro.html`.

Executing queries without the ORM

You should first know that it is possible to execute a query without the ORM. Using it is supposed to simplify your life but it is not compulsory. In some cases, for instance changes affecting many rows, you should not even use the ORM. Another instance is when you want to empty a table:

```
// --- Executing queries without the ORM
\DB::query('TRUNCATE TABLE `projects`;')->execute();
\DB::query('TRUNCATE TABLE `tasks`;')->execute();
// \DBUtil::truncate_table('projects'); is also possible
```

Creating new objects

The following example shows how to create new projects:

```
// --- Creating new objects
$project = Model_Project::forge(); // = new Model_Project()
$project->name = 'First project';
$project->save();

// You can also set properties when calling the forge method
$project = Model_Project::forge(
    array('name' => 'Second project')
);
$project->save();
```

Finding specific objects

This is how you find the first object in a table:

```
// --- Finding specific objects
$project = Model_Project::find('first');
\Debug::dump('first', $project);
```

If you refresh your web page now, you should see the following gray box:

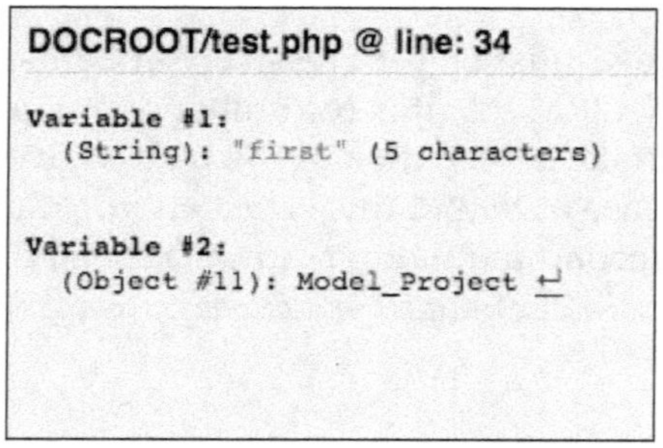

DOCROOT/test.php @ line: 34

```
Variable #1:
  (String): "first" (5 characters)

Variable #2:
  (Object #11): Model_Project ↵
```

If you unfold **Model_Project** by clicking on ↵, and then **_data**, you should see that this is indeed the first project:

```
Variable #2:
  (Object #11): Model_Project ↵

    protected _properties (Array, 4 elements) ↵
    protected _observers (Array, 2 elements) ↵
    protected _has_many (Array, 1 element) ↵
    protected _primary_key (Array, 1 element) ↵
    protected _to_array_exclude (Array, 0 elements)
    protected _table_names_cached (Array, 1 element) ↵
    protected _properties_cached (Array, 1 element) ↵
    protected _views_cached (Array, 0 elements)
    protected _relations_cached (Array, 1 element) ↵
    protected _observers_cached (Array, 1 element) ↵
    protected _cached_objects (Array, 1 element) ↵
    protected _valid_relations (Array, 4 elements) ↵
    protected to_array_references (Array, 0 elements)
    protected _is_new (Boolean): false
    protected _frozen (Boolean): false
    protected _sanitization_enabled (Boolean): false
    protected _data (Array, 4 elements) ↵
         name (String): "First project" (13 characters)
         updated_at (Integer): 1411384397
         created_at (Integer): 1411384397
         id (String): "1" (1 characters)
```

If you take a look at the console, you can also confirm this by seeing the executed SQL request:

```
SELECT … FROM `projects` AS `t0` ORDER BY `t0`.`id` ASC
LIMIT 1
```

You can also load the last object:

```
$project = Model_Project::find('last');
\Debug::dump('last', $project);
```

The executed request should be as follows:

```
SELECT … FROM `projects` AS `t0` ORDER BY `t0`.`id` DESC
LIMIT 1
```

Or you can load a project by specifying an ID:

```
$project = Model_Project::find(1);
\Debug::dump('with id = 1', $project);
```

You can note here that no request was executed. That is because the ORM caches loaded objects and the project has already been loaded in a previous request. Otherwise, the following request should have been executed:

```
SELECT … FROM `projects` AS `t0` WHERE `t0`.`id` = 1
LIMIT 1
```

Updating an object

Here is how we update an existing object (here, we change the name of the project with `id = 1`):

```
// --- Updating an object
$project = Model_Project::find(1); // Load project with id = 1
$project->name = 'First one';
$project->save();
```

Executed request:

```
UPDATE `projects` SET `name` = 'First one' WHERE `id` = '1'
```

Deleting an object

We can delete a project by calling:

```
// --- Deleting an object.
$project = Model_Project::find(1); // Load project with id = 1
$project->delete();
```

Executed request:

```
DELETE FROM `projects` WHERE `id` = '1' LIMIT 1
```

Loading several objects

We can load several objects at once. The following example shows how we can load all project instances:

```
// --- Loading several objects
// First creating an additional project for a more interesting
// result
$project = Model_Project::forge();
$project->name = 'Third project';
$project->save();

// Finding all projects
$projects = Model_Project::find('all');
\Debug::dump('all', $projects);
```

In that case, `$projects` will be an associative array of projects, the key being the project's ID, and the value being the associated project. The executed request is as follows:

```
SELECT … FROM `projects` AS `t0`
```

Using method chaining

The `query` method is an equivalent of the `find` method, but allows you to fetch objects using method chaining.

Here is how you can find all the project instances using the `query` method:

```
$projects = Model_Project::query()->get();
\Debug::dump('all (using query)', $projects);
```

The executed request is the same as previously executed:

```
SELECT … FROM `projects` AS `t0`
```

More complex requests

It is also possible to execute much more complex requests. First, let's add various tasks:

```
// Creating sample tasks
Model_Task::forge(array('name' => 'Marketing plan',
    'status' => 0, 'rank' => 0, 'project_id' => 2))->save();

Model_Task::forge(array('name' => 'Update website',
    'status' => 1, 'rank' => 1, 'project_id' => 2))->save();

Model_Task::forge(array('name' => 'Improve website template',
    'status' => 1, 'rank' => 2, 'project_id' => 2))->save();

Model_Task::forge(array('name' => 'Contact director',
    'status' => 0, 'rank' => 0, 'project_id' => 3))->save();

Model_Task::forge(array('name' => 'Buy a new computer',
    'status' => 1, 'rank' => 1, 'project_id' => 3))->save();
```

Now that we have created various tasks, we will be able to test the second parameter of the `find` method.

Let's get the first task with `project_id = 2`:

```
$task = Model_Task::find('first',
    array(
        'where' => array(
            array('project_id' => 2)
        )
    )
);
\Debug::dump('first with project_id = 2', $task);
```

Or using the `query` method:

```
$task = Model_Task::query()
    ->where('project_id', 2)
    ->order_by('id', 'asc') // Will be introduced shortly
    ->get_one();
\Debug::dump('first with project_id = 2 (using query)', $task);
```

Executed request:

```
SELECT … FROM `tasks` AS `t0` WHERE (`t0`.`project_id` = 2)
ORDER BY `t0`.`id` ASC LIMIT 1
```

Let's now get all tasks with `project_id = 2`:

```
$tasks = Model_Task::find('all',
    array(
        'where' => array(
            array('project_id' => 2)
        )
    )
);
\Debug::dump('project_id = 2', $tasks);
```

Or using the `query` method:

```
$tasks = Model_Task::query()
    ->where('project_id', 2)
    ->get();
\Debug::dump('project_id = 2 (using query)', $tasks);
```

Executed request:

```
SELECT … FROM `tasks` AS `t0` WHERE (`t0`.`project_id` = 2)
```

It is also possible to get all tasks with `project_id = 2` and `status = 1`:

```
$tasks = Model_Task::find('all',
    array(
        'where' => array(
            array('project_id' => 2),
            array('status' => 1)
        )
    )
);
\Debug::dump('project_id = 2 & status = 1', $tasks);
```

Or using the `query` method:

```
$tasks = Model_Task::query()
    ->where('project_id', 2)
    ->where('status', 1)
    ->get();
\Debug::dump('project_id = 2 & status = 1 (using query)', $tasks);
```

Executed request:

```
SELECT … FROM `tasks` AS `t0` WHERE (`t0`.`project_id` = 2)
AND (`t0`.`status` = 1)
```

This is how we get all tasks with `project_id > 2` and `status = 1`:

```
$tasks = Model_Task::find('all',
    array(
        'where' => array(
            array('project_id', '>', 2),
            array('status' => 1)
        )
    )
);
\Debug::dump('project_id > 2 & status = 1', $tasks);
```

Or using the `query` method:

```
$tasks = Model_Task::query()
    ->where('project_id', '>', 2)
    ->where('status', 1)
    ->get();
\Debug::dump('project_id > 2 & status = 1 (using query)', $tasks);
```

Executed request:

```
SELECT … FROM `tasks` AS `t0` WHERE `t0`.`project_id` > 2
AND (`t0`.`status` = 1)
```

This is how we get tasks with `project_id > 2` or `status = 1`:

```
$tasks = Model_Task::find('all',
    array(
        'where' => array(
            array('project_id' => 2),
            'or' => array('status' => 1)
        )
    )
);
\Debug::dump('project_id = 2 or status = 1', $tasks);
```

Or using the `query` method:

```
$tasks = Model_Task::query()
    ->where('project_id', '=', 2)
    ->or_where('status', 1)
    ->get();
\Debug::dump('project_id = 2 or status = 1 (query)', $tasks);
```

Executed request:

```
SELECT … FROM `tasks` AS `t0` WHERE (`t0`.`project_id` = 2) OR
 ((`t0`.`status` = 1))
```

This is how we get tasks that name contains the word `website`:

```
$tasks = Model_Task::find('all',
    array(
        'where' => array(
            array(
                'name',
                'LIKE',
                '%website%'
            ),
        )
    )
);
\Debug::dump('name contains "website"', $tasks);
```

Or using the `query` method:

```
$tasks = Model_Task::query()
    ->where('name', 'LIKE', '%website%')
    ->get();
\Debug::dump('name contains "website" (using query)', $tasks);
```

Executed request:

```
SELECT … FROM `tasks` AS `t0` WHERE `t0`.`name` LIKE
'%website%'
```

You can also specify an order:

```
$tasks = Model_Task::find('all',
    array(
        'where' => array(
            array(
                'name',
                'LIKE',
                '%website%'
            ),
        ),
        'order_by' => array(
            'rank' => 'ASC'
        ),
    )
);
\Debug::dump(
    'name contains "website" ordered by the rank column',
    $tasks
);
```

Or using the `query` method:

```
$tasks = Model_Task::query()
    ->where('name', 'LIKE', '%website%')
    ->order_by('rank', 'ASC')
    ->get();
\Debug::dump(
    'name contains "website" ordered by the rank column (query)',
    $tasks
);
```

Executed request:

```
SELECT … FROM `tasks` AS `t0` WHERE `t0`.`name` LIKE
'%website%' ORDER BY `t0`.`rank` ASC
```

You have probably noticed that using the `query` method generally allows you to write a much more concise and readable code. Therefore, you are recommended to use the `query` method for complex requests. In most cases though, using `find` or `query` doesn't make much difference, so use your best judgment.

As already stated, this is just a very small introduction to the ORM. There are many more keys other than `where` and `order_by`, and we will see some of those later (as the `related` key for instance). You are recommended to take a look at the official documentation of the ORM package at `http://fuelphp.com/docs/packages/orm/intro.html`.

We also used the `Debug` and `DB` classes. Knowing them can be useful. Again, feel free to read their official documentation, which is available at the following links:

- `http://fuelphp.com/docs/classes/debug.html`
- `http://fuelphp.com/docs/classes/database/db.html`

ORM relations

It is time for us to define the relationship between tasks and projects. As we explained earlier, defining them activates useful features that make the job of the developers easy and improve performance. Relations must be defined inside a model. For instance, we will define a relation in the **Project** model in order to access each project's tasks, and we will also define another relation in the **Task** model in order to access each task's associated project. There are 4 relation types:

- **Belongs To**: When you define a *belongs to* relationship in model A toward model B, each model A's instance can only be associated with one model B's instance. You will generally need to create a column in model A's table that will be used to connect instances. In this chapter, the **Task** model has a *belongs to* relationship with the **Project** model. Indeed, each task is associated with only one project, and the `project_id` column in the tasks' table is used to connect each instance. A concrete example is that a task with `project_id = 1` will belong to the project with `id = 1`.

- **Has many**: When you define a *has many* relationship in model A toward model B, each model A's instance can be associated with many model B's instances. You will generally need to create a column in model B's table that will be used to connect instances. In this chapter, the **Project** model has a *has many* relationship with the **Task** model; indeed, each project can have many tasks, and the `project_id` column in the tasks' table is used to connect each instance. A concrete example is that a project with `id = 1` can have many tasks with `project_id = 1`.
- **Has one**: A way to understand this relation is to think of it as a special case of a has many relationship, except that each model A's instance can be associated with only one model B's instance. If we defined a *has one* relationship (instead of has many) in the **Project** model toward the **Task** model, we would still need to define the `project_id` column inside the tasks' table, but in that case only a single task could be associated to each project.
- **Many to Many**: When you define a *many to many* relationship in model A toward model B, each model A's instance can be associated with many model B's instances and each model B's instance can be associated with many model A's instances. In that case, you will need to create an intermediary table.

You are recommended to read the official documentation about relations at `http://fuelphp.com/docs/packages/orm/relations/intro.html`.

Defining relations inside the models

Now that we have introduced the different types of relations, let's define them in our model.

First, open `APPPATH/classes/model/task.php` and add the following attribute in the `Model_Task` class:

```
protected static $_belongs_to = array('project');
```

Note that this is equivalent to the following code:

```
protected static $_belongs_to = array(
    'project' => array(
        'model_to'          => 'Model_Project',
        'key_from'          => 'project_id',
        'key_to'            => 'id',
        'cascade_save'      => true,
        'cascade_delete'    => false,
    )
);
```

In the first case, the `model_to`, `key_from`, and `key_to` keys are inferred from the array value (`'project'`). If not defined, `cascade_save` default value is `true` and `cascade_delete` default value is `false`. These keys define the following relation characteristics:

- The `model_to` key: The model across the relation (model B)
- The `key_from` key: The model's (model A's) column used to connect instances
- The `key_to` key: The model across the relation's (model B's) column used to connect instances
- The `cascade_save` key: If true, each time a model's instance is saved, the related instances will also be saved
- The `cascade_delete` key: If true, each time a model's instance is deleted, the related instances will also be deleted. Beware of this feature, as you could end up deleting more information than you really want.

Now, open `APPPATH/classes/model/project.php` and add the following attribute in the `Model_Project` class:

```
protected static $_has_many = array('tasks');
```

As with the `belongs_to` relation, it is equivalent to the following code:

```
protected static $_has_many = array(
    'tasks' => array(
        'model_to'          => 'Model_Task',
        'key_from'          => 'id',
        'key_to'            => 'project_id',
        'cascade_save'      => true,
        'cascade_delete'    => false,
    )
);
```

Testing the relations

To better illustrate this, let's test how these relations work by appending code in our `public/test.php` file.

Getting objects' relations

First let's load a task's instance with `id = 1`, and then its related project. You can notice that we set the `from_cache` parameter to `false`. This has been done to prevent FuelPHP to load the instance from the cache because we want to display all executed requests. In most cases, you are not recommended to use this parameter.

```
$task = Model_Task::find(1, array('from_cache' => false));
$project = $task->project;
\Debug::dump('Project of task with id = 1', $project);
```

In the second line, we loaded the task's project by accessing the `project` attribute. This is the relation name we declared in the `Model_Task` class. In a general manner, if you want to access a related instance through the relation `RELATION_NAME`, you can get it using `$item->RELATION_NAME`.

You can see that the following two requests were executed:

1. The first request was executed in the `find` method in order to load the task with `id = 1`.

   ```
   SELECT … FROM `tasks` AS `t0` WHERE `t0`.`id` = 1
      LIMIT 1
   ```

2. The second request was executed when getting `$task->project`: in this case the project with `id = $task->project_id` was retrieved:

   ```
   SELECT … FROM `projects` AS `t0` WHERE `t0`.`id` =
      '2' LIMIT 1
   ```

Let's load a project's instance with `id = 2`, and then its related tasks:

```
$project = Model_Project::find(
    2,
    array('from_cache' => false)
);
$tasks = $project->tasks;
\Debug::dump('Tasks of project with id = 2', $tasks);
```

Two requests have been executed:

1. The first request loads the project's instance:

   ```
   SELECT … FROM `projects` AS `t0` WHERE `t0`.`id` = 2
      LIMIT 1
   ```

2. The second request loads the project's associated tasks:

   ```
   SELECT … FROM `tasks` AS `t0` WHERE
      `t0`.`project_id` = '2'
   ```

When relations are defined, the `find` method allows you to improve performance by reducing the number of SQL requests. For instance, if you do the following:

```
$projects = Model_Project::find(
    'all',
    array('from_cache' => false)
);
foreach ($projects as $project) {
    \Debug::dump(
        'LOOP 1: Tasks of project with id = '.$project->id,
        $project->tasks
    );
}
```

Three requests will be executed, which are given as follows:

- One for loading all the projects

  `SELECT … FROM `projects` AS `t0``

- Two for loading `$project->tasks` for each project in `$projects`

```
SELECT … FROM `tasks` AS `t0` WHERE
  `t0`.`project_id` = '2'

SELECT … FROM `tasks` AS `t0` WHERE
  `t0`.`project_id` = '3'
```

Three requests don't seem a lot, but if you load 100 projects this means that you will execute 101 requests and this can lead to serious performance issues.

The `find` method allows you to address this issue through the `related` key:

```
$projects = Model_Project::find(
    'all',
    array(
        'related' => 'tasks'
    )
);
foreach ($projects as $project) {
    \Debug::dump(
        'LOOP 2: Tasks of project with id = '.$project->id,
        $project->tasks
    );
}
```

Here, only one request has been executed. The FuelPHP's ORM has loaded the relation when executing the find method by joining the tasks' table in the request.

Executed request:

```
SELECT … FROM `projects` AS `t0` LEFT JOIN
`tasks` AS `t1` ON (`t0`.`id` = `t1`.`project_id`)
```

Updating objects' relations

If you want to update a relation, you can simply update the column supporting it. For instance, the following code loads the task with `id = 1` and makes it belong to the project with `id = 3`:

```
$task = Model_Task::find(1, array('from_cache' => false));
$task->project_id = 3;
$task->save();
```

Two requests will be executed, which are given as follows:

1. The first request loads the task:

   ```
   SELECT … FROM `tasks` AS `t0` WHERE `t0`.`id` = 1 LIMIT 1
   ```

2. The second updates the `project_id` column of the task:

   ```
   UPDATE `tasks` SET `project_id` = '3',
       `updated_at` = 1404729671 WHERE `id` = '1'
   ```

Though it executes more SQL requests, we could also have written the following:

```
$task = Model_Task::find(1, array('from_cache' => false));
$task->project = Model_Project::find(
    3,
    array('from_cache' => false)
);
$task->save();
```

Four requests will be executed, which are given as follows:

1. The first request loads the task (executed by `Model_Task::find(...)`):

   ```
   SELECT … FROM `tasks` AS `t0` WHERE `t0`.`id` = 1 LIMIT 1
   ```

2. The second request loads the project we want to associate to the task (executed by `Model_Project::find(...)`):

   ```
   SELECT … FROM `projects` AS `t0` WHERE
       `t0`.`id` = 3 LIMIT 1
   ```

3. The third request loads the existing project associated to the task (executed by `$task->project`):

   ```
   SELECT … FROM `projects` AS `t0` WHERE
      `t0`.`id` = '2' LIMIT 1
   ```

4. The fourth request updates the `project_id` column of the task (executed by `$task->save()`):

   ```
   UPDATE `tasks` SET `project_id` = '3',
      `updated_at` = 1404729671 WHERE `id` = '1'
   ```

It is also possible to affect a new project to a task:

```
$task = Model_Task::find(1, array('from_cache' => false));
$task->project = Model_Project::forge();
$task->project->name = 'Fourth project';
$task->save();
```

In that case, the ORM will create a new project and then assign the correct ID to the `project_id` attribute.

Four requests will be executed, which are given as follows:

1. The first request loads the task (executed by `Model_Task::find(...)`):

   ```
   SELECT … FROM `tasks` AS `t0` WHERE `t0`.`id` = 1 LIMIT 1
   ```

2. The second request loads the existing project associated to the task (executed by `$task->project`):

   ```
   SELECT … FROM `projects` AS `t0` WHERE
      `t0`.`id` = '3' LIMIT 1
   ```

3. The third request creates the new project (executed by `$task->save()`):

   ```
   INSERT INTO `projects` (`name`, `created_at`,
      `updated_at`) VALUES ('Fourth project', 1404729796,
      1404729796)
   ```

4. The fourth request updates the `project_id` column of the task (executed by `$task->save()`):

   ```
   UPDATE `tasks` SET `project_id` = '4', `updated_at`
      = 1404729796 WHERE `id` = '1'
   ```

Similarly, it is possible to affect a new task to a project:

```
$project = Model_Project::find(
    2,
    array('from_cache' => false)
```

```
);
$task                = Model_Task::forge();
$task->name          = 'Buy a new mouse';
$task->status        = 0;
$task->rank          = 2;
$project->tasks[]    = $task;
$project->save();
```

Three requests will be executed, which are given as follows:

1. The first request loads the project (executed by `Model_Project::find(...)`):

   ```
   SELECT … FROM `projects` AS `t0` WHERE `t0`.`id` = 2
      LIMIT 1
   ```

2. The second request loads the existing tasks associated to the project (executed by `$project->tasks`):

   ```
   SELECT … FROM `tasks` AS `t0` WHERE
      `t0`.`project_id` = '2'
   ```

3. The third request creates the new task (executed by `$project->save()`):

   ```
   INSERT INTO `tasks` (`name`, `status`, `rank`,
      `project_id`, `created_at`, `updated_at`) VALUES
      ('Buy a new mouse', 0, 2, '2', 1404731559, null)
   ```

If you take a precise look at `$project->tasks`, you will notice that it is an associated array, the keys being the instances ID and the values being the instances. Thus, this is how you can update a specific task through relations:

```
$project = Model_Project::find(
    2,
    array('from_cache' => false)
);
$project->tasks[6]->name = 'Buy an optical mouse';
$project->save();
```

It will change the name of the task with `id = 6` to `'Buy an optical mouse'` (if this task exists and its `project_id` is equal to 2).

Three requests will be executed, which are given as follows:

1. The first request loads the project (executed by `Model_Project::find(...)`):

   ```
   SELECT … FROM `projects` AS `t0` WHERE `t0`.`id` = 2
      LIMIT 1
   ```

2. The second request loads the existing tasks associated to the project (executed by `$project->tasks`):

   ```
   SELECT … FROM `tasks` AS `t0` WHERE
      `t0`.`project_id` = '2'
   ```

3. The third request updates the task's `name` column (executed by `$project->save()`):

   ```
   UPDATE `tasks` SET `name` = 'Buy an optical mouse',
      `updated_at` = 1404732349 WHERE `id` = '6'
   ```

It is also possible to disconnect two related items. This example is not adapted or useful for our project, but it is important to know that you can do this. Let's try to disconnect the task with `id = 4` from the project with `id = 3`:

```
$project = Model_Project::find(
    3,
    array('from_cache' => false)
);
unset($project->tasks[4]);
$project->save();
```

Executed requests:

1. The first request loads the project (executed by `Model_Project::find(...)`):

   ```
   SELECT … FROM `projects` AS `t0` WHERE `t0`.`id` = 3 LIMIT
     1
   ```

2. The second request loads the existing tasks associated to the project (executed by `$project->tasks`):

   ```
   SELECT … FROM `tasks` AS `t0` WHERE
      `t0`.`project_id` = '3'
   ```

3. The third request attempts to disconnect the task with `id = 4` from the project (executed by `$project->save()`):

   ```
   UPDATE `tasks` SET `project_id` = null,
      `updated_at` = 1404803182 WHERE `id` = '4'
   ```

If you take a look at the executed requests, this code is not adapted to our project because:

- For it to correctly work, we should allow the `project_id` column to be null, and that isn't the case right now
- In our application, a task belonging to no project would make no sense

In other cases, doing that can be legitimate though. Again, this is only a short introduction to the ORM's relations, and you are recommended to read the official documentation at `http://fuelphp.com/docs/packages/orm/relations/intro.html`.

Observers and events

You have probably noticed in the previous section that, when saving an object, some additional values were saved in the `created_at` and `updated_at` columns without us specifying anything. For instance:

```
INSERT INTO `projects` (`name`, `created_at`, `updated_at`) VALUES
 ('Third project', 1404729796, 1404729796);
```

This happens because of the observers defined in the models. Observers override some model behaviors; for example, they can change properties' values before committing the changes to the database, or prevent the object from being saved if some conditions are met. Let's take a look at the observers defined in `Model_Project`:

```
protected static $_observers = array(
    'Orm\Observer_CreatedAt' => array(
        'events' => array('before_insert'),
        'mysql_timestamp' => false,
    ),
    'Orm\Observer_UpdatedAt' => array(
        'events' => array('before_save'),
        'mysql_timestamp' => false,
    ),
);
```

You can notice that two observers are defined: `Orm\Observer_CreatedAt` and `Orm\Observer_UpdatedAt`. They handle the `created_at` and `updated_at` columns, respectively, setting their value to the current timestamp when the object is created or updated. Observers can have custom parameters such as `mysql_timestamp`, which defines if a MySQL timestamp is saved instead of a UNIX one.

The `events` parameter is common to all observers and defines which events they should be connected to. Events are methods called in behaviors when something happens to an object; for instance, when you save an object, the ORM will try to call its behaviors' `before_save` method before changes are committed to the database. There are several events, such as `after_create` or `after_save`. You can read the full descriptive list in the official documentation at `http://fuelphp.com/docs/packages/orm/observers/creating.html#/event_names`

In order to learn more, you are also recommended to read the introduction to observers in the official documentation at `http://fuelphp.com/docs/packages/orm/observers/intro.html`

Implementation of the to-do list

Now that we explained the essential ORM features and implemented our relations, it is finally time to build our to-do list. This section assumes you have executed the complete `public/test.php` script at least once.

Allowing the user to see and change tasks' status

First, we will display the associated tasks when viewing a project's details. For instance, this web page should display all tasks of project with `id = 2` after the project's name:

`http://mytodolists.app/project/view/2`

In order to do that, we can, as we did in *Chapter 1, Building Your First FuelPHP Application*, dissect the URL and deduce that, in this case, the view action of the **Project** controller is executed. The action displays `project/view`; thus, we have to edit `APPPATH/views/project/view.php`. Add the following code under the first paragraph displaying the project's name:

```
<?php echo render('task/list', array('project' => $project)); ?>
```

The `render(...)` method is an alias for `View::forge(...)->render()`, and thus the preceding code displays the `task/list` view. Create the `APPPATH/views/task/list.php` view file (you have to create the `task` folder) and set its content to:

```
<ul id="todo_list" data-project_id="<?php echo $project->id; ?>">
    <?php foreach ($project->tasks as $task) {
            $input_id = 'todo_item_'.$task->id;
    ?>
        <li>
            <input
                type="checkbox"
                autocomplete="off"
                id="<?php echo $input_id; ?>"
                data-task_id="<?php echo $task->id; ?>"
                <?php echo $task->status ? 'checked' : ''; ?>
            >
```

```
            <label for="<?php echo $input_id; ?>">
                <?php echo $task->name; ?>
            </label>
        </li>
    <?php } ?>
</ul>
```

This code should be pretty straightforward; it displays an HTML list of the project's tasks. Each item displays the name in a label linked to a checkbox displaying its status. We can make the two following observations:

- We defined the `data-project_id` attribute inside the `ul` element. It will be later used by our JavaScript code to easily retrieve the project's ID. The same goes for the `data-task_id` attribute for each checkbox.
- You can notice we printed `$task->name` without escaping the string. You could think that this is a security breach because `$task->name` could contain HTML tags such as the `<script>` tag and therefore would be prone to XSS injections. However, it isn't because when you use the `View::forge` method, all parameters (even model properties) are, by default, processed (escaped) to prevent such security flaws. You can disable this behavior though (we will see in *Chapter 3, Building a Blog Application*, that sometimes we have to), and in that case FuelPHP provides the `e` method to manually escape variables.

> It is recommended to separate your views into small view files, each displaying a specific area of your web page. We just did it by creating an additional view for displaying the task lists. We could have gone even further by creating a view file that displays a single task and then rendering it for each item in the tasks' list.

We can now see our to-do items. But if we click on our checkboxes, it doesn't synchronize with our server, and if we refresh our web page, we can see that items are back to their old status. We will use a bit of JavaScript and jQuery in order to synchronize the checkboxes with the website.

Create a JavaScript file at `public/assets/js/website.js`.

We first have to include it in the template. Open `APPPATH/views/template.php` and add before the end of the `head` tag the following:

```
<?php
echo Asset::js(array(
    'http://code.jquery.com/jquery-1.11.2.min.js',
```

```
        'http://code.jquery.com/ui/1.11.2/jquery-ui.min.js',
        'website.js'
));
?>
```

The preceding code includes three JavaScript files into the template:

- The first two lines are the jQuery and jQuery UI scripts that we will need.
- The third one is the script containing our JavaScript code. Note that you didn't have to write the complete path. The `Asset::js` method automatically searches for the file in the `public/assets/js` folder. You should know it is possible to specify additional directories to search JavaScript and CSS files using the `Asset::add_path` method if necessary. You are recommended to read the official documentation at `http://fuelphp.com/docs/classes/asset/usage.html`.

As we will need to know our base URL in our JavaScript code in order to send AJAX requests, add the following just before the code we previously added:

```
<script type="text/javascript">
<?php
echo 'var uriBase = '.Format::forge(Uri::base())->to_json().';';
?>
</script>
```

This code creates a JavaScript variable named `uriBase` containing the base URL obtained from `Uri::base()` and encoded to a JavaScript string by `Format::forge(...)->to_json()`. You are recommended to read the official documentation about these classes at the following URLs:

- `http://fuelphp.com/docs/classes/uri.html`
- `http://fuelphp.com/docs/classes/format.html`

> This `uriBase` variable was implemented for those of you that created your project inside your webserver root directory without using virtual hosts: in that case, sending AJAX requests using only relative URLs will cause issues. An alternative is to use the base HTML tag, as we will see in *Chapter 5, Building Your Own RESTful API.*

Now that our JavaScript file and its dependencies are included in the template, we have to implement the checkbox synchronization. Open the JavaScript file we created earlier at `public/assets/js/website.js` and set its content to:

```
$(document).ready(function() {

    // Checkbox synchronization
    $('#todo_list input[type=checkbox]').change(function() {
        var $this = $(this);
        $.post(
            uriBase + 'project/change_task_status',
            {
                'task_id': $this.data('task_id'),
                'new_status': $this.is(':checked') ? 1 : 0
            }
        );
    });
});
```

For those unfamiliar with jQuery, the code does the following:

- When the document DOM is ready, the script will look for checkboxes inside our to-do list and track their changes.
- When a checkbox is changed, it sends a `POST` request to the `project/change_task_status` action with the task's ID and its new status.
- It does not handle errors; if there is a connection problem, the user will think the web page is synchronized with the server though it isn't. It could be an axis of improvement.

Now, we have to handle this request on the server side, so we need to create the `change_task_status` action inside the **Project** controller.

Note that, for the sake of simplicity, we decided to create the action in the **Project** controller, though it handles tasks and should therefore be created inside a **Task** controller. For your real projects, it is highly recommended not to do this. It is easy to fall into the trap of having a single controller handling your whole website, and though for small projects it might be 'OK', you will have serious maintainability issues as your features add up.

Open the **Project** controller and add the following action:

```
public function action_change_task_status()
{
    if (Input::is_ajax()) {
        $task = Model_Task::find(intval(Input::post('task_id')));
        $task->status = intval(Input::post('new_status'));
        $task->save();
    }
    return false; // we return no content at all
}
```

You can notice we used `Input::post` instead of the `$_POST` global variable; it gets the same value, except you can define a default value in the second parameter of `Input::post` in case the key is not defined. The same applies for `Input::get` and `$_GET`.

We also checked using `Input::is_ajax` if it is an Ajax request. Note though there is no safe ways to detect if the request was made via Ajax (never trust data coming from the client).

The synchronization should now work; any status change should be saved and preserved if you refresh the web page.

Allowing the user to add tasks

Now that we can see and change the status of projects' tasks, it could be useful to add new ones. We will add a form for doing that under the to-do list.

First open `APPPATH/views/task/list.php` and add, at the end, the following:

```
<?php echo render('task/create', array('project' => $project)); ?>
```

Then create a view file located at `APPPATH/views/task/create.php` and set its content to:

```
<h3>Create a new task:</h3>
<?php
echo Form::open();
echo Form::input(
    'task_name',
    null,
    array('placeholder'=>'Task name')
);
```

```
echo Form::submit('task_submit', 'Create');
echo Form::close();
?>
```

Nothing spectacular here, we just display a form with a text input (for the task title) and a **Create** button. We use the `Form` class for doing that, but we could have written that in HTML code as well. For more detail about this class, you are recommended to read the official documentation at `http://fuelphp.com/docs/classes/form.html`.

Note that no parameter was passed to `Form::open`; the consequence is that the form will submit information to the current URL (and that is how we will know which project the new task must be associated with). Thus, we have to handle the form in the view action of the **Project** controller. Inside the action, add the following:

```
// Checking first if we received a POST request
if (Input::method() == 'POST')
{
    // Getting the task name. If empty, we display an
    // error, otherwise we attempt to create the new
    // task
    $task_name = Input::post('task_name', '');
    if ($task_name == '') {
        // Setting the flash session variable named
        // error. Reminder: this variable is displayed
        // in the template using Session::get_flash
        Session::set_flash(
            'error',
            'The task name is empty!'
        );
    } else {
        $task = Model_Task::forge();
        $task->name = $task_name;
        $task->status = 0;
        $task->rank = 0; // temporary
        $data['project']->tasks[] = $task;
        $data['project']->save();
        // When the task has been saved, we redirect
        // the browser to the same webpage. This
        // prevents the form from being submitted
        // again if the user refreshes the webpage
        Response::redirect('project/view/'.$id);
    }
}
```

Before:

```
$this->template->title = "Project";
```

If you read the comments, the changes we made should be pretty straightforward.

Allowing the user to change tasks' order

Return back to the JavaScript file located at `public/assets/js/website.js`, and add at the end of the `$(document).ready` callback method:

```
var $todoList = $('#todo_list');
$todoList.sortable();
$todoList.disableSelection();
```

Now, if you request a project view page, you should be able to change the tasks' order by dragging the labels. This is done using the `sortable` method. The `disableSelection` method prevents the user from selecting text inside the list, because it can sometimes cause user interface issues when dragging an item.

However, the order is not synchronized, so if you refresh the web page, your custom order will be forgotten. In order to save the changes, replace `$todoList.sortable();` with the following:

```
$todoList.sortable({
    // The stop event is called when the user drop an item
    // (when the sorting process has stopped).
    'stop': function() {
        // Collecting task ids from checkboxes in the
        // new order.
        var ids = [];
        $todoList.find('input[type=checkbox]').each(function() {
            ids.push($(this).data('task_id'));
        });
        // Sending the ordered task ids to the server.
        $.post(
            uriBase + 'project/change_tasks_order',
            {
                'project_id': $todoList.data('project_id'),
                'task_ids': ids
            }
        );
    }
});
```

For more information, you are recommended to read the official documentation of the `sortable` method of jQuery UI at `http://api.jqueryui.com/sortable/`.

We now have to handle requests sent to the `change_tasks_order` action of the **Project** controller. Add the following method to the controller:

```
public function action_change_tasks_order() {
    if (Input::is_ajax()) {
        $project = Model_Project::find(
            intval(Input::post('project_id'))
        );
        // Changing the rank property according to the
        // list of ids received by the controller
        $task_ids = Input::post('task_ids');
        for ($i = 0; $i < count($task_ids); $i++) {
            $task_id = intval($task_ids[$i]);
            $project->tasks[$task_id]->rank = $i;
        }
        $project->save();
    }
    return false; // we return no content at all
}
```

And, in the view action, replace:

```
$task->rank = 0; // temporary
```

with the following:

```
// Appending the task at the end of the to-do list
$task->rank = count($data['project']->tasks);
```

If you check the task's table, the tasks' rank column is now updated when dragging tasks to new positions. But if you refresh the web page, the order is still lost; this is because we don't sort the project's tasks when we display them. In order to do that, replace the following inside the view action:

```
if ( ! $data['project'] = Model_Project::find($id))
```

with the following:

```
$data['project'] = Model_Project::find($id, array(
    'related' => array(
        'tasks' => array(
            'order_by' => 'rank',
        ),
    ),
));
if ( ! $data['project'])
```

As explained in the previous section, the `related` key allows the developer to load relations when retrieving objects. More than allowing you to improve your website's performance, it also allows you to sort or add conditions to your relations. You even can add again a `related` key to load your relations' relations.

Axis of improvements

Many features can still be added to the application. You can implement them to improve your skill:

- Allow the user to delete a task. This could be done by adding a delete icon next to each task.
- Add a dashboard to give the user a general overview of the project and their remaining tasks.
- Improve the visual interface.
- A bit trickier: add support for a multiuser environment. What happens if two users change the tasks order at the same time for instance? How to prevent loss of information?

Summary

In this chapter, we have built our first real project and learnt to use important FuelPHP features such as the ORM and debugging tools. You should begin to feel confident about implementing simple projects. In the next chapter, we are going to use more advanced FuelPHP features such as modules and presenters.

3
Building a Blog Application

Now that we have seen FuelPHP's elementary features in the previous chapters, it is time to use more advanced ones. In this chapter, we will build a typical blog application managed via a secured administration interface. We will implement it as a module since this is a convenient way in FuelPHP to improve code reusability.

By the end of the chapter, you should know:

- How to generate an administration interface
- How to create your own module
- What are CSRF attacks and how to protect your website from them
- How to create and use tasks
- How and when to use presenters
- How to easily create pagination
- How to use the slug observer
- What are the **Auth** and **Email** packages and how to use them
- How to parse markdown
- How to use **WYSIWYGS** editors and display their content

The aim of this chapter is also to consolidate your acquired knowledge, and thus the implementation will be a little longer and more repetitive than usual. Please take your time to analyze and understand how each part works, and play around by tweaking or adding features.

Specifications

First, let's define what should be expected in our final application:

- A blog displays posts. A post is described by a title, a small description (that acts as a summary), the post's content, a category, a publication date, and an author.
- The blog's home page displays a paginated list of posts. If the user clicks on the title, he should be able to see the full version of the post.
- By clicking on the post category, a similar list should appear, but only displaying the posts belonging to this category.
- Posts and categories should only be created and edited by authenticated users in the administration interface.
- The length of the post's small description should be limited to 200 characters and edited in the Markdown syntax.
- The content should be edited with a WYSIWYG plugin.
- The administrators should be able to moderate comments.
- Each time someone writes a comment, an email should be sent to the post's author.
- We want to be able to easily install a new blog on other websites.

Conception

Let's try to determine our models from the preceding specifications. Post is obviously a model, as it is the main feature of our blog (we display posts). Each post is created and updated by an authenticated user, meaning that users have to be saved into the database; therefore, we also have a **User** model. There can be posts without comments, and categories without any posts, meaning they belong to distinct models; therefore, there is also a **Category** and a **Comment** model.

That sums up to four models:

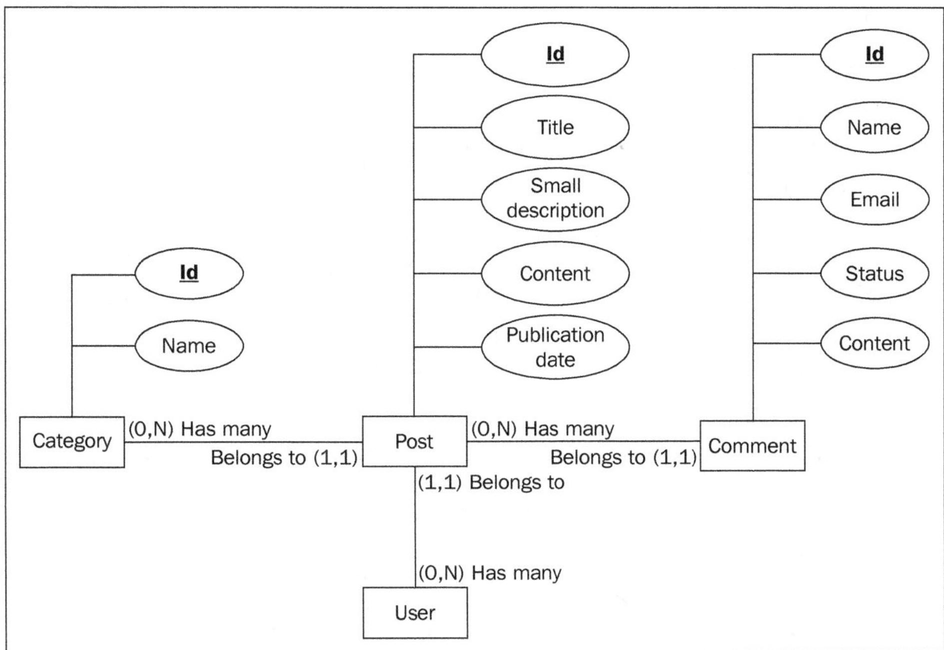

Entity Relationship diagram (Min-Max notation)

- **Post**: This model has the following properties: title, small description, content, and publication date. A post is linked to a unique category and each category has many posts, so we will add an additional column here, named `category_id`. Similarly, each post belongs to a user (the author), so we will add the `user_id` column.
- **Category**: This model only has a name property.
- **Comment**: This model has the following properties: name, email, status and content. Since a comment belongs to a unique post and each post can have many comments, we will also add a `post_id` column. When a comment is posted by a visitor, its status value will be `pending`, since it has not been reviewed. The administrator can publish or hide each comment by changing their status in the administration panel to `published` or `not_published`.

We will not generate a **User** model. We will use the one from the Auth package, that will manage users and their authentication for us.

Preliminary steps

You first need to:

1. Install a new FuelPHP instance
2. Configure Apache and your host file to handle it: in this chapter, we will access our application by requesting the `http://myblog.app` URL.
3. Update Composer if necessary
4. Create a new database for your application
5. And configure FuelPHP in order to allow your application to access this database

These steps have been covered in *Chapter 1, Building Your First FuelPHP Application*, so you might want to take a look at it.

This project will also need the ORM and Auth packages. We have already used the ORM package, and as written earlier, the Auth package will allow us to manage our users and their authentication. Since both packages are already installed, we just need to enable them. For doing this, simply open the `APPPATH/config/config.php` file and insert at the end of the returned array the following code:

```
'always_load'  => array(
    'packages'  => array(
        'orm',
        'auth',
    ),
),
```

Or you can uncomment the appropriate lines. This will load the `ORM` and `Auth` package every time a FuelPHP instance is loaded.

You can also load a package in an ad hoc manner, using the `Package::load` method. This will be addressed later in this chapter when we will use the `Email` package.

We also need to change few configuration items for the `Auth` package. First, copy the `PKGPATH/auth/config/auth.php` configuration file to `APPPATH/config/auth.php` (this configuration file will overwrite the one of the `Auth` package) and replace:

```
'driver' => 'Simpleauth',
```

By:

```
'driver' => 'Ormauth',
```

One reason we chose to use the `Ormauth` driver is that it has a much more fine-grained ACL system than the `Simpleauth` driver. `Ormauth` is more flexible and manages users, groups, roles, and permissions, whereas `Simpleauth` only manages users, groups, and roles. Another reason is that `Ormauth` already contains migrations and models managing all these components. In a nutshell, we mainly chose this driver because it is easy to set up and shows the whole scope of what is possible. However, it is important to point out that we will only use a very small fraction of its features and we could have limited ourselves to the `Simpleauth` driver.

Finally, copy the `PKGPATH/auth/config/ormauth.php` configuration file to `APPPATH/config/ormauth.php`, and set the value of `login_hash_salt` to a random string (for security precautions).

Scaffolding the posts

We will now, as we did in *Chapter 1, Building Your First FuelPHP Application* and *Chapter 2, Building a To-do List Application*, generate the necessary code to handle our posts. Since posts should only be created and edited by authenticated administrators in an administration panel, we will generate the scaffold using `admin` (alias `admin/orm`):

```
php oil generate admin post title:string slug:string small_
description:string[200] content:text category_id:int user_id:int
```

The command should output the following:

```
Creating controller: APPPATH/classes/controller/base.php
Creating controller: APPPATH/classes/controller/admin.php
Creating views: APPPATH/views/admin/template.php
Creating views: APPPATH/views/admin/dashboard.php
Creating views: APPPATH/views/admin/login.php
Creating migration: APPPATH/migrations/001_create_posts.php
Creating model: APPPATH/classes/model/post.php
Creating controller: APPPATH/classes/controller/admin/post.php
Creating view: APPPATH/views/admin/post/index.php
Creating view: APPPATH/views/admin/post/view.php
Creating view: APPPATH/views/admin/post/create.php
Creating view: APPPATH/views/admin/post/edit.php
Creating view: APPPATH/views/admin/post/_form.php
Creating view: APPPATH/views/template.php
```

You will notice that additional files have been created compared to `scaffold/orm`. These files fall into two broad categories:

- The first five generated files have been generated to handle the administration panel in a general manner (authentication and layout).
- The other ones, except the last one, have been generated to specifically handle the post administration.

You can notice that we haven't yet generated the categories and comments, we will come back to that later. Our priority right now is to make the administration panel work to see what we are dealing with.

Migrating part 1

Now, execute the migration file that has been generated:

```
php oil refine migrate
```

If you request the URL `http://myblog.app/admin` and try to log in, an error will be thrown because no table handling our users exist. To create this table (and all the other ones necessary for the `Ormauth` driver), you have to execute the `Auth` package migrations. This is done using the following command:

```
php oil refine migrate --packages=auth
```

The `oil refine migrate` command allows you to specify which modules and packages you want to migrate. You can even choose to execute all migrations (from your applications, modules, and packages) with the following command:

```
php oil refine migrate -all
```

Though in our case it doesn't make any difference, be aware that it will execute even migrations for packages that are not defined in the `always_load.packages` key of the `APPPATH/config/config.php` configuration file. Some of you might have expected this behavior, but we felt that it was an important point to stress.

The administration panel

Once the migrations have been executed, request the following URL:

`http://myblog.app/admin`

During the migration, the `Auth` package created a default user with the following credentials:

- Username: admin
- Password: admin

If you log in using these credentials, the administration panel welcome page will be displayed, as shown in the following screenshot:

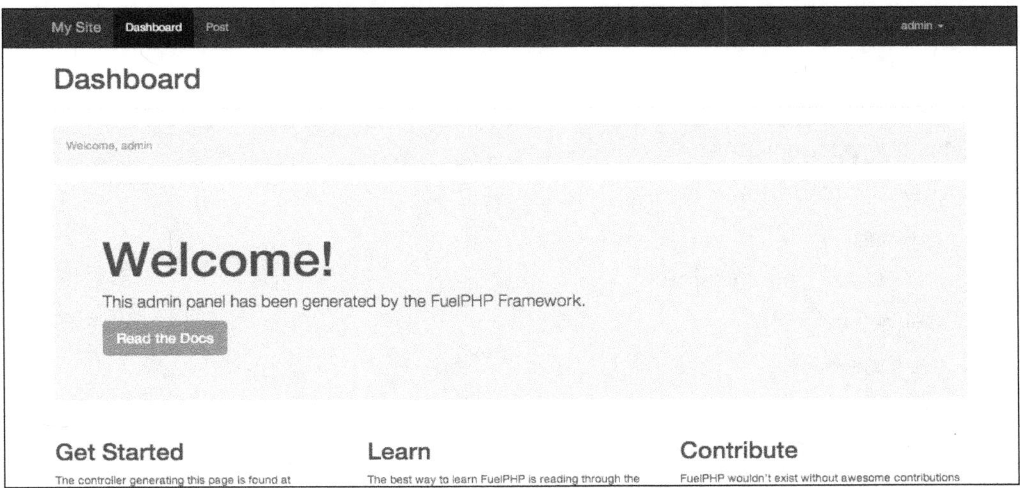

It is very similar to the default welcome page; the major difference is the upper navigation bar. As you can see in the `APPPATH/views/admin/template.php` generated file, the navigation bar automatically detects controllers in the `APPPATH/classes/controller/admin` folder and create links toward their index action. Since the `Controller_Admin_Post` controller has been generated, there is a link toward the posts list. If you click on it, you should see a CRUD scaffold pretty similar to the one generated by `scaffold/orm`:

The Auth package

If you take a look at your database now, you should see that many tables with names that are prefixed by the **users** keyword, have been created:

- users
- users_clients
- users_groups
- users_group_permissions
- users_group_roles
- users_metadata
- users_permissions
- users_providers
- users_roles
- users_role_permissions
- users_scopes
- users_sessions
- users_sessionscopes
- users_user_permissions
- users_user_roles

The `Ormauth` driver of the `Auth` package manages these tables, and some of them are linked to models located at `PKGPATH/auth/classes/model/auth`. As explained earlier, the driver provides a much more complete solution than a simple authentication system, as it manages users, groups, roles, and permissions.

It is important to point out that two other drivers exist:

- `Simpleauth`, which is a much simpler driver than `Ormauth` and only manages users, groups and roles.
- `Opauth`, which allows users to connect using `OAuth` or `OpenID` providers including Facebook, Twitter, or Google.

As we will use only a very small part of the package, explaining it to its full extent would be out of scope. For more details, you are recommended to read the official documentation at `http://fuelphp.com/docs/packages/auth/intro.html` (It can be accessed through the FuelPHP website by navigating to **DOCS** | **TABLE OF CONTENTS** | **Auth** | **Introduction**)

It would be good practice to change your admin password, as the current setting (username and password both set to `admin`) will be a major security flaw when publishing your project to the production server. You can change it using the `Auth::change_password` method, and for doing that you are recommended to read the method's official documentation at `http://fuelphp.com/docs/packages/auth/ormauth/usage.html#/method_change_password` (It can be accessed through the FuelPHP website by navigating to **DOCS** | **TABLE OF CONTENTS** | **Auth** | **Ormauth** | **Usage**).

We suggest that you execute this method in the console of **Oil** or inside a migration file (it is better if you want to propagate the change to other instances).

You could also add new users by using the `Auth::create_user` method. Note however that, for the long run, creating or using a user management system could be a good idea.

Creating the Blog module

By creating the post administration interface, we have now completed the first step of our project. Before generating and implementing our other features, it is important to remember that one additional objective is to easily install blogs on other websites by reusing the same code. For doing that, we will create a blog module, and this is where we should implement our code.

Moving files to the Blog module

The first step is to specify to FuelPHP where to look for modules. At the end of the `APPPATH/config/config.php` configuration file returned array, add (or uncomment appropriate lines):

```
'module_paths' => array(
    APPPATH.'modules'.DS
),
```

We then need to create our blog module folders. Create a folder located at `APPPATH/modules/blog` with the following subfolders:

- `classes`
- `classes/controller`
- `classes/controller/admin`
- `classes/model`

- config
- migrations
- views
- views/admin

You can also generate all these folders using the following `oil` command line:

```
php oil generate module blog -folders=classes/controller/admin,classes/model,config,migrations,views/admin
```

The next step is to move the files we generated earlier to the blog module. As it can be a bit long to complete (some code also need to be changed), we implemented an open source task for that. The repository can be found here:

https://github.com/sdrdis/move_scaffold_to_module

To install this task, simply save:

https://raw.githubusercontent.com/sdrdis/move_scaffold_to_module/master/movescaffoldtomodule.php

Into the `APPPATH/tasks/` repository.

Before executing the task and moving all the files, it is important to underline that we will also move the `001_create_posts.php` migration file to the blog module. As a consequence, the `oil` utility will consider this migration file as a new one and try to execute it. We could leave it as it is; since the migration checks if the `posts` table exists before trying to create it, it will successfully be executed, though it won't do anything. But the `oil` utility will have saved that a `001_create_posts.php` migration has been executed in the application folder, so this isn't the cleanest solution. Since we haven't entered any relevant post right now, let's first undo this migration by executing:

```
php oil refine migrate:down
```

Then execute the following command line:

```
php oil r moveScaffoldToModule -scaffold=post -module=blog
```

The command should output (`BLOGPATH` being the path of the blog module):

```
Creating controller: BLOGPATH/classes/controller/admin/post.php
Deleting controller: APPPATH/classes/controller/admin/post.php
Creating model: BLOGPATH/classes/model/post.php
Deleting model: APPPATH/classes/model/post.php
```

```
Creating view: BLOGPATH/views/admin/post/create.php
Creating view: BLOGPATH/views/admin/post/edit.php
Creating view: BLOGPATH/views/admin/post/index.php
Creating view: BLOGPATH/views/admin/post/view.php
Creating view: BLOGPATH/views/admin/post/_form.php
Deleting views: APPPATH/views/admin/post
Creating migration: BLOGPATH/migrations/001_create_posts.php
Deleting migration: APPPATH/migrations/001_create_posts.php
```

This task was created for making your life easier when implementing this project. Please note, it supposes that the code was directly generated from the `oil` utility and that you didn't make any changes inside it. It can certainly be improved.

Hopefully, it won't be needed anymore in FuelPHP 1.8 as a `--module` option might be implemented in the `oil generate scaffold` and `oil generate admin` commands, allowing developers to directly generate scaffolds inside a module.

Now, let's execute the migration file inside the blog module:

```
php oil refine migrate --modules=blog
```

Improving the navigation bar

You might have noticed that, though our post administration panel can be accessed by requesting the following URL:

`http://myblog.app/blog/admin/post`

It doesn't appear in the upper navigation bar anymore. If we take a look at the administration template located at `APPPATH/views/admin/template.php`, we can see that those links are generated by the following code:

```
<?php
    $files = new GlobIterator(APPPATH.'classes/controller/admin/*.
php');
foreach($files as $file)
    {
        $section_segment = $file->getBasename('.php');
        $section_title = Inflector::humanize($section_segment);
        ?>
```

```
<li class="<?php echo Uri::segment(2) == $section_segment ? 'active' :
'' ?>">
<?php echo Html::anchor('admin/'.$section_segment, $section_title) ?>
</li>
<?php
    }
?>
```

As you can see, the links are currently created according to files located at `APPPATH/classes/controller/admin/`. However, we would like to support modules by looking for files in the `classes/controller/admin` subdirectory of each module. For doing this, replace this code by the following:

```
<?php
// Get the navigation bar's links from an helper. We moved
// the code there because it is a bit long.
$links = Helper::get_navigation_bar_links();

foreach ($links as $link) {
    // A link will be active if the current url starts with
    // its url. For instance, we want the post link to be
    // active when requesting these urls:
    // http://myblog.app/blog/admin/post
    // http://myblog.app/blog/admin/post/create
    // http://myblog.app/blog/admin/post/view/1
    // ...
    $active = Str::starts_with(
        Uri::current(),
        Uri::base().$link['url']
    );
    ?>
<li class="<?php echo $active ? 'active' : '' ?>">
<?php echo Html::anchor(
            $link['url'],
            $link['title']
        ) ?>
</li>
<?php
}
?>
```

Create the helper at the location `APPPATH/classes/helper.php` and add the following content (read the comments for more information):

```
<?php
class Helper {
    static function get_navigation_bar_links() {
        // This method will return a list of links. Each
        // link will contain a title and a url.
        $links = array();

        // For all admin controllers of our application
        $files = new GlobIterator(
            APPPATH.'classes/controller/admin/*.php'
        );
        foreach($files as $file)
        {
            // Url and title are deducted from the file
            // basename
            $section_segment = $file->getBasename('.php');
            $links[] = array(
                'title' => Inflector::humanize(
                    $section_segment
                ),
                'url' => 'admin/'.$section_segment,
            );
        }

        // Currently, only one path is defined:
        // APPPATH/module. But this could to change.
        $module_paths = \Config::get('module_paths');
        foreach ($module_paths as $module_path) {
            // For each admin controller of each module
            $files = new GlobIterator(
                $module_path
                .
                '*/classes/controller/admin/*.php'
            );
            foreach($files as $file)
            {
                // We get the module name from the path...
                $exploded_path = explode(
                    '/',
                    $file->getPath()
```

```
                    );
                    $module = $exploded_path[
                        count($exploded_path) - 4
                    ];
                    $section_segment = $file->getBasename('.php');
                    $links[] = array(
                        'title' => Inflector::humanize(
                            $section_segment
                        ),
                        'url' => $module.'/admin/'.$section_segment,
                    );
                }
            }

            return $links;
        }
    }
```

Note that the above code supposes that all modules containing at least an admin controller can be requested.

If you refresh your administration panel, the **Post** link should appear in the upper navigation toolbar.

One caveat of this solution is that you have to perform the same changes on each new project if you want to display the **Post** link in the navigation toolbar. However, the solution is universal in the sense that, if you add other modules and admin controllers, their links will automatically appear. Moreover, if you don't use this solution, you will still be able to manage posts via the following URL:

`http://myblog.app/blog/admin/post`

Scaffolding the rest of our project

Now that the post administration panel is working and inside the blog module, it is time to generate our other models.

Scaffolding categories

Let's first take care of the Category model.

Generating files

This step is quite straightforward; as we did previously, we will use the `oil` command to generate our scaffold:

```
php oil generate admin/orm category name:string -s
```

Note that we added the `-s` (`s` for skip) parameter, as some files have already been generated previously and we don't want to replace them. This command line should output:

```
Creating migration: APPPATH/migrations/002_create_categories.php
Creating model: APPPATH/classes/model/category.php
Creating controller: APPPATH/classes/controller/admin/category.php
Creating view: APPPATH/views/admin/category/index.php
Creating view: APPPATH/views/admin/category/view.php
Creating view: APPPATH/views/admin/category/create.php
Creating view: APPPATH/views/admin/category/edit.php
Creating view: APPPATH/views/admin/category/_form.php
```

Don't launch the generated migration though; we will first move the code to our blog module.

Moving categories to the blog module

Let's use the `moveScaffoldToModule` task to move the category scaffold into the blog module:

```
php oil r moveScaffoldToModule -scaffold=category -module=blog
```

The command should output (`BLOGPATH` being the path of the blog module):

```
Creating controller: BLOGPATH/classes/controller/admin/category.php
Deleting controller: APPPATH/classes/controller/admin/category.php
Creating model: BLOGPATH/classes/model/category.php
Deleting model: APPPATH/classes/model/category.php
Creating view: BLOGPATH/views/admin/category/create.php
Creating view: BLOGPATH/views/admin/category/edit.php
Creating view: BLOGPATH/views/admin/category/index.php
```

```
Creating view: BLOGPATH/views/admin/category/view.php
Creating view: BLOGPATH/views/admin/category/_form.php
Deleting views: APPPATH/views/admin/category
Creating migration: BLOGPATH/migrations/002_create_categories.php
Deleting migration: APPPATH/migrations/002_create_categories.php
```

Migrating

Now we just have to execute our migration file. To do that, enter the following command line:

```
php oil refine migrate --modules=blog
```

If you access your administration panel, you should now be able to manage categories.

Scaffolding comments

This section is quite similar to the previous one. First, generate the scaffold:

```
php oil generate admin/orm comment name:string email:string content:text
status:string post_id:integer -s
```

This command should output the following:

```
Creating migration: APPPATH/migrations/002_create_comments.php
Creating model: APPPATH/classes/model/comment.php
Creating controller: APPPATH/classes/controller/admin/comment.php
Creating view: APPPATH/views/admin/comment/index.php
Creating view: APPPATH/views/admin/comment/view.php
Creating view: APPPATH/views/admin/comment/create.php
Creating view: APPPATH/views/admin/comment/edit.php
Creating view: APPPATH/views/admin/comment/_form.php
```

Then, move the scaffold to the blog module:

```
php oil r moveScaffoldToModule -scaffold=comment -module=blog
```

This command should output the following:

```
Creating controller: BLOGPATH/classes/controller/admin/comment.php
Deleting controller: APPPATH/classes/controller/admin/comment.php
Creating model: BLOGPATH/classes/model/comment.php
Deleting model: APPPATH/classes/model/comment.php
```

```
Creating view: BLOGPATH/views/admin/comment/create.php
Creating view: BLOGPATH/views/admin/comment/edit.php
Creating view: BLOGPATH/views/admin/comment/index.php
Creating view: BLOGPATH/views/admin/comment/view.php
Creating view: BLOGPATH/views/admin/comment/_form.php
Deleting views: APPPATH/views/admin/comment
Creating migration: BLOGPATH/migrations/003_create_comments.php
Deleting migration: APPPATH/migrations/002_create_comments.php
```

Before launching the migration file, we will improve it by changing the `status` column type to `ENUM`, since there are only three possible values: `not_published`, `pending`, and `published`. To do that, edit the `BLOGPATH/migrations/003_create_comments.php` file and replace the following line:

```
'status' => array('constraint' => 11, 'type' => 'int'),
```

By:

```
'status' => array(
    'constraint' => "'not_published','pending','published'",
    'type' => 'enum',
    'default' => 'pending'
),
```

And finally, launch the migration file using oil:

```
php oil refine migrate --modules=blog
```

Comments should now be manageable in the administration interface.

Scaffolding posts (front)

In order to have a starting point, we are going to generate the scaffold of posts for the front. We will, of course, change the controller a lot, because we don't want visitors to edit and create posts.

Before doing anything, check that no file has been generated at `APPPATH/views/template.php` (as I write, `oil generate admin/orm` seems to generate an incorrect file at that location). If that is the case, delete that file: it will be regenerated later by oil.

Enter the following command:

```
php oil generate scaffold/orm post title:string slug:string small_
description:string[200] content:text category_id:int user_id:int
```

It should output:

```
Creating migration: APPPATH/migrations/002_create_posts.php
Creating model: APPPATH/classes/model/post.php
Creating controller: APPPATH/classes/controller/post.php
Creating view: APPPATH/views/post/index.php
Creating view: APPPATH/views/post/view.php
Creating view: APPPATH/views/post/create.php
Creating view: APPPATH/views/post/edit.php
Creating view: APPPATH/views/post/_form.php
```

Now move the scaffold to the blog module by entering the following command:

```
php oil r moveScaffoldToModule -scaffold=post -module=blog
```

This should print the following output:

```
Creating controller: BLOGPATH/classes/controller/post.php
Deleting controller: APPPATH/classes/controller/post.php
Deleting model: APPPATH/classes/model/post.php
Creating view: BLOGPATH/views/post/create.php
Creating view: BLOGPATH/views/post/edit.php
Creating view: BLOGPATH/views/post/index.php
Creating view: BLOGPATH/views/post/view.php
Creating view: BLOGPATH/views/post/_form.php
Deleting views: APPPATH/views/post
Deleting migration: APPPATH/migrations/002_create_posts.php
```

Note that, as a migration file with as similar file name was already in the blog module, the task simply removed the one in the application directory (without copying it into the blog module). This is the expected behavior since a migration that creates the posts table already exists in the module.

You should be able to access the scaffold by requesting the following URL:

```
http://myblog.app/blog/post
```

Refining the administration panel

Now that all the scaffolds have been created, it is time to refine our administration panel:

- As categories are very simple models (they only have a `name` attribute), the **View** link doesn't give the user more information than in the listing, so we will remove it. We will also display the number of posts associated with each category in the categories list; it will give us an idea of the most used categories.
- We don't need to create new comments inside the administration panel, so we need to remove the associated links and actions. We also need to do some improvements in the edition form and in the listing.
- Same for the posts; we will remove most columns when listing posts, we will add a WYSIWYG editor, a markdown editor and a category select box inside the post creation and edition forms.

Note that there could be a lot of other improvements. You are recommended to add the changes you deem necessary.

Refining the posts administration panel

Let's start with the posts administration panel. You might want to add some categories for the purpose of testing. Note that you should be able to test your application again at the end of each section.

Improving the post creation and edition forms

We will begin with the creation/edition form. We generated it and, as we saw in the previous chapters, the view managing this form can be found at: `BLOGPATH/views/admin/post/_form.php`.

Removing and automatically filling the slug

The **slug** property should only depend on the title, and it will be used in URLs for improving the SEO. Its value will be automatically filled from the title, so we don't need its related field in the form. Therefore, remove the second `div` with the class `form-group` along with its content (which contains the `slug` input).

To automatically fill its value, we will use an observer (as for the `created_at` and `updated_at` columns); `Orm\Observer_Slug`. In a model's instance, this observer takes a property value and saves its slug version into a second property. In the default case, without any additional configuration, it will take the value of `title` and save its slug version into `slug`. This is exactly our case, so it will be pretty simple, but you are recommended to read the official documentation for more information:

`http://fuelphp.com/docs/packages/orm/observers/included.html#os_slug`

(It can be accessed through FuelPHP website by navigating to **DOCS** | **TABLE OF CONTENTS** | **ORM** | **Observers+** | **Included observers**)

Open the **Post** model located at `BLOGPATH/classes/model/post.php` and add the following at the end of the `$_observers` property:

```
'Orm\\Observer_Slug',
```

Finally, we have to remove all elements related to the **Slug** field processing.

First, in the `validate` method of the **Post** model, remove:

```
$val->add_field('slug', 'Slug', 'required|max_length[255]');
```

Then, open the **Post** controller located at `BLOGPATH/classes/controller/admin/post.php` and remove:

```
'slug' => Input::post('slug'),
```

And:

```
$post->slug = Input::post('slug');
```

And:

```
$post->slug = $val->validated('slug');
```

Changing the small description input to a textarea

We want to change the small description input into a `textarea`, because though its length is limited to 200 characters, the standard input isn't user friendly. Replace:

```
<?php echo Form::input('small_description', ... ); ?>
```

By:

```
<?php
echo Form::textarea(
    'small_description',
    Input::post(
```

```
        'small_description',
isset($post) ? $post->small_description : ''
    ),
    array(
        'class' => 'col-md-4 form-control',
        'placeholder' => 'Small description',
        'rows' => 4,
        'maxlength' => 200,
    )
);
?>
```

We want to write content using the markdown syntax (take a look at `https://en.wikipedia.org/wiki/Markdown` if you are not familiar with it) and display the formatted small description in our front end, but we won't need to change anything else for now since this formatting process will happen in our front views. Though, you could add a JavaScript markdown plugin here to make this `textarea` even more user-friendly.

Editing the post content using a WYSIWYG editor

The next form item is the content and we want to edit it with a WYSIWYG editor. We just have to add a JavaScript plugin. We will use **TinyMCE**, a well-known open source WYSIWYG editor.

First, you will need to include the TinyMCE JavaScript file. Open the template file located at `APPPATH/views/admin/template.php` and add:

```
'//tinymce.cachefly.net/4.1/tinymce.min.js'
```

At the end of the `Asset::js` first array parameter.

> Note that we used the JavaScript file hosted on TinyMCE's recommended CDN at the time this book was written. Depending on when you read this book and your requirements, you might want to use a different URL or host TinyMCE on your servers.

Next, we need to specify to TinyMCE which `textarea` has to be transformed to WYSIWGs. Inside the same template, add the following at the end of the first `script` tag:

```
// Transforms textareas with the wysiwyg class to wysiwygs
tinymce.init({selector:'textarea.wysiwyg'});
```

Finally, we need to add the `wysiwyg` class to our content `textarea`. Return to the file located at `APPPATH/views/admin/post/_form.php`, search for `Form::textarea('content'` and inside this method call, replace:

```
'class' => 'col-md-8 form-control'
```

By:

```
'class' => 'col-md-8 form-control wysiwyg'
```

Replacing the category input by a select box

The next item in the form is **Category id**. Setting the category id manually is not user friendly for the administrator; the best would be to display a select box, so that categories can be chosen by their title.

First, create a view file at `BLOGPATH/views/admin/category/selector.php`, and add the following content:

```
<?php
/*
Loading the list of all categories here, since it doesn't
depend on the post being created / edited. (Temporary)
*/
$categories = \Blog\Model_Category::find('all');

$options = array();
foreach ($categories as $category) {
    $options[$category->id] = $category->name;
}
echo Form::select('category_id', $category_id, $options);
```

Then, back on the `BLOGPATH/views/admin/post/_form.php` view file, fix the category field title by replacing:

```
Form::label('Category id', 'category_id'
```

With:

```
Form::label('Category', 'category_id'
```

And include our select box by replacing:

```
<?php echo Form::input('category_id', ... ) ?>
```

With:

```
<div>
<?php
$select_box = \View::forge('admin/category/selector');

// Other way to set a view parameter; sets the $category_id
// variable.
$select_box->set(
    'category_id',
    Input::post(
        'category_id',
        isset($post) ? $post->category_id : null
    )
);

echo $select_box;
?>
</div>
```

If you test the form, the select box should be working. But there is a small issue; when we created the selector view, we loaded a list of categories inside the view. This isn't respecting the MVC pattern, as we are loading models inside a view. But it would not make sense to load these objects inside the **Post** controller, because the view doesn't actually depend on any post; we always load all categories, no matter the context. As written earlier in *Chapter 1, Building Your First FuelPHP Application*, we should use a presenter in that case. Luckily, we don't need to make many changes.

First, create the presenter file at `BLOGPATH/classes/presenter/admin/category/selector.php` and add the following content:

```
<?php
namespace Blog;

class Presenter_Admin_Category_Selector extends \Presenter
{
    public function view()
    {
        $this->categories = Model_Category::find('all');
    }
}
```

Then, edit the BLOGPATH/views/admin/post/_form.php view file to replace the following line:

```
$select_box = \View::forge('admin/category/selector');
```

By:

```
$select_box = \Presenter::forge('admin/category/selector');
```

And finally, edit the BLOGPATH/views/admin/category/selector.php view and remove the following line:

```
$categories = \Blog\Model_Category::find('all');
```

Though we won't need them immediately, we will add the relations between the post and category models. Since each post can only have one category, and each category can be related to many posts, there is a belongs_to relationship between posts and categories, and a has_many relationship between categories and posts.

First, open the **Post** model located at BLOGPATH/classes/model/post.php, and add the following code inside the class:

```
protected static $_belongs_to = array('category');
```

Then, open the **Category** model located at BLOGPATH/classes/model/category.php, and add the following code inside the class:

```
protected static $_has_many = array('posts');
```

Replacing the user_id field by author

The last field in our form is the **user_id field**. We will replace this field by an author field. This field won't be editable; the author of a post will simply be the authenticated user that creates it.

We first need to add the relation between posts and users; since each post can only be related to a single user, and users can have as many posts as they want, the relation's type is belongs_to.

Open the **Post** model located at BLOGPATH/classes/model/post.php and add the following at the end of the $_belongs_to array:

```
'author' => array(
    'model_to'          => 'Auth\Model\Auth_User',
    'key_from'          => 'user_id',
    'key_to'            => 'id',
    'cascade_save'      => true,
```

```
        'cascade_delete'     => false,
    ),
```

Next, we will change how the field is displayed in the creation/edition form. Open `BLOGPATH/views/admin/post/_form.php`, and first replace:

```
<?php echo Form::label('User id', ... ); ?>
```

By:

```
<?php echo Form::label('Author'); ?>
```

And then replace:

```
<?php echo Form::input('user_id', ... ); ?>
```

By:

```
<div>
<?php
/*
This field is not editable, so we simply display the author.
current_user is a global variable that defines the current
logged user.
*/
$author = isset($post) ? $post->author : $current_user;
echo $author->username;
?>
</div>
```

And finally, we need the **Post** controller to reflect that behavior. For doing that, we first change how the `user_id` attribute is saved in the create and edit actions. Open the **Post** controller located at `BLOGPATH/classes/controller/admin/post.php`, and, inside the create action, replace the following:

```
'user_id' => Input::post('user_id'),
```

By:

```
'user_id' => $this->current_user->id,
```

And inside the edit action, simply delete the following line:

```
$post->user_id = Input::post('user_id');
```

And:

```
$post->user_id = $val->validated('user_id');
```

Though, you still won't be able to create a new post now, as the following message will appear: **The field User Id is required and must contain a value**. This is happening because of the **Post** model `validate` method. The remaining thing to do is to remove the `user_id` validation. Open the **Post** model located at `BLOGPATH/classes/model/post.php`, and remove the following line inside the `validate` method:

```
$val->add_field('user_id', ... );
```

Removing the View link

Since we are not interested in keeping the detailed view of posts, we can remove the `View` link. Open `BLOGPATH/views/admin/post/edit.php` and remove the following code:

```
<?php echo Html::anchor(..., 'View'); ?> |
```

The posts' list

If you have tested the form we improved to create new posts, you have probably noticed that the listing is not well adapted.

Removing the Slug, Small description and Content columns

The first issue is that the **Slug**, **Small description**, and **Content** columns are displayed, though their value's length can be important. Since this can have a terrible effect on the table layout, we will have to remove them. Open the listing view located at `BLOGPATH/views/admin/post/index.php` and remove the following lines:

```
<th>Slug</th>
<th>Small description</th>
<th>Content</th>
```

And:

```
<td><?php echo $item->slug; ?></td>
<td><?php echo $item->small_description; ?></td>
<td><?php echo $item->content; ?></td>
```

Displaying the category and author names

The second issue is that we are displaying the categories' and users' ids, though displaying their associated names would be more convenient.

First, change the table titles accordingly by replacing:

```
<th>Category id</th>
```

By:

```
<th>Category</th>
```

And the following line:

```
<th>User id</th>
```

By:

```
<th>Author</th>
```

And change each line value by replacing:

```
<td><?php echo $item->category_id; ?></td>
```

By:

```
<td><?php echo $item->category->name; ?></td>
```

And the following line:

```
<td><?php echo $item->user_id; ?></td>
```

By:

```
<td><?php echo $item->author->username; ?></td>
```

You could leave the code as it is, since the correct information will appear in the listing. But if you activate the profiler, you will notice that if you have several posts, a lot of SQL requests will be executed. As we saw before, this is because we are calling `$item->category` and `$item->author`, and, if not cached, each call executes a SQL request. In order to optimize the number of requests being made, we will use the `related` key. Open the **Post** controller located at `BLOGPATH/classes/controller/post.php` and, inside the index action, replace the following line:

```
$data['posts'] = Model_Post::find('all');
```

By:

```
$data['posts'] = Model_Post::find(
    'all',
    array(
        'related' => array(
            'category',
            'author',
        ),
    )
);
```

Removing the view link

Since we are implementing the administration panel, we can reduce the code to what is strictly necessary. The post edition and visualization is redundant, since we have access to the post information when we are editing it. Thus, we will remove the **View** link. Simply remove the following line:

```
<?php echo Html::anchor(..., 'View'); ?> |
```

It is a good idea to remove the **View** action inside the **Post** controller as well as the view located at `BLOGPATH/admin/post/view.php`, since they are now useless code.

Refining the categories administration panel

Let's now focus on the categories administration panel. The **Category** model is quite simple, so there is not much to do. As a matter of fact, we will almost only change the listing page.

Removing the View link

Since the model only has one attribute that is already displayed on the list, the view link and page are not of much use. First, delete the **View** link inside the view located at `BLOGPATH/views/admin/category/index.php` by removing:

```
<?php echo Html::anchor(..., 'View'); ?> |
```

You can then remove the **View** action inside the **Category** controller and the view located at `BLOGPATH/views/admin/category/view.php`, since they are now useless code.

We also have to remove the **View** link inside the edition form. Open `BLOGPATH/views/admin/category/edit.php` and remove the following code:

```
<?php echo Html::anchor(..., 'View'); ?> |
```

Adding the number of post's column

One challenge of this section is to display how many posts there are for each category. This is not simple and there is no ideal solution.

Let's first add our column into our table. Under:

```
<th>Name</th>
```

Add:

```
<th>Number of posts</th>
```

And under:

```
<td><?php echo $item->name; ?></td>
```

Add:

```
<td><?php /* Depends on solution */ ?></td>
```

Now let's test different options.

Solution 1: using count

The first solution is quite straightforward; we use the `count` method. Replace:

```
<td><?php /* Depends on solution */ ?></td>
```

By:

```
<td>
<?php
echo \Blog\Model_Post::count(
    array(
        'where' => array(
            array('category_id' => $item->id)
        )
    )
);
?>
</td>
```

Though the solution is quite simple, there are major drawbacks. Firstly, it doesn't respect the MVC pattern. Secondly, it will generate a request for each category displayed. Don't use this if you have a lot of categories.

Solution 2: using related

Another solution is to use the `related` key. First, open the **Category** controller located at `BLOGPATH/classes/controller/admin/category.php` and, inside the index action, replace the following line:

```
$data['categories'] = Model_Category::find('all');
```

By:

```
$data['categories'] = Model_Category::find(
    'all',
    array(
        'related' => array(
            'posts',
        ),
    )
);
```

And back to the `BLOGPATH/views/admin/category/index.php` view, replace:

```
<td><?php /* Depends on solution */ ?></td>
```

By:

```
<td><?php echo count($item->posts); ?></td>
```

On the one hand, this solution limits the number of requests but, on the other hand, it might load a lot of useless post instances into the memory, so this is not ideal either. Don't use this if you have a lot of posts.

Solution 3: using DB::query

Another solution is to load categories using `DB::query`. First, open the **Category** controller located at `BLOGPATH/classes/controller/admin/category.php` and, inside the index action, replace the following line:

```
$data['categories'] = Model_Category::find('all');
```

By:

```
$data['categories'] = Model_Category::find_all_with_nb_posts();
```

Then add the following method inside the **Category** model:

```
public static function find_all_with_nb_posts() {
    return \DB::query(
        'SELECT
            `categories`.*,
            count(`posts`.`id`) as nb_posts
        FROM `categories`
        LEFT JOIN `posts` ON (
            `posts`.`category_id` = `categories`.`id`
        )
        GROUP BY `categories`.id'
```

```
        )
        ->as_object('\Blog\Model_Category')
        ->execute()
        ->as_array();
}
```

> It is possible to execute a custom query and then transform the result into model's instances thanks to the `as_object` method. In this request, we add a custom column, `nb_posts`, that counts the number of posts for each category. This column is accessible in our categories instances under the `nb_posts` attribute.

And back to the `BLOGPATH/views/admin/category/index.php` view, replace:

```
<td><?php /* Depends on solution */ ?></td>
```

By:

```
<td><?php echo $item->nb_posts ?></td>
```

This solution is interesting for its performance: no additional queries or memory usage. Its drawback is that it doesn't use the ORM, and this solution might be tricky to implement for more complex problems.

For this instance though, we are recommending this solution.

Refining the comments administration panel

We also need to make some adjustments here. You are recommended to manually add some comments now, because you won't be able to after we change the interface (there would be no point in adding comments through the administration interface, since any user will be able to do it on the website).

Improving the comments listing

First, we will improve the comments listing.

Removing the view and adding a new comment link

As we won't need those features, we will remove their links, actions and views.

First, open the `BLOGPATH/views/admin/comment/index.php` view file and remove:

```
<?php echo Html::anchor(..., 'View'); ?> |
```

And:

```
<?php echo Html::anchor(..., 'Add new Comment', ...); ?>
```

And you are also recommended to remove the create and view action of the **Comment** controller, as well as the `BLOGPATH/views/admin/comment/create.php` and `BLOGPATH/views/admin/comment/view.php` files.

Removing the Email and Content columns

We will remove these two columns because they can take too much space. For doing that, open `BLOGPATH/views/admin/comment/index.php` and remove the following lines:

```
<th>Email</th>
<th>Content</th>
```

And:

```
<td><?php echo $item->email; ?></td>
<td><?php echo $item->content; ?></td>
```

Replacing the Post id column by Post

It would be more convenient to know the title of the post the comment is related to, instead of the post's id.

First, replace:

```
<th>Post id</th>
```

By:

```
<th>Post</th>
```

And then replace:

```
<td><?php echo $item->post_id; ?></td>
```

By:

```
<td>
<?php
echo $item->post ? $item->post->title : '<i>Post deleted</i>';
?>
</td>
```

But if we want this to work, we have to define the relations between posts and comments. Open the **Post** model located at `BLOGPATH/classes/model/post.php`, and add the following property:

```
protected static $_has_many = array('comments');
```

And then open the **Comment** model located at `BLOGPATH/classes/model/comment.php`, and add the following property:

```
protected static $_belongs_to = array('post');
```

Now, you are able to display the listing again. But, you might notice that if you have several comments, a lot of requests are executed. Again, we need to use the `related` key to prevent that. Open the `Comment` controller located at `BLOGPATH/classes/controller/admin/comment.php` and, inside the index action, replace:

```
$data['comments'] = Model_Comment::find('all');
```

By:

```
$data['comments'] = Model_Comment::find(
    'all',
    array(
        'related' => array('post'),
        // display last comments first
        'order_by' => array('id' => 'DESC'),
    )
);
```

Improving the comment edition form

We will improve two fields in the comment edition form; `Status`, and `Post id`.

Changing the Status input to a select box

Since there are only three possible statuses, we will replace the input by a select box. Open the form located at `BLOGPATH/views/admin/comment/_form.php`, and replace:

```
<?php echo Form::input('status', ...); ?>
```

By:

```
<div>
<?php
echo Form::select(
    'status',
    $comment->status,
    array(
        'not_published' => 'not_published',
        'pending' => 'pending',
        'published' => 'published',
    )
);
?>
</div>
```

Replacing Post id by Post

Again, displaying a post's id is not relevant for the administrator; the best would be to display the post's title.

First, replace:

```
<?php echo Form::label('Post id', ...); ?>
```

By:

```
<?php
echo Form::label(
    'Post',
    null, // No associated input
    array('class' => 'control-label')
);
?>
```

And then replace:

```
<?php echo Form::input('post_id', ...); ?>
```

By:

```
<div><?php echo $comment->post ? $comment->post->title : '<i>Post
deleted</i>'; ?></div>
```

We then need to prevent any change in the `post_id` property when processing the form. Open the **Comment** controller and, inside the `action_edit` method, remove the following line:

```
$comment->post_id = Input::post('post_id');
```

And:

```
$comment->post_id = $val->validated('post_id');
```

Finally, we need to remove the `post_id` validation. Open the **Comment** model and remove the following line:

```
$val->add_field('post_id', ...);
```

Removing the View link

Since there is no view action anymore, we have to remove the **View** link. Open `BLOGPATH/views/admin/comment/edit.php` and remove the following code:

```
<?php echo Html::anchor(..., 'View'); ?> |
```

Protecting your website against CSRF attacks

You would certainly like to prevent hackers from changing your website content, as the consequences could be disastrous. Although the risks are limited as long as you are the only one to access an administration panel you implemented yourself, you might want to protect your website against **Cross-Site Request Forgery (CSRF)** attacks.

CSRF attacks are based on the trust a website has in a user's browser. Let's illustrate these attacks with an example. Suppose you logged yourself into your administration interface. If you access, a bit later, a webpage on another website that contains the following code:

```
<html>
    <head>
        <title>My attack</title>
    </head>
    <body>
        <img src="http://myblog.app/blog/admin/post/delete/1" />
    </body>
</html>
```

In your website, the delete action of the **Post** controller will get called and the post with `id = 1` will be deleted (if it exists), without your approval or any notification. The hacker that created the webpage has then succeeded in his CSRF attack by exploiting the fact that you were logged in to your administration panel. It worked because your action didn't verify that the request was legitimate. More advanced attacks can even submit forms, and you could then find yourself with unwanted content on your website.

Luckily, FuelPHP allows you to easily protect your website by including a security token in links or forms. This security token is later checked when the action is called. That process ensures that the client requested the action from the website, and not from somewhere else.

Protecting links

First, let's protect the delete links in the post listing.

Open the `BLOGPATH/views/admin/post/index.php` view file and replace:

```
'blog/admin/post/delete/'.$item->id
```

By:

```
'blog/admin/post/delete/'.$item->id.
'?'.\Config::get('security.csrf_token_key').
'='.\Security::fetch_token()
```

If you refresh the webpage, the delete links should now point to a URL looking like:

```
http://myblog.app/blog/admin/post/delete/ID?fuel_csrf_token=215be7bad
7eb4999148a22341466f66395ce483d12b17cae463b7bf4b6d6d86233ce38ce6b145c
08bf994e56610c1502158b32eca6f6d599a5bb3527d019c324
```

Now that we call the delete action of the **Post** controller with the CSRF token as a `get` parameter, we just have to check if its value is correct before deleting the post. In order to do that, open the **Post** controller and, inside the delete action, replace:

```
if ($post = Model_Post::find($id))
```

By:

```
if (($post = Model_Post::find($id)) and \Security::check_token())
```

Your delete action is now protected. You should do the same with the delete links of the **Category** and **Comment** administration interfaces. In general, it is even recommended to add this protection to any link that executes an important or critical action.

Protecting forms

We will now use a very similar technique to protect our post creation and edition forms. First, open the `BLOGPATH/views/admin/post/_form.php` view file and add:

```
<?php echo Form::csrf(); ?>
```

Just after:

```
<?php echo Form::open(array("class"=>"form-horizontal")); ?>
```

The `Form::csrf` method will automatically add a hidden input to your form containing the token. If you display the HTML code of the post creation or edition webpage, you should see that this method returned a string similar to:

```
<input name="fuel_csrf_token"
  value="2411b0a6b942105fb80aa0cb1aaf89
  ca91e0ea715f5641bbfbb5ded23221fcecbbfe701
  6c8dbd922a19b12274989e67f71d266300ad14ebd9730c3ec604ec4f5"
  type="hidden" id="form_fuel_csrf_token" />
```

Now, let's check that this token is correct before making any change to the database.

Open the **Post** controller and, inside the create action, replace:

```
if ($post and $post->save())
```

By:

```
if (\Security::check_token() and $post and $post->save())
```

And inside the edit action, replace:

```
if ($post->save())
```

By:

```
if (\Security::check_token() && $post->save())
```

For the sake of this section's conciseness, we do not display a special error message when the token doesn't have the expected value, but you are recommended to add this feature.

Anyway, your post creation and edition forms are now protected too. You should do the same with the creation and edition forms of the **Category** and **Comment** administration interfaces. In general, it is even recommended to add this protection to all your forms.

Refining the front-end

We now have to refine the front-end of our website, that is to say what visitors will see.

Refining the posts' listing

If you request the following URL:

```
http://myblog.app/blog/post
```

You will see the scaffold we generated earlier with `scaffold/orm`.

Deleting useless features

The first important thing to do is to prevent any edition on our posts. As we did several times for the administration panel, remove the create, edit and delete actions of the **Post** controller and their associated views. Note that, here, we are talking about the **Post** controller located at `BLOGPATH/classes/controller/post.php`, since we are working on the website's front-end. You can also delete the `BLOGPATH/views/admin/post/_form.php` view file, as it is only called from the create and edit views.

Changing how the posts' listing is displayed

Currently, the posts' listing is displayed in a table and, for our blog, we want to display the list more linearly, as most blogs are displayed.

The simplest way is to replace the view located at `BLOGPATH/post/index.php` by:

```
<?php if ($posts): ?>
<?php foreach ($posts as $item): ?>
<div class="post" id="post_<?php echo $item->id; ?>">
<h2>
<?php
echo Html::anchor('blog/post/view/'.$item->id, $item->title);
?>
</h2>
<?php
/*
As we will display the same information when visualizing a
post, we will implement different views in order
to easily reuse them later in BLOGPATH/views/post/view.php
*/
echo \View::forge(
```

```
        'post/small_description',
        array('post' => $item)
    );
    echo \View::forge(
        'post/additional_informations',
        array('post' => $item)
    );
    ?>
    </div>
    <?php endforeach; ?>
    <?php else: ?>
    <p>No Posts.</p>
    <?php endif; ?>
```

As we are displaying additional content in separated views (see comments), we need to create these views. Create the `BLOGPATH/views/post/small_description.php` view file and set its content with the following:

```
<div class="post_small_description">
<?php
echo \Markdown::parse($post->small_description)
?>
</div>
```

And create the `BLOGPATH/views/post/additional_informations.php` view file and set its content by the following:

```
<div class="post_date">
<?php
echo \Date::forge($post->created_at)->format('us_full');
?>
</div>
<div class="post_category">
    Category:
<?php echo $post->category->name ?>
</div>
<div class="post_author">
    By
<?php echo $post->author->username ?>
</div>
```

Finally, in order to optimize the number of requests being made, open the **Post** controller (the one for the front-end), and replace:

```
$data['posts'] = Model_Post::find('all');
```

By:

```
$data['posts'] = Model_Post::find(
    'all',
    array(
        'related' => array(
            'author',
            'category',
        ),
    )
);
```

Adding pagination

If you add a lot of posts, you will notice that the list becomes very long. To prevent this behavior, we will now add the `Pagination` feature.

At the beginning of the index action of the **Post** controller, add the following code in order to create a `Pagination` instance:

```
// Pagination configuration
$config = array(
    'total_items'    => Model_Post::count(),
    'per_page'       => 10,
    'uri_segment'    => 'page',
);

// Create a pagination instance named 'posts'
$pagination = \Pagination::forge('posts', $config);
```

Here, we set the main options of the `Pagination` configuration, but you are recommended to take a look at the official documentation, as there are many more options:

`http://fuelphp.com/docs/classes/pagination.html`

(It can be accessed through FuelPHP website by navigating to **DOCS** | **Core** | **Pagination**)

If you don't have a lot of posts, you can lower the `per_page` value in order to test the pagination.

Now when we retrieve the posts, we have to take into account the pagination. Replace:

```
$data['posts'] = Model_Post::find(...);
```

By:

```
$data['posts'] = Model_Post::find(
    'all',
    array(
        'related' => array(
            'author',
            'category',
        ),
        'rows_offset' => $pagination->offset,
        'rows_limit' => $pagination->per_page,
    )
);
```

We need to pass the pagination instance we created to our view in order to display it. At the end of the action, add the following code:

```
$this->template->content->set('pagination', $pagination);
```

This will have the same effect as setting a `pagination` key inside the `$data` parameter.

Open the `BLOGPATH/views/post/index.php` view file, and under:

```
<?php endforeach; ?>
```

Add:

```
<?php echo $pagination; ?>
```

Now, if you refresh your listing page and have enough posts, you will see that your pagination appears but is escaped, in the sense that it displays the HTML code. This is because view parameters are escaped by default and we didn't notify FuelPHP not to escape the `pagination` parameter. Open the **Post** controller again and, inside the index action, replace:

```
$this->template->content->set('pagination', $pagination);
```

By:

```
$this->template->content->set('pagination', $pagination, false);
```

Using posts' slug

If you display the listing, everything should look just fine. But if you click on the title of one post, the view page will be shown but the URL will look like this:

`http://myblog.app/blog/post/view/1`

This is not great for the SEO, because we don't use the slug we created earlier. To fix that, first open the `BLOGPATH/views/post/index.php` view file, and replace:

```
echo Html::anchor('blog/post/view/'.$item->id, $item->title);
```

By:

```
echo Html::anchor(
    'blog/post/view/'.$item->slug,
    $item->title
);
```

Now that the link is pointing to the right URL, the view action has to handle this new behavior. Open the **Post** controller and first replace the following line:

```
public function action_view($id = null)
```

By:

```
public function action_view($slug = null)
```

And then replace the view action's content by:

```
is_null($slug) and Response::redirect('blog/post');

$data['post'] = Model_Post::find(
    'first',
    array(
        'where' => array(
            array('slug' => $slug),
        ),
    )
);
if ( ! $data['post'])
{
    Session::set_flash(
        'error',
        'Could not find post with slug: '.$slug
    );
```

```
        Response::redirect('blog/post');
    }

    $this->template->title = "Post";
    $this->template->content = View::forge('post/view', $data);
```

Listing posts by categories

One interesting additional feature would be to list posts belonging to each category. For instance, if we request the following URL:

```
http://myblog.app/blog/post/category/1
```

We would like to display posts belonging to the category with `id = 1`.

> The best would have been to use a slug, as we did for posts. We didn't implement it for the sake of this chapter's conciseness, but you are recommended to do so.

First, open the `BLOGPATH/views/post/additional_informations.php` and replace:

```
<?php echo $post->category->name ?>
```

By:

```
<?php
echo Html::anchor(
    'blog/post/category/'.$post->category->id,
    $post->category->name
);
?>
```

If you think about it, the list of posts displayed for a category is similar to the one where no category is filtered. The view and even the requests are similar.

We could have written a category action inside the **Post** controller and, in that case, the index and category actions could have called a same common method; this solution would have been acceptable and even recommended in most cases.

But we will take a different approach here. Since the actions have a lot in common, we will reroute:

```
http://myblog.app/blog/post/category/category_id
```

To:

```
http://myblog.app/blog/post/index
```

And add the category processing inside the index action.

First, create and open the `BLOGPATH/config/routes.php` file, and set its content to:

```
<?php
return array(
    'blog/post/category/:category_id' => 'blog/post/index',
);
```

Now we have to add the category processing inside our index action in the **Post** controller. First, in the index action of the **Post** controler, replace:

```
$config = array(...);
```

By:

```
$config = array(
    'per_page'       => 10,
    'uri_segment'    => 'page',
);

// Get the category_id route parameter
$category_id = $this->param('category_id');
if (is_null($category_id)) {
    $config['total_items'] = Model_Post::count();
} else {
    $config['total_items'] = Model_Post::count(
        array(
            'where' => array(
                array('category_id' => $category_id),
            ),
        )
    );
}
```

Then, replace:

```
$data['posts'] = Model_Post::find(...);
```

By:

```
$data['posts'] = Model_Post::query()
    ->related(array('author', 'category'))
    ->rows_offset($pagination->offset)
    ->rows_limit($pagination->per_page);

if (!is_null($category_id)) {
    $data['posts']->where('category_id', $category_id);
}

$data['posts'] = $data['posts']->get();
```

You can notice we used the `query` method here as it was more convenient than the `find` method in this case.

Adding indexes

In order to optimize our website, we will add some indexes to our tables. For doing that, create a migration file located at `BLOGPATH/migrations/004_create_indexes.php` and set its content to:

```
<?php

namespace Fuel\Migrations;

class Create_indexes
{
  public function up()
  {
        // For optimizing relations
        \DBUtil::create_index('comments', 'post_id');
        \DBUtil::create_index('posts', 'category_id');
        \DBUtil::create_index('posts', 'user_id');

        // For optimizing slug retrieval
        \DBUtil::create_index('posts', 'slug');
  }
```

```
    public function down()
    {
            \DBUtil::drop_index('comments', 'post_id');
            \DBUtil::drop_index('posts', 'category_id');
            \DBUtil::drop_index('posts', 'user_id');
            \DBUtil::drop_index('posts', 'slug');
    }
}
```

Don't forget to execute the migration file.

Refining the posts' visualization webpage

When clicking on a post's title in the listing page, you will see that the visualization webpage is not perfect. We need to improve how it is displayed, to display the post's validated comments, and to display and process the comment form.

Changing the post layout

In order to improve how a post is displayed, open the `BLOGPATH/views/post/view.php` view file and set the following content:

```
<div class="post_view">
<h2>
<?php echo $post->title; ?>
</h2>

<?php
// Reusing views we created earlier
echo \View::forge(
    'post/small_description',
    array('post' => $post)
);
?>
<div class="post_content">
<?php echo $post->content; ?>
</div>
<?php
echo \View::forge(
    'post/additional_informations',
    array('post' => $post)
);
?>
</div>
<?php echo Html::anchor('blog/post', 'Back'); ?>
```

Now, if you visualize a post with a content containing HTML elements, you will see that it will be escaped (you will see the HTML code). This is because any parameter sent to a view is by default filtered.

> The way each parameter is by default filtered can be changed in the `APPPATH/config/config.php` configuration file, using the `security.output_filter` key. Its default value is `array('Security::htmlentities')`, explaining why the HTML code is escaped. You could change this value to `array('Security::xss_clean')` to solve this issue, but you should know that it can potentially cause a performance hit.

For solving that, inside the view action of the **Post** controller, add:

```
$this->template->content->set(
'post_content',
$data['post']->content,
false
);
```

After:

```
$this->template->content->set(
    'post_content',
    $data['post']->content,
    false
);
```

And, in the `BLOGPATH/views/post/view.php` view file, replace:

```
<?php echo $post->content; ?>
```

By:

```
<?php echo \Security::xss_clean($post_content); ?>
```

You should be cautious when disabling the `filter` parameter, as it can add security issues. Since the posts are edited only by administrators, it is less risky, but this doesn't prevent us from taking extra measures. That is why we used the `Security::xss_clean` method to limit potential issues.

You are probably wondering why we set the post content in an additional unfiltered view parameter, instead of just setting the `filter` parameter of `View::forge` to false. The reason is that, in that case, we would have sent a totally unfiltered `post` object (since all objects properties are filtered when `filter` is set to true). This would have forced us to manually escape most other properties we display on views, resulting in many more changes.

If you decide, in another case, to disable the `filter` parameter directly in `View::forge`, beware of an important detail; when the `filter` parameter is enabled, it escapes all passed objects' properties and therefore, changes them in the process. Consequently, the objects will be irreversibly changed after any `View::forge` with the `filter` parameter set to `true`. Thus, even if you set the `filter` parameter to false when calling `View::forge` in the controller, your objects' attributes might still get escaped if you are displaying sub views with `filter` set to `true`, so be sure to disable `filter` in that case too.

Adding the comment form

We also want the user to be able to post comments. To do that, we will first implement the comment creation form (derived from the one of the administration panel). Create the `BLOGPATH/views/comment/_form.php` view file and set its content to:

```
<h3>Add a comment</h3>
<?php echo Form::open(array("class"=>"form-horizontal")); ?>

  <fieldset>
    <div class="form-group">
<?php
echo Form::label(
    'Name',
    'name',
    array('class' => 'control-label')
);

echo Form::input(
    'name',
    Input::post(
        'name',
    isset($comment) ? $comment->name : ''
    ),
    array(
```

```
            'class' => 'col-md-4 form-control',
            'placeholder' => 'Name'
        )
    );
    ?>

        </div>
        <div class="form-group">
    <?php
    echo Form::label(
        'Email',
        'email',
        array('class' => 'control-label')
    );

    echo Form::input(
        'email',
        Input::post(
            'email',
            isset($comment) ? $comment->email : ''
        ),
        array(
            'class' => 'col-md-4 form-control',
            'placeholder' => 'Email'
        )
    );
    ?>

        </div>
        <div class="form-group">
    <?php
    echo Form::label(
        'Content',
        'content',
        array('class' => 'control-label')
    );

    echo Form::textarea(
        'content',
        Input::post(
            'content',
            isset($comment) ? $comment->content : ''
        ),
        array(
```

```
            'class' => 'col-md-8 form-control',
            'rows' => 8,
            'placeholder' => 'Content'
        )
);
?>

        </div>
        <div class="form-group">
          <label class='control-label'> </label>
<?php
echo Form::submit(
    'submit',
    'Save',
    array('class' => 'btn btn-primary')
);
?>
</div>
  </fieldset>
<?php echo Form::close(); ?>
```

As mentioned earlier, it is a derived version of the comment form in the administration panel, except we removed the **Status** and **Post** fields. Now, add the following line at the end of `BLOGPATH/views/post/view.php` to display the form when showing a post:

```
<?php echo View::forge('comment/_form'); ?>
```

We now have to process it. Open the **Post** controller and, inside the view action, before the following line:

```
$this->template->title = "Post";
```

Add:

```
// Is the user sending a comment? If yes, process it.
if (Input::method() == 'POST')
{
    $val = Model_Comment::validate('create');

    if ($val->run())
    {
        $comment = Model_Comment::forge(array(
            'name' => Input::post('name'),
            'email' => Input::post('email'),
```

```
            'content' => Input::post('content'),
            'status' => 'pending',
            'post_id' => $data['post']->id,
        ));

        if ($comment and $comment->save())
        {
            Session::set_flash(
                'success',
                e('Your comment has been saved, it will'.
                 ' be reviewed by our administrators')
            );
        }

        else
        {
            Session::set_flash(
                'error',
                e('Could not save comment.')
            );
        }
    }
    else
    {
        Session::set_flash('error', $val->error());
    }
}
```

This is derived from the generated scaffold code, so there is nothing that you have not already seen. If you try to validate the comment form, you will notice that the `status` validation prevents the comment object from being saved. Open the `BLOGPATH/model/comment.php` model file, and replace:

```
$val->add_field('status', 'Status',
  'required|max_length[255]');
```

By:

```
// We require status only if we are editing the comment (thus
// we are on the administration panel).
if ($factory == 'edit') {
    $val->add_field(
        'status',
        'Status',
```

```
            'required|max_length[255]'
        );
    }
```

Displaying comments

Now that the user is able to create comments, it would be nice to display them. A small correction; it would be nice to display those that have been validated by the administrator. We don't want to display all comments, but only those with their `status = published`. In order to make our work easier, we will first add a relation to the **Post** model that only retrieves published comments. Open the **Post** model, and add the following at the end of the `$_has_many` property:

```
'published_comments' => array(
    'model_to'          => '\Blog\Model_Comment',
    'conditions' => array(
        'where' => array(
            array('status' => 'published'),
        ),
    ),
),
```

As you can see, it is also possible to add default conditions (and orders) to relations. From now on, `$post->published_comments` will retrieve the post's comments with `status = published`.

Let's use this relation to display our published comments. Open `BLOGPATH/views/post/view.php` and before:

```
<?php echo View::forge('comment/_form'); ?>
```

Add:

```
<div class="comments">
<?php
foreach ($post->published_comments as $comment):
    echo \View::forge(
        'comment/item',
        array('comment' => $comment)
    );
endforeach;
?>
</div>
```

Finally, create the `BLOGPATH/views/comment/item.php` view file and set its content to:

```
<div class="comment">
<div class="comment_content">
<?php echo $comment->content; ?>
</div>
<div class="comment_date">
<?php
echo \Date::forge($comment->created_at)->format('us_full');
?>
</div>
<div class="comment_name">
        By
<?php echo $comment->name; ?>
</div>
</div>
```

Notifying the author when a new comment is posted

As comments require a validation from the administrator, we will send an email to the post's author when a new comment is posted.

We will do that with the `Email` package. This package is located at the `PKGPATH/email` directory. You can adapt the package configuration file by copying `PKGPATH/email/config/email.php` to `APPPATH/config/email.php` and changing the returned array, depending on your local configuration. You must at least set the `defaults.from.email` and `defaults.from.name` values.

You can choose between several email drivers. The default driver is `mail` and, as we could expect, simply use the `mail` PHP method. The `sendmail` driver is also commonly chosen and use the open source `sendmail` utility. The `smtp` driver connects to the email server using sockets. Other drivers, such as `mailgun` or `mandrill`, allow you to use external services to send your emails.

You should read the official documentation at

`http://fuelphp.com/docs/packages/email/introduction.html`

(It can be accessed through FuelPHP website by navigating to **DOCS** | **TABLE OF CONTENTS** | **Email** | **Introduction**)

> If you want to send emails from your local system, you will probably have to change additional configuration files, such as `php.ini`. Feel free to search the web for more information, as there are countless resources on the topic.

In order to send those emails, open the **Post** controller and, inside the view action, just before:

```
Session::set_flash('success', ...);
```

Add:

```
// Manually loading the Email package
\Package::load('email');

$email = \Email::forge();

// Setting the to address
$email->to(
    $data['post']->author->email,
    $data['post']->author->username
);

// Setting a subject
$email->subject('New comment');

// Setting the body and using a view since the message is long
$email->body(
    \View::forge(
        'comment/email',
        array(
            'comment' => $comment,
        )
    )->render()
);

// Sending the email
$email->send();
```

Finally, create the `BLOGPATH/views/comment/email.php` view file and set its content to:

```
Hi,

A new comment has been posted.


Author: <?php echo $comment->name; ?>


Email: <?php echo $comment->email; ?>


Content:
<?php echo $comment->content; ?>



Go to the administration panel to accept / reject it.
<?php echo Uri::base().'admin' ?>


Thanks,
```

Clearing rejected comments

If your blog gets spammed and you find yourself with a lot of comments with status set as `not_published`, you might want to remove all these comments to clean your comments database. We could simply implement a link and an action but, for the sake of the example, let's implement a task for doing that.

Tasks are classes that can be executed through the command line using the `oil` utility. They are generally used for background processes or cron jobs. Sometimes, they can also be used for generating or modifying existing code, like the task we previously used for moving scaffolds to modules.

Let's generate our task file using the `oil` utility:

```
php oil generate task clearComments
```

It should output:

```
No tasks actions have been provided, the TASK will only create default
task.
    Preparing task method [Index]
Creating tasks: APPPATH/tasks/clearcomments.php
```

If you now open the task file located at `APPPATH/tasks/clearcomments.php`, you should see the following class:

```
<?php
namespace Fuel\Tasks;

class Clearcomments
{
    // ...
  public function run($args = NULL)
  {
    // ...
  }

    // ...
  public function index($args = NULL)
  {
    // ...
  }
}
```

The `oil` utility generated a class named `Clearcomments`, with two methods: `run` and `index`. Each method can be called using the `oil` utility.

The following command executes the `run` method:

```
php oil refine clearComments:run
```

The following command executes the `index` method:

```
php oil refine clearComments:index
```

If you add a public method named `my_method`, it will also be called when executing:

```
php oil refine clearComments:my_method
```

The `run` method is the default method and can therefore be called this way:

```
php oil refine clearComments
```

It is possible to pass additional parameters to the task. For instance:

```
php oil refine clearComments:run param_1 param_2
```

In that case, the `oil` utility will call `Clearcomments::run('param_1', 'param_2')`.

You should read the official documentation at:

`http://fuelphp.com/docs/packages/oil/generate.html#/tasks`

(It can be accessed through FuelPHP website by navigating to **DOCS** | **TABLE OF CONTENTS** | **Oil** | **Generate**)

`http://fuelphp.com/docs/general/tasks.html`

(It can be accessed through FuelPHP website by navigating to **DOCS** | **TABLE OF CONTENTS** | **FuelPHP** | **General** | **Tasks**)

Replace the class content by the following:

```
public function run()
{
    \DB::query(
        'DELETE FROM comments WHERE status="not_published";'
    )->execute();
    return 'Rejected comments deleted.';
}
```

Now, if you run:

```
php oil refine clearComments
```

It should delete all rejected comments.

You can execute this task manually or you can set up a cron job to execute it regularly.

Additional improvements

Many additional improvements are possible. Some edge cases need to be handled: for instance, try to successfully display the administration panel when post or categories are deleted. You can set the route configuration so that your welcome page shows your posts' listing. When visualizing a post, you can optimize the SQL requests being sent, by using the related parameter. You could even send an e-mail to all commenters when a new comment is being posted, and allow them to unsubscribe if they want to. You should add the improvements you deem necessary, this can only have a beneficial effect on your FuelPHP skills.

We have one additional suggestion about modules. In this chapter, for the sake of simplicity and conciseness, we created a single module, blog, to manage posts, comments and categories. Yet, depending on the website, developers might want to disable (for instance, disable comments), change these features or even add new ones.

We could handle this issue by creating a configuration file defining whether or not a specific feature should be enabled, or the way some features should operate. It can do the trick but, if your module accumulates many features, your code could become unmaintainable.

A better way to solve this issue is to create several smaller modules that handle each feature. After all, comments can also be used on product pages, for instance. There can also be multiple ways to display a list of posts, so separating models and controllers/views into distinct modules can also be a good idea. You should always aim for simple and small modules that interact with each other, instead of a big module that does everything.

Summary

In this chapter, we have built a complex project with many features. By trying to make the code as maintainable as possible (by using modules for instance), we have provided a snapshot of how projects should be implemented so that adding new features remains easy. We have also addressed some common ORM issues, learnt how to easily paginate a listing, and used the Auth and Email packages. You certainly don't know everything about the FuelPHP framework, but implementing most projects should not be a problem for you now.

In the next chapter, you will learn how to add reusable features by installing an external package as well as creating your own.

4 Creating and Using Packages

In this chapter, you will learn how to install, use, and create FuelPHP packages. For illustration purposes, we suppose that we want to prevent spammers and bots from polluting our website, and we will explore two different solutions for solving this issue. We will first use an existing package (recatpcha), and then we will create our own package.

By the end of this chapter, you will know:

- What are CAPTCHAs
- How to install an external package manually or with the oil command line
- What is reCAPTCHA and how to use the associated FuelPHP package
- How to create your own package
- What is a bootstrap file and how to use it

What are CAPTCHAs?

CAPTCHAs (**Completely Automated Public Turing test to tell Computers and Humans Apart**) are generally used to prevent bots or programs from accessing some features of a website. For instance, in a blog, you may want to prevent bots from adding unsolicited and unrelated ads in the comments section. If you want your users to pay a membership fee to access your content, you might also want to prevent programs from aspiring this restricted content.

You have probably already seen a lot of CAPTCHAs, generally displayed as distorted text inside images. A well-known service is reCAPTCHA, whose verification form looks like the following image:

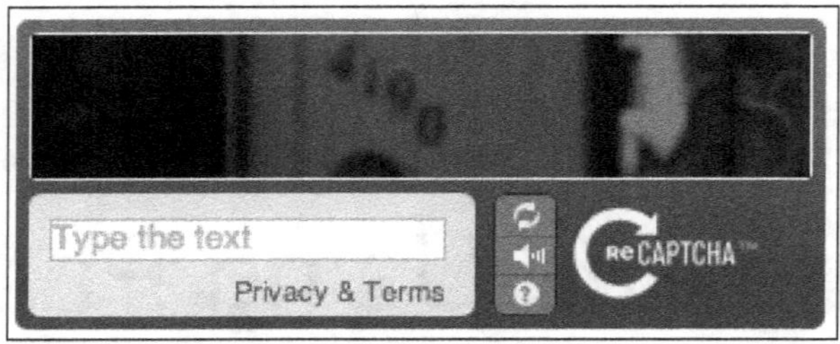

Unfortunately, since there are a lot of incentives to create Spam bots, no CAPTCHA system is perfect, but at least they make the bots' work more difficult.

Preliminary steps

You first need to follow the given steps:

1. Install a new FuelPHP instance.
2. Configure Apache and your host file to handle it. In this chapter, we will access our application by requesting `http://mytest.app`.
3. Update Composer if necessary.
4. Create a new database for your application.
5. Configure FuelPHP in order to allow your application to access this database.

These steps have been covered in *Chapter 1, Building Your First FuelPHP Application,* so you might want to take a look at it.

Generating the sample application

In order to test our packages, we will create a simple application that will handle dummy items. Just to be perfectly clear, we are not interested here by the ultimate goal of the application; this is just a test application. Most of the work will be done inside the packages. The user interface and the model will therefore be very simple and will be fully generated by the scaffold command of the `oil` utility. The packages will later be connected to the creation and edition features to determine whether or not the visitor is human.

First, generate the scaffold using the following command:

```
php oil generate scaffold/crud item name:string
```

It will print the following output:

```
Creating migration: APPPATH/migrations/001_create_items.php
Creating model: APPPATH/classes/model/item.php
Creating controller: APPPATH/classes/controller/item.php
Creating view: APPPATH/views/item/index.php
Creating view: APPPATH/views/item/view.php
Creating view: APPPATH/views/item/create.php
Creating view: APPPATH/views/item/edit.php
Creating view: APPPATH/views/item/_form.php
Creating view: APPPATH/views/template.php
```

Then, execute the generated migration file by executing the following command:

```
php oil refine migrate
```

If you now request the following URL, our test application should work perfectly:

`http://mytest.app/item`

The reCAPTCHA solution

The first method for integrating a CAPTCHA system into your website is to use FuelPHP's **recaptcha package**. This is a convenient solution, since there is not much to be implemented and it allows you to integrate a well-known CAPTCHA system that your visitors are used to dealing with.

Installing the recaptcha package

First, we will install the recaptcha package, which easily integrates the **reCAPTCHA service** into your FuelPHP application.

The reCAPTCHA service is a popular and free service provided by Google that allows you to check whether or not your visitor is a bot by asking him/her to enter words seen in distorted text images on screen. An interesting fact is that it helps to digitize the text of actual images and books.

Installing the package is very simple. Visit the following URL:

`https://github.com/fuel-packages/fuel-recaptcha`

Now, click on the **Download ZIP** button and then unzip the file inside the `PKGPATH` directory (`fuel/packages`).

There are alternative ways of downloading packages. You can use the `oil` utility using the following command:

```
php oil package install recaptcha
```

It is recommended that you read the official documentation about this `oil` feature available at the following URL:

`http://fuelphp.com/docs/packages/oil/package.html`

(Can be accessed through the FuelPHP website by navigating to **DOCS** | **TABLE OF CONTENTS** | **Oil** | **Package**)

Some packages can also be installed through the Composer utility.

Configuring the recaptcha package

Before proceeding, you need to create an account on the reCAPTCHA website:

`http://www.google.com/recaptcha`

Once this is done, you have to copy the `PKGPATH/fuel-recaptcha/config/recaptcha.php` configuration file to `APPPATH/config/recaptcha.php` and set inside the new file the `private_key` and `public_key` keys provided in the reCAPTCHA website.

Integrating the recaptcha package

Now that we have installed and configured the recaptcha package in our FuelPHP instance, we just have to integrate it into our creation and edition forms. Open the `APPPATH/views/item/_form.php` file, and between the two `div` elements with the `form-group` class, add the following code:

```
<div class="form-group">
<?php
echo Form::label('Please verify that you are human');

// It is how we display the recaptcha form as you can read
// in the package readme file.
echo ReCaptcha::instance()->get_html();
?>
</div>
```

At the beginning of the `create` and `edit` action of the `Item` controller, add the following line of code:

```
Package::load('fuel-recaptcha');
```

If you display the creation or edition form, the reCAPTCHA validation system will appear as shown in the following screenshot:

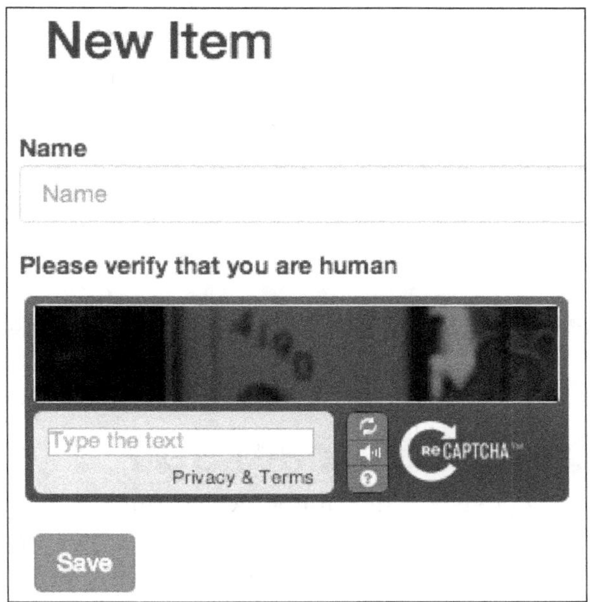

All we have to do now is to check whether the value entered by the user is correct. Open the `Item` controller, and in the `create` and `edit` actions, surround the following code:

```
$val = Model_Item::validate(/* 'create' or 'edit' */);

if ($val->run())
// And the following if else statement content
```

By:

```
if (static::is_captcha_correct())
{
    // Code to be surrounded
} else {
    Session::set_flash(
```

```
            'error',
            'You have entered an invalid value for the CAPTCHA'
        );
    }
```

In the `Item` controller, add the CAPTCHA verification method:

```
public static function is_captcha_correct() {
    // This is how a CAPTCHA is checked according to the
    // package readme file.
    return ReCaptcha::instance()
        ->check_answer(
            Input::real_ip(),
            Input::post('recaptcha_challenge_field'),
            Input::post('recaptcha_response_field')
    );
}
```

Any item addition/edition will now fail if you enter an invalid value for the CAPTCHA.

Creating your own package

The solution we saw previously can be implemented quickly, but there is a major flaw; reCAPTCHA is very well known, and there are various online services that offer to decode thousands of them for a few dollars (they can use Optical Character Recognition or even actual human solvers). In fact, any well-known system has the same problem, so sometimes the best solution lies more in the originality of the system than its absolute robustness. Indeed, even if the new system is much simpler, it will force spammers to specifically create new bots if they want to pollute your website, thus creating a kind of resistance (as long as your website is not popular).

We will therefore build a new CAPTCHA package in order to create our own original solution. Instead of displaying an image containing distorted text, we will simply ask the visitor to calculate a simple addition.

Please note that the solution is only implemented to demonstrate how a package can be built. We will therefore, choose a very simple solution that can potentially be easily decoded. You are welcome to adapt this modest package to create your own robust verification system.

Conception

As we need to check whether the user has entered the correct number on the server, we will save the expected answer in the database. For doing this, we will generate the `Captcha_Answer` model that will only contain the `id`, `expected_value`, and `created_at` attributes.

Generating the package

We will again use the `oil` command to generate a scaffold for our package:

```
php oil generate package captcha
```

This will print the following output:

```
Creating file: PKGPATH/captcha/classes/captcha.php
Creating file: PKGPATH/captcha/config/captcha.php
Creating file: PKGPATH/captcha/bootstrap.php
```

You can see that several files have been generated. If you open the `Captcha` class located at `PKGPATH/captcha/classes/captcha.php`, you will see that the class is in the `Captcha` namespace and several methods are already implemented:

```
<?php
namespace Captcha;

class CaptchaException extends \FuelException {}

class Captcha
{
    // ...
    protected static $_defaults = array();
    // ...
    protected $config = array();
    // ...
    public static function _init()
    {
        \Config::load('captcha', true);
    }
    // ...
    public static function forge($config = array())
    {
        $config = \Arr::merge(
            static::$_defaults,
```

```
            \Config::get('captcha', array()),
            $config
        );
        $class = new static($config);
        return $class;
    }
    // ...
    public function __construct(array $config = array())
    {
        $this->config = $config;
    }
    // ...
    public function get_config($key, $default = null)
    {
        return \Arr::get($this->config, $key, $default);
    }
    // ...
    public function set_config($key, $value)
    {
        \Arr::set($this->config, $key, $value);
        return $this;
    }
}
```

- There are five methods, as follows: The constructor, where you pass the package configuration as a parameter.
- The static `forge` method, which gets the package configuration file located at `PKGPATH/captcha/config/captcha.php` and passes it to the constructor. This means that if you create a `Captcha` object using the `forge` method, its configuration will automatically be loaded from the configuration file, whereas if you create it using the constructor, you will have to define the package configuration manually.
- The `get_config` and `set_config` methods are self-explanatory.
- The `_init` method, which is called when the `Captcha` class is initialized. In a general manner, in any class, if you define a static `_init` method, it will be called when the class is loaded by FuelPHP. In our class, the method loads the configuration file located at `PKGPATH/captcha/config/captcha.php`.

The `PKGPATH/captcha/config/captcha.php` configuration file is currently an empty array, but you are free to add as many parameters as you wish.

The `captcha` package we generated also has a `bootstrap` file located at `PKGPATH/captcha/bootstrap.php`. This `bootstrap` file is executed when the package is loaded. Similarly, the `APPPATH/bootstrap.php` file is executed when your application is loaded (almost each time a web page is requested).

If you open the `PKGPATH/captcha/bootstrap.php` file, you will see the following code:

```
<?php

Autoloader::add_core_namespace('Captcha');

Autoloader::add_classes(array(
  'Captcha\\Captcha' => __DIR__ . '/classes/captcha.php',
  'Captcha\\CaptchaException' => __DIR__ . '/classes/captcha.php',

));
```

The `Autoloader::add_classes` method specifies to the Autoloader where classes can be found. For instance, after executing the `bootstrap` file, FuelPHP will know that the `Captcha\Captcha` class is located in the `PKGPATH/captcha/classes/captcha.php` file.

The `Autoloader::add_core_namespace` method specifies to the `Autoloader` a namespace that needs to be added to the core namespace. In practical terms, after executing the `bootstrap` file, `\Captcha\Captcha` and `\Captcha` will both refer to the same class.

It is recommended that you read the Autoloader official documentation that can be found at:

`http://fuelphp.com/docs/classes/autoloader.html`

(This can be accessed by navigating to the FuelPHP website at **DOCS** | **TABLE OF CONTENTS** | **Core** | **Autoloader**)

It is also recommended that you read the official documentation about packages:

`http://fuelphp.com/docs/general/packages.html`

(This can be accessed by navigating to the FuelPHP website at **DOCS** | **TABLE OF CONTENTS** | **FuelPHP** | **General** | **Packages**.)

Generating the Captcha_Answer model

For speeding up the process, we will again use the `oil` command line:

```
php oil generate model captcha_answer expected_value:int created_at:int
--crud
```

This will print the following output:

```
Creating model: APPPATH/classes/model/captcha/answer.php
Creating migration: APPPATH/migrations/002_create_captcha_answers.php
```

Before doing anything else, you need to move these files into our package:

- Move `APPPATH/classes/model/captcha/answer.php` to `PKGPATH/captcha/classes/model/captcha/answer.php`.
- Also, move `APPPATH/migrations/002_create_captcha_answers.php` to `PKGPATH/captcha/migrations/001_create_captcha_answers.php` (don't forget to rename the file).

Once it is done, open `PKGPATH/captcha/classes/model/captcha/answer.php` and add the following at the beginning of the file (after `<?php`):

```
namespace Captcha;
```

You also need to add the following property inside the model, in order to automatically fill the `created_at` property:

```
protected static $_created_at = 'created_at';
```

Open the `bootstrap` file located at `PKGPATH/captcha/bootstrap.php`, and add the following code at the end of the array passed to `Autoloader::add_classes`:

```
    'Captcha\\Model_Captcha_Answer' => __DIR__ .
      '/classes/model/captcha/answer.php',
```

Migrating the package

We now need to execute the migration file in the `Captcha` package. In order to do this, simply enter the following command:

```
php oil refine migrate --packages=captcha
```

Integrating the package into our application

In this section, for the sake of clarity, we will assume that you haven't implemented the reCAPTCHA solution. Although, it is worth noting that this new implementation will clearly be inspired from it. Thus, if you have implemented the reCAPTCHA solution, simply replace the old code by the new one as you go.

First, add the following methods in the `Captcha` class located at `PKGPATH/captcha/classes/captcha.php`:

```
public function check_answer($id, $answer) {
    return true;
}

public function get_html() {
    return '<div>Will be implemented in the next section</div>';
}
```

You can notice we didn't implement anything inside those methods; these are just dummy methods. As they are a little bit complex, we will complete them in the next section, but for now we will connect them to the test application. Open the `APPPATH/views/item/_form.php`, and between the two `div` elements with the `form-group` class, add the following lines of code:

```
<div class="form-group">
<?php
echo Form::label('Please verify that you are human');

// Displaying the captcha form
echo Captcha::forge()->get_html();
?>
</div>
```

At the beginning of the `create` and `edit` action of the `Item` controller, add the following code:

```
Package::load('captcha');
```

We have now to check whether the value entered by the user is correct. Open the `Item` controller, and in the `create` and `edit` actions, surround the following code:

```
$val = Model_Item::validate(/* 'create' or 'edit' */);

if ($val->run())
// And the following if else statement content
```

By:

```
if (static::is_captcha_correct())
{
    // Code to be surrounded
} else {
    Session::set_flash(
        'error',
        'You have entered an invalid value for the captcha'
    );
}
```

Finally, still in the `Item` controller, add the CAPTCHA verification method:

```
public static function is_captcha_correct() {
    // Checking the captcha
    return Captcha::forge()
        ->check_answer(
            Input::post('captcha_id'),
            Input::post('captcha_answer')
    );
}
```

If you now test your application, the message **Will be implemented in the next section** will appear under **Please verify that you are human**, and any item will be added or updated without any checking, as shown in the following screenshot:

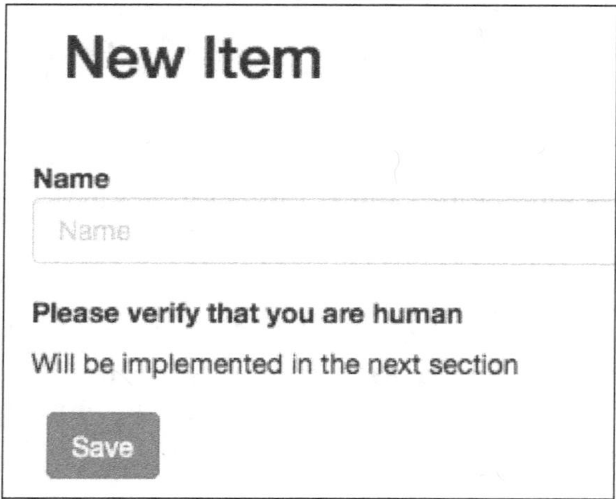

Implementing the get_html method

Open the `Captcha` class and replace the `get_html` method by the following:

```
/**
* Returns the CAPTCHA form
*
* @return string the CAPTCHA form html code
*/
public function get_html() {

    // Getting configuration
    $min_number = $this->get_config('min_number');
    $max_number = $this->get_config('max_number');

    // Generating two random numbers
    $number_1 = rand($min_number, $max_number);
    $number_2 = rand($min_number, $max_number);

    // Computing the correct answer
    $answer = $number_1 + $number_2;

    // Saving the expected answer
    $captcha_answer = Model_Captcha_Answer::forge();
    $captcha_answer->expected_value = $answer;
    $captcha_answer->save();


    return \View::forge(
        'captcha',
        array(
            'number_1' => $number_1,
            'number_2' => $number_2,
            'captcha_answer' => $captcha_answer,
        )
    )->render();
}
```

As you can see, we are calling the `captcha` view inside the `get_html` method. Thus, we need to implement it. Create the `PKGPATH/captcha/views/captcha.php` view file and add the following content:

```
<div class="captcha_area">
    <div class="captcha_instruction">
        <?php echo $number_1; ?> + <?php echo $number_2; ?> ?
    </div>
    <div class="captcha_fields">
        <input type="hidden" name="captcha_id"
               value="<?php echo $captcha_answer->id; ?>" />
        <input type="text" name="captcha_answer"
               value="" class="col-md-4 form-control" />
    </div>
</div>
```

Finally, as you probably noticed in the `new get_html` method, we get `min_number` and `max_number` from the configuration file, so we need to define these values (feel free to change them). Open the `PKGPATH/captcha/config/captcha.php` configuration file, and replace its content by the following lines of code:

```
<?php

return array(
    'min_number' => 1,
    'max_number' => 9,
);
```

If you reload the creation or edition form, you will now see the CAPTCHA verification form:

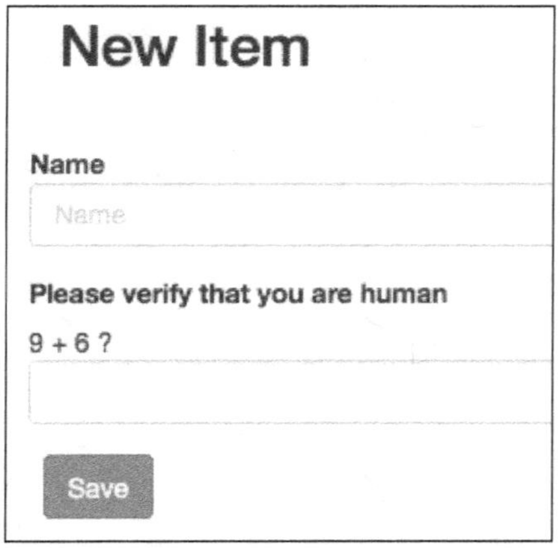

Implementing the CAPTCHA verification method

The `check_answer` method is pretty simple; as we saved the expected answer into a `Model_Captcha_Answer` instance, we just have to retrieve it and check whether the posted answer is correct. In the `Captcha` class, replace the `check_answer` method by the following code:

```
/**
* Check if the captcha is valid
*
* @param int $id id of the CAPTCHA answer
* @param string $answer answer given by the visitor
* @return boolean is the answer correct ?
*/
public function check_answer($id, $answer) {
    // Model::find_by_pk finds an instance by its
    // Primary Key (in our case, id).
    $captcha_answer = Model_Captcha_Answer::find_by_pk(
        intval($id)
    );
    $correct = $captcha_answer->expected_value == $answer;

    // The answer has been checked, so no need to keep the
    // expected answer
    $captcha_answer->delete();

    return $correct;
}
```

Cleaning old captchas

As you might have noticed, each time we display a CAPTCHA, we add a new row into the `captcha_answers` table, and this row will be cleared when, or rather if, the user submits their answer. If the user leaves the form without submitting it, the row will never be deleted. A good practice would be to periodically delete these rows. We could use the model's delete method for this, but since there can be several rows to be removed, we will instead simply execute a SQL request.

Still in the `Captcha` class, add the following method:

```
/**
* Clean the old captchas
*/
public function clean_old_captchas() {
    \DB::query('
        DELETE FROM `captcha_answers`
        WHERE `created_at` < '.
       intval(\Date::forge()->get_timestamp()
        - $this->get_config('captcha_expiration'))
        .';')
        ->execute();
}
```

You can then add the following at the beginning of the `get_html` and `check_answer` methods:

```
$this->clean_old_captchas();
```

Since we are using `$this->get_config('captcha_expiration')` to determine when a CAPTCHA expires, we need to define the `captcha_expiration` key in the `PKGPATH/captcha/config/captcha.php` configuration file:

```
// Captcha are expired 4 hours after generation
'captcha_expiration' => 3600 * 4,
```

Possible improvements

As we explained in the beginning of this section, the package can certainly be improved. Instead of displaying the addition in plain text, you could display it inside an image. You could then make it a little difficult to read, for example, by adding noise and alternating colors. This is out of scope of this chapter, since we want to focus on packages, but it is recommended that you add such features to improve your PHP and FuelPHP skills.

Summary

The main focus of this chapter was packages: how to install external packages and how to create your own packages. You have therefore learned how to create and use reusable code. We have used the **fuel-recaptcha** package, but if you go to the URL `https://github.com/fuel-packages?tab=repositories`, you will see there are a lot of different packages available. Since FuelPHP also uses Composer, you can look into `https://packagist.org/search/?q=fuel` and install additional packages using Composer.

When you think about adding a new feature in your application, it is always a good idea to see if there is an existing project fulfilling your needs. If you can't find one, you can improve a close enough package or create your own, as we did with our custom `Captcha` package. Once finished, consider sharing it, for instance, by publishing it on GitHub; you can then give back to the community who brought you this amazing framework.

In the next chapter, you will see how you can create an application providing and using its own API. We will also tackle how you can automatically test your application to prevent unwanted regressions.

5
Building Your Own Restful API

In this chapter, we will create our own microblogging application similar to Twitter. The social component will be fairly simple: users will post on their walls messages containing up to 140 characters. The real input of this chapter will reside in setting up a JSON API that can be accessed by external applications and adding automated tests that will allow you to track regressions. In order to limit the amount of data exchanged, we will make our application use this API as often as possible.

By the end of the chapter, you should know:

- How to create a signup form
- How to implement a JSON API without duplicating any code
- What is the `Parser` package
- What are language-agnostic template systems and why use such systems
- What is the Mustache engine and how to implement views using it
- What is a magic migration
- How to implement unit tests and run them

Specifications

It is possible for visitors to subscribe to our micro blogging application. Once they do, they are able to write small posts of 140 characters which will be displayed on their profile page. Anyone, even non-users, can see a user's profile page.

In order to avoid authentication issues and keep this project simple, we will only provide a read-only JSON API. Also, we won't track applications using our API and therefore no limitations will be implemented (this could be an important point if you are thinking of publishing your own API). Therefore, only the users' profile information (username, creation date, and so on) and published posts will be available through the API.

Conception

We will need the following two models:

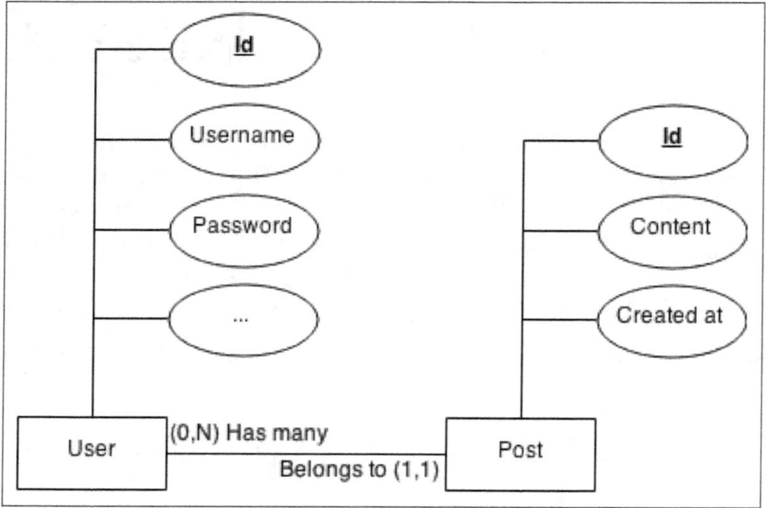

Entity Relationship diagram (Min-Max notation)

- **User**: Since the model's table will be generated from the `Auth` package's migration, the columns will already be generated. The columns we need are `username` and `password`.
- **Post**: Each post has a `content` and a `created_at` property. Since each post can only be published by a single user and each user can publish many posts, there is a `belongs_to` relationship between posts and users and a `has_many` relationship between users and posts. Thus, an additional `user_id` property must be added for the relationship.

FuelPHP installation and configuration

You first need to perform the following steps:

1. Install a new FuelPHP instance.
2. Configure Apache and the host file to handle it. In this chapter, we will access our application by requesting the `http://mymicroblog.app` URL.
3. Update Composer if necessary.
4. Create a new database for your application.
5. Finally, configure FuelPHP in order to allow your application to access this database.

This project will also need the `ORM`, the `Auth`, and the `Parser` packages. We used the `ORM` and the `Auth` packages in previous chapters, but we never used the `Parser` package; we will explain its role later in *The Parser package and template engines* section. Since they are already installed, we just need to enable them. For doing this, simply open the `APPPATH/config/config.php` file and insert the following lines of code at the end of the returned array:

```
'always_load'  => array(
    'packages'  => array(
        'orm',
        'auth',
        'parser',
    ),
),
```

Alternatively, you can uncomment the appropriate lines. This will load the `ORM`, the `Auth`, and the `Parser` package every time a FuelPHP instance is loaded. We also need to change a few configuration items for the `Auth` package.

First, copy the file located at `PKGPATH/auth/config/auth.php` to `APPPATH/config/auth.php` and `PKGPATH/auth/config/simpleauth.php` to `APPPATH/config/simpleauth.php`.

Then, open the configuration file `APPPATH/config/auth.php` and change the `salt` value to a random string (this is a security precaution). We will use the `Simpleauth` driver here, as we don't need many features in our authentication system.

Then, open the file `APPPATH/config/simpleauth.php` and set the value of `login_hash_salt` to a random string (again, for security precaution). Install the `Auth` tables by executing their migration files:

```
php oil refine migrate --packages=auth
```

If you take a look at the database, you should see that several tables have been generated:

- `users`
- `users_clients`
- `users_providers`
- `users_scopes`
- `users_sessions`
- `users_sessionscopes`

However, as expected, there are much fewer tables generated than for the `Ormauth` driver.

The Parser package and template engines

You may notice that we added the `parser` package into the `always_load.package` key. Thanks to this package, instead of writing our view in PHP, we are able to use template engines. For those of you that are not familiar with template engines, they allows us to write our view files in a different syntax.

For instance, a list of items might be displayed by writing the following code in PHP:

```
<h1>Items</h1>
<?php foreach ($items as $item) { ?>
    <li><?php echo $item->title ?></li>
<?php } ?>
<a href="item/create">Create an item</a>
```

But, using the HAML template engine, it can be written like this:

```
%h1 Items
- foreach ($items as $item)
  %li
    = $item->title
%a(href="item/create") Create an item
```

Alternatively, by using the Mustache template engine, it can be written like this:

```
<h1>Items</h1>
{{#items}}
  <li>{{title}}</li>
{{/items}}
<a href="item/create">Create an item</a>
```

There are various reasons you might want to use template engines:

- It allows you to write much more concise and elegant code, for example as in the HAML language.
- It allows you to keep a consistent code format.
- It forces you to separate logic from presentation. Thus, you can easily hand your code to a designer who can change it without having to understand any PHP.

For our project, we are going to use the Mustache template engine, but for none of the preceding reasons.

A major benefit of language-agnostic template engines

If you open the main web page of the Mustache template engine (`http://mustache.github.io/`), you are going to see that the engine is available in many different languages (Ruby, JavaScript, Python, Node.js, PHP, Java, C++, ASP, C#, and so on). However, it doesn't matter which language you are going to use the engine: the syntax of the template will remain the same and the language won't have any influence on the code you will write. This is because Mustache is a language-agnostic template engine. This is a great advantage if you work with a team using many different languages such as PHP, JavaScript, Ruby, or Python; your views can be written in the same common markup language. We are going to use this feature to our own advantage.

The following diagram shows the most common way that websites work right now:

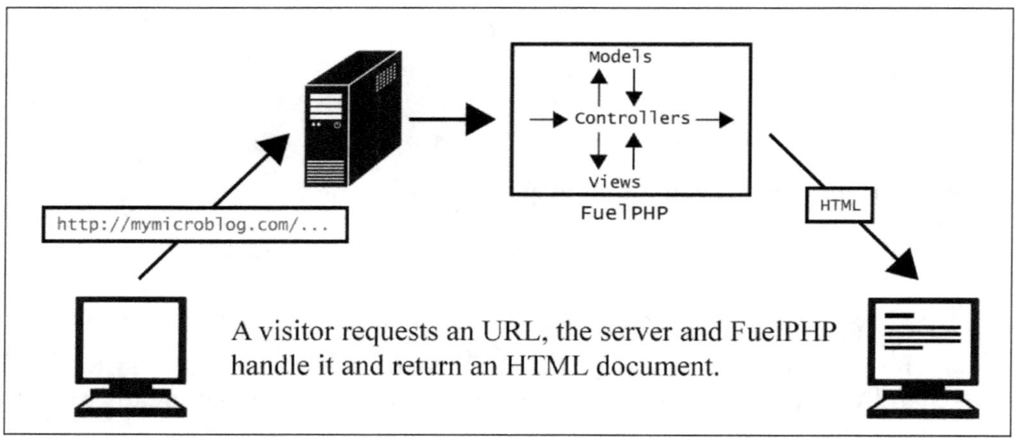

But you often need to dynamically load new content once your webpage is displayed in your browser:

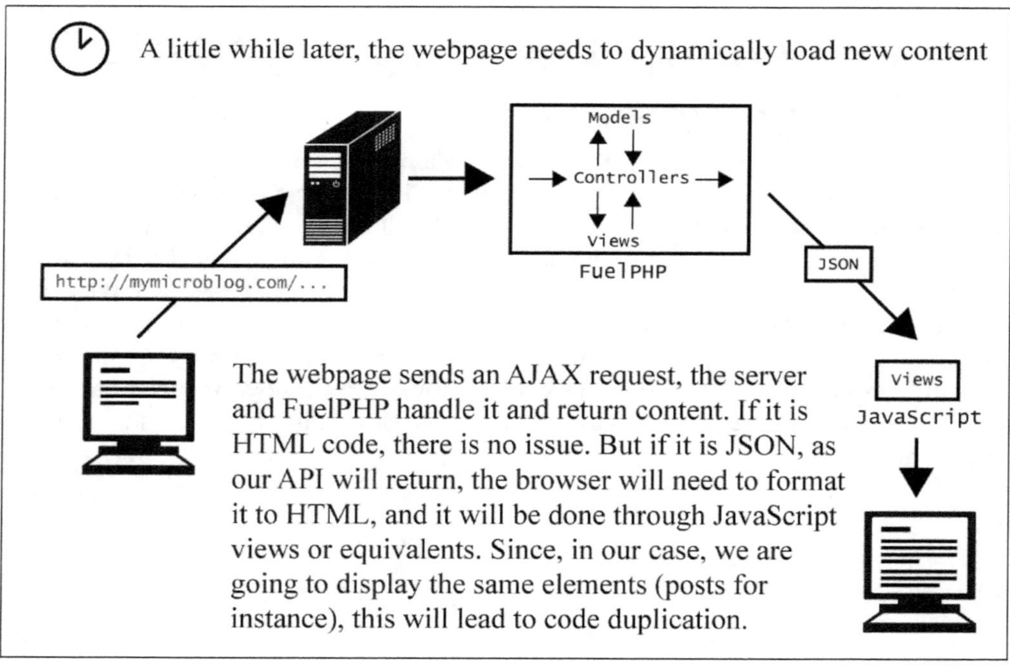

A little while later, the webpage needs to dynamically load new content
Models
Controllers
Views
FuelPHP
JSON
http://mymicroblog.com/...
Views
JavaScript
The webpage sends an AJAX request, the server and FuelPHP handle it and return content. If it is HTML code, there is no issue. But if it is JSON, as our API will return, the browser will need to format it to HTML, and it will be done through JavaScript views or equivalents. Since, in our case, we are going to display the same elements (posts for instance), this will lead to code duplication.

In order to further illustrate this, let's say we are displaying a user's profile page, and thus displaying its list of posts. If the user has already published 1000 posts, we won't display them all at once. We will first display the last 30 posts, for instance, using PHP views, so at some point the web page should look like this:

```
...
<div class="posts_list">
    <div class="post" id="post_232">
       <div class="post_author">first_user</div>
       <div class="post_content">My last post.</div>
       <div class="post_date">5 minutes ago</div>
    </div>
    <div class="post" id="post_214">
       <div class="post_author">first_user</div>
       <div class="post_content">Hello everyone.</div>
       <div class="post_date">21 minutes ago</div>
    </div>
    ...
</div>
...
```

When the visitor will scroll through the bottom of the web page, it will send an AJAX request to the server API that will replace the 30 previous posts, but in JSON format. The returned code should look like this:

```
{
    ...
    "posts": [
        {
            "id": 142,
            "content": "previous post.",
            "created_at": 1409741475,
            "author": {
                "id": 24,
                "username": "first_user"
            }
        },
        {
            "id": 125,
            "content": "very old post.",
            "created_at": 1209751372,
            "author": {
                "id": 24,
                "username": "first_user"
            }
        },
        ...
    ]
    ...
}
```

We have all the necessary data, but we need to transform it to HTML code so that the user can see it. Whether you use jQuery or direct DOM manipulations, you will need to use JavaScript code to do this (that code will act as JavaScript views). This will lead to code duplication, in the sense that, if you change the way posts are displayed in the PHP views, you will need to change the JavaScript code as well. For large projects, this will quickly become unmanageable. However, all this can change if we use the mustache template engine

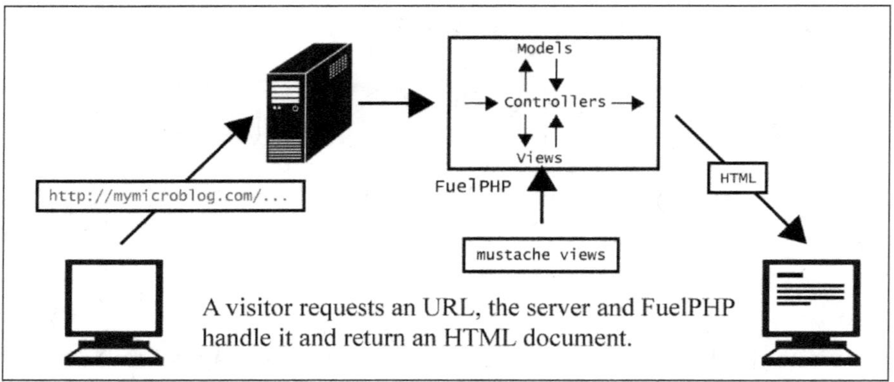
Models
Controllers
Views
FuelPHP
HTML
http://mymicroblog.com/...
mustache views
A visitor requests an URL, the server and FuelPHP handle it and return an HTML document.

Nothing exceptional here. However, the process is improved when loading dynamic content:

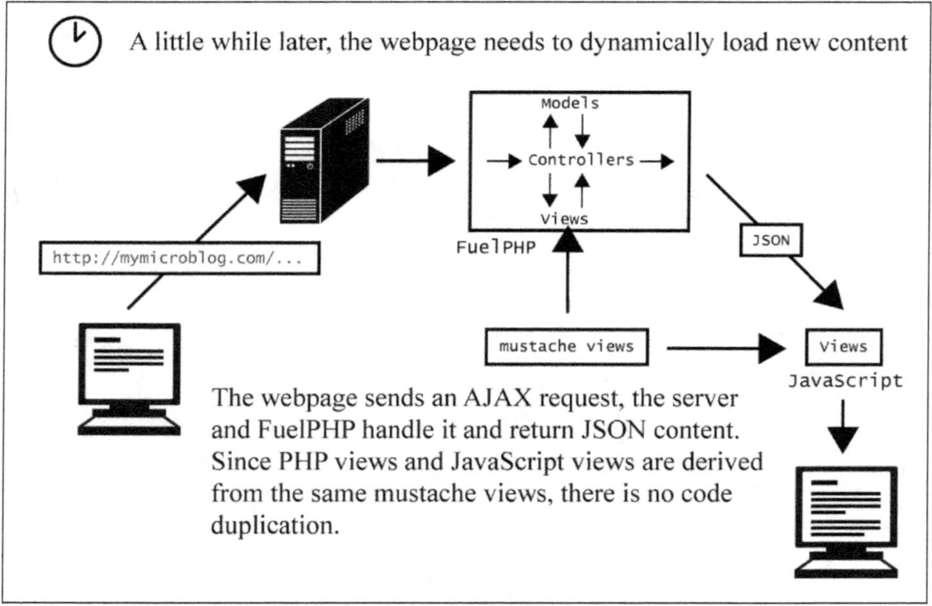
A little while later, the webpage needs to dynamically load new content
Models
Controllers
Views
FuelPHP
JSON
http://mymicroblog.com/...
mustache views
Views
JavaScript
The webpage sends an AJAX request, the server and FuelPHP handle it and return JSON content. Since PHP views and JavaScript views are derived from the same mustache views, there is no code duplication.

Since the Mustache template engine is language agnostic, it is possible to interpret a single template in both PHP and JavaScript. If we want to change, let's say, how posts are displayed, all we have to do is to change this one template. No duplication always means a more robust and maintainable application.

Of course, we could always write a full JavaScript application that would load data from the API without using any PHP views. This way, no template engine would be necessary, as we would only write JavaScript views. However, being able to return HTML content directly from the server has two benefits. First, if the client doesn't support JavaScript—as is the case for most search engines—it will still be able to access the website (so the indexing of your application will be better). Secondly, when the client is accessing your website for the first time, you can speed up the process by returning the cached HTML code of the requested web page.

In order to use the Mustache template engine, we need to install it. In the `composer.json` file, add the following line in the `require` list (don't forget to add a comma in the previous line):

```
"mustache/mustache": "2.7.0"
```

Then update Composer.

> We chose the Mustache engine mainly because of its simplicity, but you have a lot of other choices. If you want to use the API strategy we are going to implement in a more complex project, I recommend you take a look at more complete solutions. For instance, though they are not per se language-agnostic template engines, you could take a look at Smarty and its JavaScript port jSmart.

Subscription and authentication features

Instead of generating entire scaffolds, we will manually create controllers and views as we won't need most CRUD features.

Implementing the subscription and authentication forms

First, let's create the user controller. Create a file at `APPPATH/classes/controller/user.php` and set its contents to:

```
<?php
class Controller_User extends Controller_Template
{

}
```

The home page, which will be handled by the `index` action of the `User` controller, displays the user's posts if the user is logged in, otherwise it will display the subscription and authentication forms.

Since we have no user in our system, nobody can log in. Thus, we will begin the subscription and authentication forms.

First, add the following method in the `User` controller:

```
public function action_index()
{
    if (false /* is the user logged ? */) {
        // @todo: handle response if user is logged.
    } else {
        $this->template->content =
            View::forge(
                'user/connect.mustache',
                array(),
                // By default, mustache escapes displayed
                // variables, so no need to escape them here
                false
            );
    }
}
```

We will come back to this action later, but so far it should be pretty straightforward for you.

As we are using `Controller_Template`, we need to define a template. Create the template view file at `APPPATH/views/template.php` and set its contents to:

```
<!DOCTYPE html>
<html>
<head>
<?php
```

```
echo '<base '.array_to_attr(array('href' => Uri::base())).' />';
?>
    <meta charset="utf-8">
    <title>My microblog</title>
    <?php echo Asset::css('bootstrap.css'); ?>
    <?php echo Asset::css('website.css'); ?>
    <style>
        body { margin: 50px; }
    </style>
    <?php echo Asset::js(array(
        'http://code.jquery.com/jquery-1.11.2.min.js',
        'bootstrap.js'
    )); ?>
    <script>
        $(function(){ $('.topbar').dropdown(); });
    </script>
</head>
<body>

    <div class="navbar navbar-inverse navbar-fixed-top">
        <div class="container">
            <div class="navbar-header">
                <a class="navbar-brand"
<?php echo array_to_attr(array('href' => Uri::base())) ?>
                >
                    My microblog
                </a>
            </div>
        </div>
    </div>

    <div class="container">
        <div class="row">
                <div class="col-md-12">
<?php if (Session::get_flash('success')): ?>
                        <div class="alert
                             alert-success
                             alert-dismissable">
                               <button
                             type="button"
                             class="close"
                             data-dismiss="alert"
                             aria-hidden="true">
                         &times;
```

```
                        </button>
                                  <p>
<?php
echo implode(
    '</p><p>',
    (array) Session::get_flash('success')
); ?>
                                  </p>
                           </div>
<?php endif; ?>
<?php if (Session::get_flash('error')): ?>
                           <div class="alert
                                alert-danger
                                alert-dismissable">
                                  <button
                                type="button"
                                class="close"
                                data-dismiss="alert"
                                aria-hidden="true">
                            &times;
                        </button>
                                  <p>
<?php
echo implode(
    '</p><p>',
    (array) Session::get_flash('error')
); ?>
                                  </p>
                           </div>
<?php endif; ?>
                      </div>
<?php echo $content; ?>
            </div>
        </div>
</body>
</html>
```

It is inspired by the admin template generated in *Chapter 3, Building a Blog Application* you can compare it to the file used for the scaffold generation located at `PKGPATH/oil/views/admin/template.php`. We use the Bootstrap framework to easily structure our web pages in a responsive way; we will use its CSS classes from time to time. You can take a look at the official documentation for Bootstrap at `http://getbootstrap.com/`.

We will also define some custom CSS classes inside the `website.css` file. Since we are already including it in our template, create the style sheet file at `public/assets/css/website.css` and set its contents to:

```
body {
    background-color: #f8f8f8;
}

h1.home {
    font-size: 45px;
    text-align: center;
}

.alert {
    margin-top: 10px;
}
```

Now, we need to create the `APPPATH/views/user/connect.mustache` view. We need to add the sign up and sign in forms there, so no rocket science:

```
<h1 class="home">
    My microblog
</h1>
<div class="signup_or_signin">
    <div class="signin col-md-1"></div>
    <div class="signup col-md-4">
        <h2>Signup</h2>
        <form action="user/signup" method="post">
            <div class="form-group">
                <input
                        type="text"
                        name="username"
                        placeholder="Username"
                        class="form-control" />
            </div>
            <div class="form-group">
                <input
                        type="email"
                        name="email"
                        placeholder="Email"
                        class="form-control" />
            </div>
            <div class="form-group">
                <input
                        type="password"
```

```
                                name="password"
                                placeholder="Password"
                                class="form-control" />
                        </div>
                        <div class="form-group">
                            <input
                                type="submit"
                                value="Signup"
                                class="btn btn-lg
                                       btn-primary
                                       btn-block" />
                        </div>
                    </form>
                </div>
                <div class="signin col-md-2"></div>
                <div class="signin col-md-4">
                    <h2>Signin</h1>
                    <form action="user/signin" method="post">
                        <div class="form-group">
                            <input
                                type="text"
                                name="username"
                                placeholder="Email or Username"
                                class="form-control" />
                        </div>
                        <div class="form-group">
                            <input
                                type="password"
                                name="password"
                                placeholder="Password"
                                class="form-control" />
                        </div>
                        <div class="form-group">
                            <input
                                type="submit"
                                value="Signin"
                                class="btn btn-lg
                                       btn-primary
                                       btn-block" />
                        </div>
                    </form>
                </div>
                <div class="signin col-md-1"></div>
            </div>
```

Since there are no dynamic parts in our view yet, you can see it is very similar to a classic PHP or HTML view.

Finally, as we want the `index` action of the `User` controller to be our home page, we need to define its URI in the `_root_` key of our `routes` configuration file. Open the `APPPATH/config/routes.php` configuration file and set its contents to:

```
<?php
return array(
  '_root_'  => 'user/index',
);
```

If you request the following URL:

`http://mymicroblog.app/`

You should see a simple yet responsive web page with sign up and sign in forms.

In the following screenshot, you can see what the web page looks like on large screens:

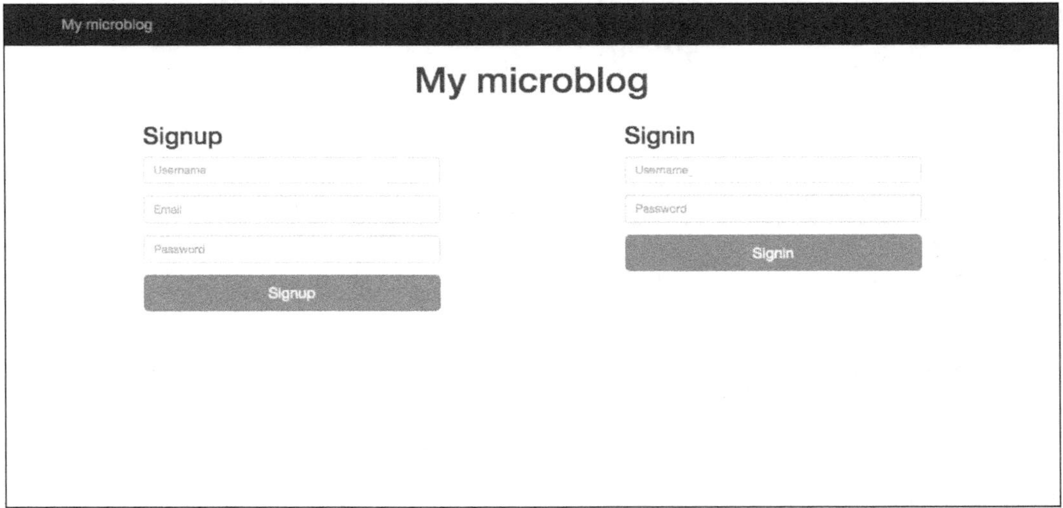

This is what the web page looks like on smaller screens and devices:

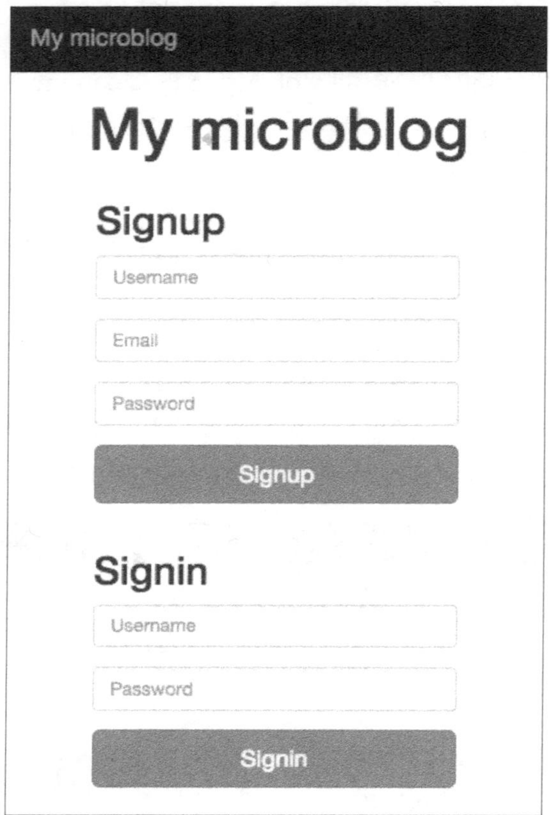

Handling the signup form

As no user exists right now, it is time to create the `signup` action in the `User` controller (targeted by the signup form) so that we can create our first user. Create the following method and read comments (you should already be familiar with all these methods):

```
public function action_signup()
{
    /*
    Validating our form (checks if the username, the
    password and the email have a correct value). We
    are using the same Validation class as we saw on
    numerous generated models
    */
```

```
$val = Validation::forge('signup_validation');
$val->add_field(
    'username',
    'Username',
    'required|valid_string[alpha,lowercase,numeric]'
);
$val->add_field(
    'password',
    'Password',
    'required|min_length[6]'
);
$val->add('email', 'Email')
    ->add_rule('required')
    ->add_rule('valid_email');

// Running validation
if ($val->run())
{
    try {
        // Since validation passed, we try to create
        // a user
        $user_id = Auth::create_user(
            Input::post('username'),
            Input::post('password'),
            Input::post('email')
        );

        /*
        Note: at this point, we could send a
        confirmation email, but for the sake of this
        chapter conciseness, we will leave the
        implementation of this feature to you as a
        training exercise.
        */

        // If no exceptions were triggered, the user
        // was succesfully created.
        Session::set_flash(
            'success',
            e('Welcome '.Input::post('username').'!')
        );
    } catch (\SimpleUserUpdateException $e) {
        // Either the username or email already exists
        Session::set_flash('error', e($e->getMessage()));
```

```
            }

        }
        else
        {
            // At least one field is not correct
            Session::set_flash('error', e($val->error()));
        }

        /*
        Sending the signup form fields information so that they
        are already filled when the user is redirected to the
        the index action (useful if the user could not be created)
        */
        Session::set_flash('signup_form', Input::post());

        // No matter what, we return to the home page.
        Response::redirect('/');
    }
```

If you now request the home page and fill the signup form correctly, a new user should be created in the `users` table. If something goes wrong (you enter an incomplete e-mail address or the username already exists for instance), an error message will be displayed but the form will be emptied since we go back to the home page. This is no big deal, but it could lower your transformation ratio. We saved the form data in the signup_form flash variable; therefore, it is now accessible in the `index` action. We will pass it to the view by replacing, in the `index` action:

```
View::forge(...);
```

with:

```
View::forge(
    'user/connect.mustache',
    array(
        'signup_form' => Session::get_flash('signup_form'),
    ),
    // By default, mustache escape displayed
    // variables, so no need to escape them here
    false
);
```

To autofill the `username` field, open the `APPPATH/views/user/connect.mustache` view file and replace the `username` input in the signup form with the following code snippet:

```
<input
        type="text"
        name="username"
        placeholder="Username"
        class="form-control"
        value="{{signup_form.username}}"/>
```

As you can see, we displayed the `$signup_form['username']` variable by writing `{{signup_form.username}}`. In a Mustache file, a `$var` variable is displayed by writing `{{var}}` and `$var['val_1']` is displayed by writing `{{var.val_1}}`. If `$var` is an object, `$var->val_1` is also displayed by writing `{{var.val_1}}`.

You can also autofill the `email` field by adding `value="{{signup_form.email}}"` in the `email` input of the signup form.

Handling the signin form

Now that we can create new users, we need to handle the signin form. We will therefore create the `signin` action in the `User` controller:

```
public function action_signin()
{
    // If already logged in, redirecting to home page.
    if (Auth::check()) {
        Session::set_flash(
            'error',
            e('You are already logged in, '.
            Auth::get_screen_name().'.')
        );
        Response::redirect('/');
    }

    $val = Validation::forge();
    $val->add('username', 'Email or Username')
        ->add_rule('required');
    $val->add('password', 'Password')
        ->add_rule('required');

    // Running validation
    if ($val->run())
    {
```

```
            $auth = Auth::instance();

            // Checking the credentials.
            if (
                Auth::check() or
                $auth->login(
                    Input::post('username'),
                    Input::post('password')
                )
            )
            {
                Session::set_flash(
                    'success',
                    e('Welcome, '.Auth::get_screen_name().'!')
                );
            }
            else
            {
                Session::set_flash(
                    'error',
                    'Incorrect username and / or password.'
                );
            }
        } else {
            Session::set_flash(
                'error',
                'Empty username or password.'
            );
        }

        // No matter what, we return to the home page.
        Response::redirect('/');
    }
```

This is again very much inspired from the `admin` controller generated by the administration panel generator in `oil`; take a look at the `login` action of the `admin` controller (used for the administration panel generation) located at `PKGPATH/oil/views/admin/orm/controllers/admin.php`.

Allowing the user to sign out

You probably noticed while testing the form that, once you successfully log in, you are unable to log out. Also, unless you have just successfully logged in, you don't have any idea whether you are logged in or not.

To solve this problem, we will display the username in the navigation bar and allow the user to sign out in a dropdown, as we did in the administration panel.

Open the template file located at `APPPATH/views/template.php`, and replace `<div class="navbar-header">...</div>` with the following lines of code:

```
<div class="navbar-header">
    <!-- Allows the navbar to collapse when
         the screen width is too small -->
    <button
            type="button"
            class="navbar-toggle"
            data-toggle="collapse"
            data-target=".navbar-collapse">
        <span class="icon-bar"></span>
        <span class="icon-bar"></span>
        <span class="icon-bar"></span>
    </button>
    <a class="navbar-brand"
<?php echo array_to_attr(array('href' => Uri::base())); ?>
    >
        My microblog
    </a>
</div>
<div class="navbar-collapse collapse">
<?php if (Auth::check()): ?>
    <ul class="nav navbar-nav pull-right">
        <li class="dropdown">
            <a
               data-toggle="dropdown"
               class="dropdown-toggle"
               href="#">
                <?php echo e(Auth::get_screen_name()) ?>
                <b class="caret"></b>
            </a>
            <ul class="dropdown-menu">
                <li>
<?php
echo Html::anchor('user/signout', 'Sign out');
?>
                </li>
            </ul>
        </li>
    </ul>
<?php endif; ?>
</div>
```

If you are logged in, your username should now appear in the upper right side of your screen. If you click on your username, the **Sign out** link should appear.

We now have to implement this `signout` action inside the `User` controller. This step is pretty simple:

```
public function action_signout()
{
    Auth::logout();
    Response::redirect('/');
}
```

Allowing the user to create and view posts

We will now allow users to create their own posts and display them in their profile page. Posts will also be the main information displayed by our API.

Generating the Post model

We need first to generate the Post model. As usual, we will use `oil`. Enter the following command line:

```
php oil generate model post content:varchar[140] user_id:int
created_at:int --no-timestamp
```

The output is as follows:

```
Creating model: APPPATH/classes/model/post.php
Creating migration: APPPATH/migrations/001_create_posts.php
```

You can see that we used the `--no-timestamp` parameter here. It simply prevents the automatic generation of the `created_at` and `updated_at` columns. Since we can have a lot of posts and the `updated_at` column then be useless, we generate the `created_at` column manually. As a consequence, we need to specify the `CreatedAt` observer ourselves. Open the Post model located at `APPPATH/classes/model/post.php` and add the following attribute:

```
protected static $_observers = array(
    'Orm\Observer_CreatedAt' => array(
        'events' => array('before_insert'),
        'mysql_timestamp' => false,
    ),
);
```

Then, simply execute your application migrations using `oil`:

```
php oil refine migrate
```

Allowing the user to create new posts

We will begin by implementing the user interface, and then we will implement the post creation action.

Implementing the user interface

First, let's add a **New post** button in the right side of the navigation bar. Open the template file located at `APPPATH/views/template.php` and just after `<ul class="nav navbar-nav pull-right">`, add the following lines of code:

```
<li>
    <a href="#"
       data-toggle="modal"
       data-target="#create_post_modal">
        <!-- Displays the pencil icon.
             http://glyphicons.com/ -->
        <span class="glyphicon glyphicon-pencil"></span>
        New post
    </a>
</li>
```

If you refresh the home page and are signed in, you should see the button appear with a pencil icon inside it on the right-hand side of the navigation bar. We extensively used the Bootstrap framework, so it is recommended that you read the official documentation at `http://getbootstrap.com/`.

The important things to notice are the two attributes declared inside the link:

```
data-toggle="modal" data-target="#create_post_modal"
```

This means that when we click on the link, we want Bootstrap to display a modal window using the content of the `div` element with `id = create_post_modal`. Thus, we need to define this `div` element. Before `</body>`, add the following lines of code:

```
<!-- Post modal window -->
<div
     class="modal fade"
     id="create_post_modal"
     tabindex="-1"
     role="dialog"
     aria-labelledby="myModalLabel"
```

```
         aria-hidden="true">
        <div class="modal-dialog">
            <div class="modal-content">
                <div class="modal-header">
                    <button
                            type="button"
                            class="close"
                            data-dismiss="modal">
                        <span aria-hidden="true">&times;</span>
                        <span class="sr-only">Close</span>
                    </button>
                    <h4 class="modal-title" id="myModalLabel">
                        Compose new Post
                    </h4>
                </div>
                <div class="modal-body">
                    <!-- Will be displayed conditionally -->
                    <div id="post_success" class="alert
                                alert-success">
                        Your post has been successfully
                        published!
                    </div>
                    <!-- Will be displayed conditionally -->
                    <div id="post_fail" class="alert
                                alert-danger"></div>

                    <textarea
                              id="post_content"
                              rows="4"
                              class="form-control"></textarea>
                </div>
                <div class="modal-footer">
                    <span id="post_remaining_characters"></span>
                    <button
                            type="button"
                            class="btn btn-primary"
                            id="post_submit_button">
                        Submit
                    </button>
                </div>
            </div>
        </div>
    </div>
```

This code was inspired from the live demo in the official documentation at http://getbootstrap.com/javascript/#modals.

Add the following style in the website.css file:

```
textarea {
    resize: none;
}

#post_success, #post_fail {
    display: none;
}

#post_remaining_characters.too_much {
    color: red;
}
```

On clicking on the **New post** button, you should now see the following modal window:

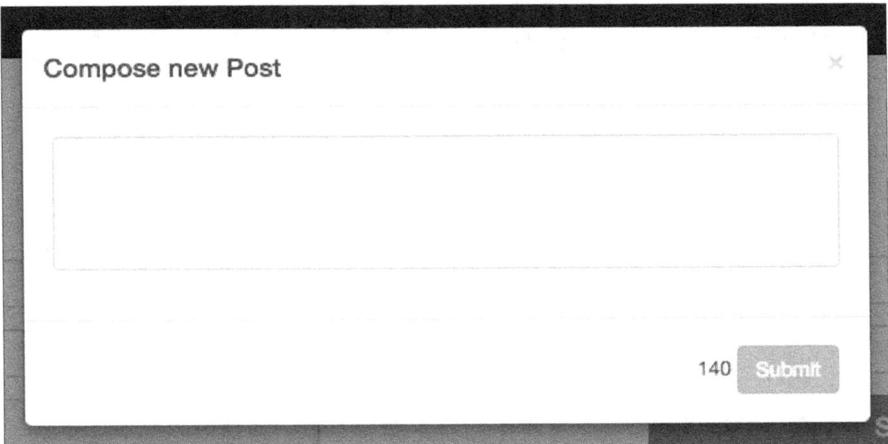

However, if you try to click on the **Submit** button, nothing will happen. We need to add some JavaScript code to do that.

Since this won't be very short, first create a new JavaScript file at public/assets/js/post_form.js and include it in the template by adding 'post_form.js', after 'bootstrap.js', inside the Asset::js call in the template.

Next, open the newly created JavaScript file and set its contents to:

```
// When the DOM is ready
$(function(){
    // jQuery elements initialization
    var $postContent = $('#post_content');
    var $postRemainingCharacters =
        $('#post_remaining_characters');
    var $postSuccess = $('#post_success');
    var $postFail = $('#post_fail');
    var $postSubmitButton = $('#post_submit_button');

    // Defining the max number of characters of a post
    var postMaxNbCharacters = 140; // will be improved

    /*
    Refreshes the remaining number of characters indicator,
    and whether or not the submission button is enabled.
    */
    function refreshPostWindow() {
        var postLength = $postContent.val().length;
        var remainingCharacters =
            postMaxNbCharacters - postLength;

        $postRemainingCharacters
        .text(remainingCharacters)
        .attr(
            'class',
            remainingCharacters >= 0 ? '' : 'too_much'
        );

        $postSubmitButton.prop(
            'disabled',
            postLength == 0 || remainingCharacters < 0
        );
    }

    // Initialization
    refreshPostWindow();

    /*
    When showing the post creation modal window, clearing
    all previous messages. Useful if a user publishes many
    posts in a row.
```

```
*/
$('#create_post_modal')
.on('show.bs.modal', function() {
    $postFail.hide();
    $postSuccess.hide();
});

// When the user type in the post textarea
$postContent.keyup(function() {
    // In case he writes two posts in a row
    $postSuccess.hide();
    // See comments above
    refreshPostWindow();
});

// When clicking on the submit button
$postSubmitButton.click(function() {

    // Sending an AJAX POST request to post/create.json
    // with the post content.
    $.post(
        'post/create.json',
        {post_content: $postContent.val()}
    )
    .done(function(data) {
        // In case the connection succeeded

        /*
        The action will define whether or not the
        post passed validation using the data.success
        variable.
        */
        if (data.success) {
            // If succeeded
            $postFail.hide();
            $postContent.val('');
            refreshPostWindow();
            $postSuccess.show();
        } else {
            // If failed, the error message will be
            // defined in data.error.
            $postFail
            .text(data.error)
            .show();
```

```
                }
            })
            .fail(function() {
                // In case the connection failed
                $postFail
                .text('Sorry, it seems there was an issue ' +
                      'somewhere. Please try again later.')
                .show();
            });
        });
    });
```

Read the comments in the preceding code. If you refresh the home page and try to submit a new post, the message **Sorry, it seems there was an issue somewhere. Please try again later.** will appear because we didn't implement the `post/create` action yet.

You might have noticed the following line:

```
var postMaxNbCharacters = 140; // will be improved
```

This line is problematic, because we are defining here the maximum number of characters a post can have, and we will need this information later when implementing our action (for validation). The best option is to define this information once so that, if we have to change it in the future, we only need to change one line. Therefore, we will write this variable in a configuration file.

Create the configuration file at `APPPATH/config/mymicroblog.php` and set its contents to:

```
<?php
return array(
    'post_max_nb_characters' => 140,
);
```

Its access will be easy later in our action, but the configuration file's content is currently inaccessible by our JavaScript code. In order to solve this issue, open the template view file located at `APPPATH/views/template.php`, and add the following lines of code after `$(function(){ $('.topbar').dropdown(); });` inside the `script` tag:

```
<?php
// Converts the mymicroblog configuration to json.
$json_configuration = Format::forge(
```

```
        \Config::load('mymicroblog', true)
    )->to_json();

    echo '              ';
    echo 'var MMBConfiguration = '.$json_configuration.";\n";
    ?>
```

Then, go back to the `post_form.js` JavaScript file and replace `var postMaxNbCharacters = 140; // will be improved` with the following lines of code:

```
var postMaxNbCharacters =
    MMBConfiguration['post_max_nb_characters'];
```

When you have some common variables and constants between your JavaScript and your PHP code, it is always a good idea to adopt a similar solution.

Implementing the post creation action

We will now handle the AJAX request, check the sent data, and create the post if everything is ok.

First, we will need to create the `Post` controller. Create the `APPPATH/classes/controller/post.php` file and, for the moment, set its contents to:

```
<?php
class Controller_Post extends Controller_Rest
{
}
```

You can see that we are extending a different controller class here; instead of `Controller_Template`, we are extending `Controller_Rest`. It is a basic controller with a RESTful support built in. It will allow us to easily implement the JSON response we will send, and it will also help us later when we will implement the API.

To illustrate this, add the following test action:

```
public function action_test() {
    return $this->response(array(
        'test_1' => 42,
        'test_2' => 'Answer to the Ultimate Question',
        'test_3' => array(
            'test_4' => array(
                'test_5', 'test_6', 'test_7'
            ),
            'test_8' => true,
```

```
            'test_9' => null,
        ),
    ));
}
```

If you request the following URL now:

`http://mymicroblog.app/post/test`

The following output should appear:

The requested REST method returned an array or object:

{ "test_1": 42, "test_2": "Answer to the Ultimate Question", "test_3": { "test_4": ["test_5", "test_6", "test_7"], "test_8": true, "test_9": null } }

If you request the following URL:

`http://mymicroblog.app/post/test.json`

It will return:

```
{
    "test_1":42,
    "test_2":"Answer to the Ultimate Question",
    "test_3":{
        "test_4":["test_5","test_6","test_7"],
        "test_8":true,
        "test_9":null
    }
}
```

If you request the following URL:

`http://mymicroblog.app/post/test.xml`

It will return:

```
<?xml version="1.0" encoding="utf-8"?>
<xml>
    <test_1>42</test_1>
    <test_2>Answer to the Ultimate Question</test_2>
    <test_3>
        <test_4>
            <item>test_5</item>
            <item>test_6</item>
            <item>test_7</item>
```

```
        </test_4>
        <test_8>1</test_8>
        <test_9/>
    </test_3>
</xml>
```

If you request the following URL:

```
http://mymicroblog.app/post/test.php
```

It will return:

```
array (
    'test_1' => 42,
    'test_2' => 'Answer to the Ultimate Question',
    'test_3' =>
    array (
        'test_4' =>
        array (
            0 => 'test_5',
            1 => 'test_6',
            2 => 'test_7',
        ),
        'test_8' => true,
        'test_9' => NULL,
    ),
)
```

You should have understood by now that, depending on the extension defined in the requested URL, the action will return a result in the associated format. I recommend you to read the official documentation at `http://fuelphp.com/docs/general/controllers/rest.html#/formats` to see which formats are supported.

The documentation can be accessed by opening the FuelPHP website and navigating to **DOCS** | **FuelPHP** | **General** | **Controllers** | **Rest**.

A specific property of the REST controllers is that they allow you to implement actions that only answer to specific HTTP methods. For instance, if we had named our `action_test` method as `get_test`, the `test` action would have only responded to `GET` requests. The same is true for `POST`, `PUT`, `DELETE`, and `PATCH` requests; you are again recommended to read the official FuelPHP documentation about REST controllers.

Delete the `test` action and add the following `create` action:

```
public function action_create()
{
    $post_content = Input::post('post_content');

    $response = array();

    if (!Auth::check()) {
        // In case the user has been signed out before
        // he submits his post.
        $response = array(
            'success' => false,
            'error' => 'You are not authenticated.',
        );
    } else {
        // Checking if the post is correct. The JavaScript
        // should have tested that already, but never trust
        // the client.
        $val = Validation::forge('post');
        $val->add_field(
            'post_content',
            'post',
            'required|max_length[140]'
        );

        if ($val->run())
        {
            // Creating the post.
            list(, $user_id) = Auth::get_user_id();
            $post = Model_Post::forge();
            $post->content = $post_content;
            $post->user_id = $user_id;
            if ($post and $post->save()) {
                $response = array(
                    'success' => true,
                );
            } else {
                $response = array(
                    'success' => false,
                    'error' => 'Internal error: Could'.
                        ' not save the post.',
                );
            }
```

```
            } else {
                // The error can only occur on the only field...
                $error = $val->error()['post_content'];
                $response = array(
                    'success' => false,
                    'error' => $error->get_message(),
                );
            }
        }

        return $this->response($response);
    }
```

Now if you try to add a new valid post, a new row should be added in the `posts` table and the following message should appear:

Your post has been successfully published!

> Though we are sending a JSON response, we don't consider the `create` action as a part of the application API. As written earlier, our API will only allow read-only access and no authentication will be required; the action doesn't observe any of those requirements. However, the fact that it returns JSON content (as well as other formats) is a good start if you want to integrate it into an API.

Implementing the profile page

Since we can create posts now, it would be great to display them. As we wrote in the specification, the user profile page displays the list of published posts, so we will implement it.

Configuring the routes

We would like to display this profile page when requesting the following URL:

`http://mymicroblog.app/USERNAME`

We could add a parameter to the `index` action of the `User` controller, but that would unnecessarily complicate the action. Instead of doing that, we are going to use routes to transparently reroute those URLs to the `show` action of the `User` controller:

`http://mymicroblog.app/user/show/USERNAME`

To do this, open the `APPPATH/config/routes.php` configuration file and add the following line at the end of the returned array:

```
'(:segment)' => 'user/show/$1',
```

Creating the user model

Inside the `show` action, we will have to request a user from the database. We will create the user model to do this more easily. Create the `APPPATH/classes/model/user.php` file and set its contents to:

```
<?php

class Model_User extends \Orm\Model
{
  protected static $_properties = array(
      'id',
      'username',
        'password',
        'group',
        'email',
        'last_login',
        'login_hash',
        'profile_fields',
        'created_at',
        'updated_at',
  );


  protected static $_table_name = 'users';

    protected static $_observers = array(
      'Orm\Observer_CreatedAt' => array(
          'events' => array('before_insert'),
          'mysql_timestamp' => false,
      ),
      'Orm\Observer_UpdatedAt' => array(
          'events' => array('before_save'),
          'mysql_timestamp' => false,
      ),
  );
}
```

Implementing the show action

We will now implement the `show` action inside the `User` controller, as we had done previously:

```
public function action_show($username) {
    // Finding a user with a similar username
    $user = Model_User::find('first', array(
        'where' => array(
            array('username' => $username),
        ),
    ));

    if (!$user) {
        Session::set_flash(
            'error',
            'The user '.e($username).' does not exists.'
        );
        Response::redirect('/');
    }

    // Finding 20 latest posts (will be improved)
    $posts = Model_Post::find('all', array(
        'related' => 'user',
        'where' => array(
            array('user_id' => $user->id),
        ),
        'order_by' => array('id' => 'DESC'),
        'limit' =>
        \Config::get('mymicroblog.pagination_nb_posts'),
    ));

    // Displaying the profile page
    $this->template->content =
        View::forge(
            'user/show.mustache',
            array(
                'user' => $user,
                /*
                As Model_Post::find returns an associative
                array, with ids as keys and posts as
                values, we need to transform it to a
                classic array, otherwise mustache will
                process as an object and not the list,
                hence the use of array_values.
```

```
                */
                'posts' => array_values($posts),
            ),
            // By default, mustache escape displayed
            // variables...
            false
        );
    }
```

There are a few more things that we need to do. First, you can see we specified `'related' => 'user'` when finding posts, but we didn't declare this relation inside the Post model. Fix that by opening the Post model and adding the following attribute:

```
protected static $_belongs_to = array('user');
```

Then, in the User model, you might have seen that we get the number of posts to load from the configuration `\Config::get('mymicroblog.pagination_nb_posts')`. We need to specify this configuration item inside the `APPPATH/config/mymicroblog.php` file. Inside the returned array, add the following line:

```
'pagination_nb_posts' => 20,
```

But there is still an issue; we haven't loaded the configuration file yet, so `\Config::get('mymicroblog.pagination_nb_posts')` will return `null`. We could load the configuration file in the same action, but since we are going to need it elsewhere, we are going to load it in the `before` method. This method is called before any action is executed. Add the following line in the beginning of the `User` controller:

```
public function before() {
    parent::before();

    \Config::load('mymicroblog', true);
}
```

If we want this action to work, we still need to implement the `user/show.mustache` view.

Implementing views

First, create the `APPPATH/views/user/show.mustache` view file and set its contents to:

```
<div class="col-md-3"></div>
<div class="col-md-6 profile">
    <div class="row profile_informations">
        <h1>
```

```
            {{user.username}}
        </h1>
    </div>
    {{> post/list}}
</div>
<div class="col-md-3"></div>
```

The only new syntax that is `{{> post/list}}`; it means we want to display the `post/list` partial, and its PHP equivalent looks like this:

```
echo \View::forge(
    'post/list.mustache',
    array(/* all current variables */),
    false
);
```

We have separated the `post` listing because we will need to display it on other actions. Therefore, the next logical step is to implement this partial. Create the `APPPATH/views/post/list.mustache` view file and set its contents to:

```
<div class="row post_list">
    {{> post/inside_list}}
</div>
```

We just implemented a simple `div` element and called another partial inside it. This new partial will only display the content of the list. Create the `APPPATH/views/post/inside_list.mustache` view file and set its contents to:

```
{{#posts}}
    <div class="post">
        <div class="post_content">{{content}}</div>
        <div class="post_additional_infos">
            By
            <a
                class="post_author"
                href="/{{user.username}}">
                {{user.username}}
            </a>
            &middot;
            <span
                class="post_date"
                data-timestamp="{{created_at}}">
            </span>
        </div>
    </div>
{{/posts}}
```

To understand this, you need to understand a new Mustache tag. The `{{#posts}}` and `{{/posts}}` tags are implemented here to loop over the `posts` array. The content within these two tags will be repeated for each post. Variables displayed inside this loop will either be previously declared variables, or the properties of the current post in the loop; for instance, `{{created_at}}` is the `created_at` attribute of the current post in the loop, but we could display `{{independent_variable}}`, which would not be an attribute of the current post but of a previously declared variable. Take a look at the official documentation to understand how variables are resolved (the second link is hosted on the repository of the PHP port of Mustache but is quite complete and clear):

- `http://mustache.github.io/mustache.5.html`
- `https://github.com/bobthecow/mustache.php/wiki/Variable-Resolution`

However, if you now try to access a profile page, only the username will be displayed even if this user created posts. This is because Mustache doesn't know where to find partials. To solve this issue, open back the `User` controller and add the following lines of code at the end of the `before` method:

```
\Parser\View_Mustache::parser()
    ->setPartialsLoader(
    new Mustache_Loader_FilesystemLoader(
        APPPATH.'views'
    )
);
```

If you plan to use Mustache on modules, you will need to set other paths when calling the `setPartialsLoader` method.

We will now add some styles. Open the `public/assets/css/website.css` file and append the following code:

```
.profile {
    border-left: 1px solid #e8e8e8;
    border-right: 1px solid #e8e8e8;
    background-color: white;
}

.profile_informations {
    text-align: center;
    padding-top: 10px;
    padding-bottom: 40px;
```

```
        border-bottom: 1px solid #e8e8e8;
    }

    .post {
        padding: 5px 10px 5px 10px;
        border-bottom: 1px solid #e8e8e8;
    }

    .post_content {
        margin-bottom: 10px;
        word-break: break-all;
        white-space: pre-wrap;
    }

    .post_additional_infos {
        color: #888;
    }
```

If you refresh the profile page, the posts' list should appear now.

There is still an issue though: no date is displayed. However, you have probably read how we displayed `created_at` in the `APPPATH/views/post/inside_list.mustache` view file, as shown in the following lines:

```
<span>
    class="post_date"
    data-timestamp="{{created_at}}">
</span>
```

Nothing is visible, but the timestamp can be accessed inside a `span` element with the `post_date` class. We want to display those dates in a relative format (for example, 5 minutes ago) and regularly update them. We will do this using JavaScript and jQuery. As this is a complex operation, we will create a new JavaScript file. Create the `public/assets/js/posts_dates.js` file and set its contents to:

```
/*
Converts a timestamp to relative format.
You could use plugins as jquery.timeago for doing that, and
it would probably be better that way, but we implemented
ourselves the method for being sure we won't have any
compatibility issues in the future. It is far from a perfect
solution: for instance, it supposes the client and the server
share the same time zone.
*/
function relativeFormat(timestamp) {
```

```
        var timeLabels = [
            {
                divider: 31536000,
                label: '(:nb) year ago',
                label_plural: '(:nb) years ago'
            },
            {
                divider: 2592000,
                label: '(:nb) month ago',
                label_plural: '(:nb) months ago'
            },
            {
                divider: 86400,
                label: '(:nb) day ago',
                label_plural: '(:nb) days ago'
            },
            {
                divider: 3600,
                label: '(:nb) hour ago',
                label_plural: '(:nb) hours ago'
            },
            {
                divider: 60,
                label: '(:nb) minute ago',
                label_plural: '(:nb) minutes ago'
            }
        ];

        var seconds = Math.floor(
            (new Date() - timestamp) / 1000);

        for (var i = 0; i < timeLabels.length; i++) {
            var nb = Math.floor(seconds / timeLabels[i].divider);

            if (nb > 0) {
                var label = timeLabels[i][
                    (nb == 1 ? 'label' : 'label_plural')];
                return label.replace('(:nb)', nb);
            }
        }
        return 'Few seconds ago';
    }

    // Refresh all posts dates
```

```
function refreshPostsDates() {
    $('.post_date').each(function() {
        var $this = $(this);
        $this.text(
            relativeFormat(
                parseInt($this.data('timestamp')) * 1000
            )
        );
    });
}

// When the DOM is ready
$(function(){
    refreshPostsDates();

    // Regularly refresh posts dates (every 30000ms = 30s)
    setInterval(refreshPostsDates, 30000);
});
```

Finally, we need to include this script inside the template located at `APPPATH/views/template.php`. Add `'posts_dates.js'`, after `'post_form.js'`.

Implementing the API

Now that we have developed the first version of the profile pages, we will begin to implement the API to access our website data.

Implementing the base controller

As we will need methods on both the `User` and `Post` controllers, we will first implement a base controller that will be extended by both controllers. Create the `APPPATH/classes/controller/base.php` file and set its contents to:

```
<?php
class Controller_Base extends Controller_Hybrid
{

}
```

You can see that `Controller_Base` is extending a new native controller named `Controller_Hybrid`. As its name suggests, it is a hybrid version implementing features from both `Controller_Template` and `Controller_Rest`. It is exactly what we need if we want an action to return JSON or HTML, depending on the context.

First, move the `before` method we implemented in the `User` controller inside this new `Base` controller.

Next, implement the following methods:

```
/*
Overriding the is_restful method to make the controller go into
rest mode when an extension is specified in the URL. Ex:
http://mymicroblog.com/first_user.json
*/
public function is_restful()
{
    return !is_null(\Input::extension());
}

/*
Handles an hybrid response: when no extension is specified
the action returns HTML code by setting the template's content
attribute with the specified view and data, and when an
extension is specified, the action returns data in the expected
format(if available).
*/
public function hybrid_response($view, $data) {
    if (is_null(\Input::extension())) {
        $this->template->content =
        View::forge(
            $view.'.mustache',
            $data,
            // By default, mustache escape displayed
            // variables...
            false
        );
    } else {
        $this->response($data);
    }
}
```

Each time we want a hybrid response (HTML, JSON, or XML depending on the extension requested), we will have to call the `hybrid_response` method.

Finally, make the `Post` and the `User` controllers extend this new `Base` controller.

Implementing your first hybrid action

Inside the `show` action of the `User` controller, replace `$this->template->content = ...;` with the following lines of code:

```
return $this->hybrid_response(
    'user/show',
    array(
        'user' => $user,
        'posts' => array_values($posts),
    )
);
```

Now if you request the following URL:

`http://mymicroblog.app/USERNAME.json`

(Or `http://mymicroblog.app/USERNAME.xml`, as browsers generally display this format better)

You will see that the data is now accessible. The problem is that you can read too much information:

- The most urgent issue is that we display all the attributes for each object. It is very problematic for user objects as we display their hashed passwords, their login hash, their e-mails, and possibly other confidential information. This is a very serious security issue.
- We don't need to display every time the same attributes of an object. For instance, we might want to release more information about a user when displaying its profile page, but only its username when displaying the `user` attribute of a post. This is less urgent, but still an important issue.

Implementing mappers to control how the information is shared

In order to control which information is sent through the API, we will implement mappers that will transform our objects to appropriate associative arrays containing only the attributes we want to show. The mappers will map differently objects depending on the context.

Create the `APPPATH/classes/mapper.php` file and set its contents to:

```
<?php
// This class will be extended by all our mappers and
// contains general purpose methods.
```

```
class Mapper
{
    /**
    * Transforms an object or objects to their mapped
    * associative arrays. No matter what mapper we
    * will use, the idea is to always call
    * Mapper_CLASS::get('CONTEXT', $objects)
    *
    * @param string $context The context
    * @param mixed $objects Array of objects or single object
    *
    * @return array Array of associative array or associative
    *               array
    */
    static function get($context, $objects) {
        if (is_array($objects)) {
            $result = array();
            foreach ($objects as $object) {
                $result[] = static::get($context, $object);
            }
            return $result;
        } else {
            return static::$context($objects);
        }
    }

    /**
    * Extracts specified properties of an object and
    * returns them as an associative array.
    *
    * @param object $object The object to convert
    * @param array $attributes The list of attributes to extract
    *
    * @return array The associative array
    */
    static function extract_properties($object, $properties) {
        $result = array();
        foreach ($properties as $property) {
            $result[$property] = $object->{$property};
        }
        return $result;
    }
}
```

We will now create the mappers for our Post and User models. First, create the `APPPATH/classes/mapper/post.php` file and set its contents to:

```
<?php
// Mapper for posts
class Mapper_Post extends Mapper
{
    static function item($post) {
        $result = static::extract_properties(
            $post,
            array('id', 'content', 'created_at')
        );
        $result['user'] = Mapper_User::get(
            'minimal',
$post->user
        );
        return $result;
    }
}
```

Then, create the `APPPATH/classes/mapper/user.php` file and set its contents to:

```
<?php
// Mapper for users
class Mapper_User extends Mapper
{
    static function minimal($user) {
        return array('username' => $user->username);
    }

    static function profile($user) {
        $result = static::extract_properties(
            $user,
            array('id', 'username', 'created_at')
        );

        /*
        profile_fields is always empty, but this is just here
        to illustrate that you can also send other information
        than object attributes.
        */
        $result['profile_fields'] = unserialize(
            $user->profile_fields
        );
        return $result;
    }
}
```

Now, we just have to use these mappers in our `show` action of the `User` controller. Inside the action, replace:

```
'user' => $user,
'posts' => array_values($posts),
```

With the following lines of code:

```
'user' => Mapper_User::get('profile', $user),
'posts' => Mapper_Post::get('item', $posts),
```

Now if you request the following URLs:

- `http://mymicroblog.app/USERNAME.json`
- `http://mymicroblog.app/USERNAME.xml`

You should see that only the useful information appears. You can always access `http://mymicroblog.app/USERNAME`, as the Mustache template engine processes objects and associative arrays in the same way.

Some open source libraries provide tools that allow you to do a similar job that we did with our `mapper` classes, but in a standardized and more sophisticated way. If you are searching for one, I recommend that you take a look at the `fractal` library at `http://fractal.thephpleague.com/`.

Improving the listing

The profile web pages are still incomplete as we only show the users' last 20 posts. It would be great to improve this listing by adding a **See more** button that allows us to read older posts.

I recommended you to generate many posts (you could do that programmatically) on a profile in order to test our interface.

Giving JavaScript access to our Mustache views

In this section, we are going to transform JSON data to HTML content using JavaScript. Indeed, when you will for instance click on the **See more** button, an AJAX request will be sent toward our API that will return JSON data. We need to transform this JSON code to HTML content so that the viewer can read it but as we don't want any code duplication, we will give the JavaScript code access to our Mustache views. This will be done by copying all the Mustache files content into an object in the `public/assets/js/templates.js` JavaScript file.

Generating the templates.js file

We will discuss two alternatives to generate the `template.js` file.

The easy and dirty way

The easy and dirty solution is to regenerate this file each time someone accesses your application in development mode. To do this, open a `APPPATH/bootstrap.php` file and add the following lines of code at the end:

```
// Executed each time the application is requested in
// development mode
if (Fuel::$env == Fuel::DEVELOPMENT && !\Fuel::$is_cli) {
    $view_directory = APPPATH.'views/';
    $extension = '.mustache';

    /*
    The following searches for mustache files in APPPATH/views/
    and saves its content into the $template associative array.
    Each key will be the template relative path; for instance,
    if a template is located at
    APPPATH/views/dir_1/file.mustache the value of the key
    will be dir_1/file.
    Each value will be the template content.
    */
    $templates = array();
    $it = new RecursiveDirectoryIterator($view_directory);
    foreach(new RecursiveIteratorIterator($it) as $file)
    {
        if (substr($file, -strlen($extension)) == $extension) {
            // Deducing the key from the filename
            // APPPATH/views/dir_1/file.mustache -> dir_1/file
            $file_key = substr(
                $file,
                strlen($view_directory)
            );
            $file_key = substr(
                $file_key,
                0,
                -strlen($extension)
            );

            $templates[$file_key] = file_get_contents($file);
        }
    }
```

```
        $template_file_content = 'MyMicroblog.templates = '.
            json_encode($templates).';';

        // Saves the templates in the templates.js file
        file_put_contents(
            DOCROOT.'assets/js/templates.js',
            $template_file_content
        );
    }
```

Even though we generate the file only on development mode, it can become unsustainable if you have a big application containing lots of templates; you will have latency and memory issues. You also might need to change some permission to allow the file to be created. In most cases, you should be ok though, and a good point of this solution is that it doesn't require any dependency.

Using guard-templates

Instead of generating the JavaScript file each time you request your application, you could use a utility such as guard-templates. The idea is that you launch this utility when you are coding your application, and that utility will track any file change and regenerate the JavaScript file when necessary.

> Please note that, at the time of writing, this utility doesn't seem to work on Ubuntu: if that is still the case when you read the book, you are recommended to use the solution we provided in the last section.

You first need Ruby and gem installed on your computer. Then, you must install the `guard-template` gem by executing:

```
sudo gem install guard-templates
```

Then execute the following command at the root of your website directory (as you did for `oil`):

```
guard init templates
```

Open the generated `Guardfile` file at the root of your website directory; it contains a sample configuration of the guard-templates utility. Replace its content with:

```
guard 'templates',
      :output => 'public/assets/js/templates.js',
      :namespace => 'MyMicroblog' do
    watch(/fuel\/app\/views\/(.*)\.mustache$/)
end
```

Understanding this configuration should be fairly easy. If you have any doubt, you can always check the official documentation at `https://github.com/thegreatape/guard-templates`.

You can then launch `guard` by executing the following command:

```
guard
```

It will then generate the JavaScript file and regenerate it each time any Mustache template is changed.

Integrating template.js and Mustache.js

Now that our Mustache templates are stored into a JavaScript file, we have to integrate it into our website.

First, we must install `mustache.js`, which is the JavaScript port of Mustache. In order to do this, go to the `mustache.js` repository at `https://github.com/janl/mustache.js`.

Clone the repository or download and unzip the archive in the `public/assets/js/mustache` folder.

We will also implement the `render` function, which is inspired from the `render` function of FuelPHP (the equivalent of `View::forge(...)->render()`). To do this, create the `public/assets/js/view.js` file and set its contents to:

```
// We need to initialize the MyMicroblog for our templates
// to work
MyMicroblog = {};

// Inspired from FuelPHP's render method
function render(view, data) {
    return Mustache.render(
        MyMicroblog.templates[view],
        data,
        MyMicroblog.templates
    );
}
```

We now need to include our JavaScript files in the template. Open the `APPPATH/views/template.php` file and add the following lines of code after the `'bootstrap.js',` line:

```
'mustache/mustache.js',
'view.js',
'templates.js',
```

Refresh your web page. If you open the JavaScript console (in your browser's developer tools) now and execute:

```
render('user/connect', {})
```

You should see that it returns the correct HTML code.

Implementing the post/list action

We will also need to retrieve the posts data from the server. For this, we will implement two actions inside the `Post` controller: the `list` and `count` actions. Add the following code at the end of the `Post` controller:

```
// Get the posts list depending on $_GET parameters
// limited to 20 posts maximum
public function action_list() {
    $query = static::get_posts_query(Input::get(), true);
    $posts = $query->limit(
        \Config::get('mymicroblog.pagination_nb_posts')
    )->get();

    return $this->response(
        Mapper_Post::get('item', $posts)
    );
}

// Get the number of posts depending on $_GET parameters
public function action_count() {
    $query = static::get_posts_query(Input::get(), false);
    return $this->response($query->count());
}
```

The `get` and `count` actions call the `static::get_posts_query` method. We need to implement this method, and we will do that in the `Base` controller:

```
// Getting the posts query
public static function get_posts_query($params) {
    $user_id = Arr::get($params, 'user_id', null);
    // id > since_id
    $after_id = intval(
        Arr::get($params, 'after_id', null)
    );
    // id < from_id
    $before_id = intval(
```

```
            Arr::get($params, 'before_id', null)
        );

        $query = Model_Post::query();
        $query->related('user');
        $query->where('user_id', '=', $user_id);
        if ($after_id != 0) {
            $query->where('id', '>', $after_id);
        }
        if ($before_id != 0) {
            $query->where('id', '<', $before_id);
        }
        $query->order_by(array('id' => 'DESC'));

        return $query;
    }
```

Now, if you request the following URL:

`http://mymicroblog.app/post/list.json?user_id=ID`

It will return the 20 latest posts of the user with `id = ID`.

If you request the following URL:

`http://mymicroblog.app/post/list.json?user_id=ID&before_id=30`

It will return the 20 latest posts with an `id` value less than `30` that have been published by the user with `id = ID`.

If you request the following URL:

`http://mymicroblog.app/post/list.json?user_id=ID&after_id=30`

It will return the 20 latest posts with an `id` value greater than `30` that have been published by the user with `id = ID`.

Now, if you request the following URL:

`http://mymicroblog.app/post/count.json?user_id=ID`

It will return the number of posts published by the user with `id = ID`.

If you request the following URL:

`http://mymicroblog.app/post/count.json?user_id=ID&before_id=30`

It will return the number of posts with an `id` value less than `30` that have been published by the user with `id = ID`.

If you request the following URL:

```
http://mymicroblog.app/post/count.json?user_id=ID&after_id=30
```

It will return the number of posts with an `id` value greater than `30` that have been published by the user with `id = ID`.

We will use the `count` action later, when we will need to know if any posts have been published since we displayed a user profile.

To limit code duplication, in the `show` action of the `User` controller, replace `$posts = Model_Post::find('all', ...);` with the following lines of code:

```
$query = static::get_posts_query(
    array('user_id' => $user->id),
    true
);
$posts = $query->limit(
\Config::get('mymicroblog.pagination_nb_posts')
)->get();
```

Preventing any duplication inside the controllers is ok, but if you need to implement a lot of code and methods similar to `get_posts_query` inside a controller, something is wrong with your implementation. You should think about moving some pieces of code in models, helpers, or libraries. I must say I hesitated a bit about where this method should be implemented, but I decided to implement it in the `Base` controller since it would be more convenient. In general, be wary of long pieces of code inside a controller, as they should not contain too much logic.

Implementing the See more button

We will need to do some changes in the views. First, open `APPPATH/views/post/inside_list.mustache` and replace `<div class="post">` with the following line:

```
<div class="post" data-post_id="{{id}}">
```

It will allow us to identify which posts are already displayed. Then, open the `APPPATH/views/post/list.mustache` view and replace `<div class="row post_list">` with the following line:

```
<div class="row post_list" data-user_id="{{user.id}}">
```

This will allow us to know the user identifier when requesting for more posts. Then, add the following lines of code after `{{> post/inside_list}}`:

```
<div class="load_more see_more">
    <button type="button" class="btn btn-default btn-lg">
        <span
            class="glyphicon glyphicon-arrow-down"></span>
        See more...
    </button>
    <div class="loading_message">
        Loading...
    </div>
</div>
```

Now that the button is added, we need to specify what will happen when we click on it so we will code it on a new JavaScript file. Create the `public/assets/js/posts_list.js` file and set its contents to:

```
// When the DOM is ready
$(function() {

// Triggered when the user clicks on the see more button
    $('body').on(
'click',
'.post_list .see_more button',
        function() {
            // JQuery elements initialization
            var $this = $(this);
            var $post_list = $this.closest('.post_list');
            var $see_more = $this.closest('.see_more');

            // Getting user_id and before_id (last displayed
            // post id)
            var user_id = $post_list.data('user_id');
            var before_id =
                $post_list.find('.post:last').data('post_id');

            /*
            Adding the loading class to the see more in order
            to tell the user we are loading older posts.
            */
            $see_more.addClass('loading');

            // Getting the older posts
            $.get(
```

```
                    'post/list.json',
                    {
                        user_id: user_id,
                        before_id: before_id
                    }
                )
                .done(function(data) {
                    if (data != null) {
                        // Displaying loaded posts
                        $see_more.before(
                            render('post/inside_list', {posts: data})
                        );
                    } else {
                        // Everything has been loaded, no need
                        // to show the See more button anymore
                        $see_more.addClass('all_loaded');
                    }
                    $see_more.removeClass('loading');

                    // Refreshing posts dates
                    refreshPostsDates();
                })
                .fail(function() {
                    $see_more.removeClass('loading');
                    alert('Sorry, it seems there was an issue ' +
                        'somewhere. Please try again later.');
                });

            }
        );

        // @note: we will add more code here later
    });
```

Don't forget to include this JavaScript file in the template. Open the template and add `'posts_list.js'`, after `'posts_dates.js'`.

Then, add the following CSS code at the end of the `public/assets/css/website.css` file:

```
    .load_more {
        padding: 10px 0px 10px 0px;
        text-align: center;
```

```
    border-bottom: 1px solid #e8e8e8;
}

.loading_message,
.load_more.loading button,
.load_more.all_loaded {
    display: none;
}

.load_more.loading .loading_message {
    display: block;
}
```

The **See more** button should now work when you have more than 20 posts in a profile page. It could be perfected in many ways. For instance, when there are less than 20 posts in a profile, the button is first visible, but if you click on it, it will simply disappear as there are no more posts to show. There are many easy ways to solve this small problem, so we will leave it to you.

One improvement that could come in handy for those readers that are not very familiar with JavaScript is infinite scrolling. Open the `public/assets/js/posts_list.js` file and replace:

```
// @note: we will add more code here later
```

With the following code:

```
// When the See more button appears in the screen, the following
// code triggers a click on it to load older posts, resulting in
// an infinite scroll
$(document).scroll(function() {
    var $this = $(this);
    var $see_more_button = $('.see_more button');
    if ($see_more_button.length > 0 &&
        $see_more_button.is(':visible')) {
        if (
            $this.scrollTop() + $(window).height() >
            $see_more_button.offset().top) {
            $see_more_button.click();
        }
    }
});
```

Redirecting the home page to the logged user's web page

When the user is connected, we want to redirect the home page to his web page so they can take a look at their posts. In order to do this, go to the `index` action of the `User` controller and in place of the following line:

```
if (false /* is the user logged ? */) {
```

Write the following lines:

```
if (Auth::check()) {
Response::redirect('/'.Auth::get_screen_name());
```

That is optional, but you might also want to change and add some `Response::redirect` calls inside the `signin` action of the `User` controller to make things a bit cleaner (without changing anything the user will be redirected twice when signing in).

Unit tests

Unit tests are particularly suitable for this project, as it is important to regularly check if the API is returning the correct data. We will in this section quickly introduce you to how unit tests are implemented in FuelPHP. These tests will be very superficial as this is just an introduction. If you are not familiar with unit tests, you can start by reading the FuelPHP documentation about unit testing at `http://fuelphp.com/docs/general/unit_testing.html`.

The documentation can be accessed at the FuelPHP website by navigating to **DOCS** | **FuelPHP** | **General** | **Unit Testing**.

For more general information, you can look at the Wikipedia web page for more references (`http://en.wikipedia.org/wiki/Unit_testing`).

To make things short, unit tests allow you to test individual units in your code, such as methods or classes, to check if they work as intended. In most cases, they are executed regularly to check if there is no regression in your project. In the Test Driven Development process, tests are even written before the code and are used as some sort type of unit specification. In that development process, developers first define how a method should work in unit tests, and then they implement the method and check that it passes all the tests and assertions (assertions are conditions that must be met) they have previously written.

Unit tests should be separated from Integration tests, that test a group of units and how they function together, Functional tests that check that your projects follow its functional requirements, and Acceptance tests that check that final features accessed by users are working as it is expected.

When writing unit tests, you should try at least to stick with the following guidelines:

- Each unit test should only test a single code unit (generally methods, but sometimes classes) at a time.
- Try to write as few assertions as possible to test features, as unnecessary assertions lead to less maintainability.
- Tests should be independent from each other. For instance, you should not write a unit test that supposes another unit test has been run before.
- Each unit test purpose should be clear: Its name should be explicit and the code should be easy to understand (don't hesitate to use comments).

Now let's see in practice how to run unit tests in FuelPHP.

First, you need to install PHPUnit. To do that, enter the following command line:

```
php composer.phar require phpunit/phpunit:4.4.*
```

While PHPUnit is downloaded and installed, create the `APPPATH/config/oil.php` configuration file and set its contents to:

```
<?php
return array(
  'phpunit' => array(
      'autoload_path' =>
             VENDORPATH.'phpunit/phpunit/PHPUnit/Autoload.php',
      'binary_path' => VENDORPATH.'bin/phpunit',
  ),
);
```

Once PHPUnit is installed, you can launch tests. First, simply execute the following command line:

```
php oil test
```

The output will be something like this:

```
Tests Running...This may take a few moments.
...
Time: 512 ms, Memory: 20.25Mb
OK (375 tests, 447 assertions)
```

As you can see, `375` tests already exist and the `php oil test` command line executed all of them. These tests are all in the FuelPHP core and can be found in the `fuel/core/tests` directory.

We are going to create our own tests. Create the `APPPATH/tests/examples.php` file and set its contents to:

```
<?php
namespace Fuel\App;

/**
 * Examples tests
 *
 * @group App
 */
class Test_Examples extends \TestCase
{
    // This method is executed before all tests are executed.
    // If your unit test require some initialization, you can
    // do it here.
    public static function setUpBeforeClass() {
        \Config::load('mymicroblog', true);

        // Executing migrations (we are on a test database)
        \Migrate::latest('auth', 'package');
        \Migrate::latest();

        // Truncating the tables since we might already have data
        \DBUtil::truncate_table('users');
        \DBUtil::truncate_table('posts');

        // Generating test data
        \Auth::create_user(
            'first_user',
            'test',
            'email@email.com'
        );
        for ($i = 1; $i < 100; $i++) {
            $post = \Model_Post::forge(array(
                'content' => 'post 1',
                'user_id' => 1
            ));
```

```
            $post->save();
        }

        // ...
    }

    /**
     * Tests the User mapper.
     *
     * @test
     */
    public function test_extract_properties() {
        $object = new \stdClass();
        $object->a = '1';
        $object->b = 2;
        $object->c = true;

        $res = \Mapper::extract_properties(
            $object,
            array('a', 'c')
        );

        $expected_res = array('a' => '1', 'c' => true);

        $this->assertEquals($res, $expected_res);

        // A lot more should be tested...
    }

    /**
     * Tests the User mapper.
     *
     * @test
     */
    public function test_user_mapper() {
        // Getting any user.
        // Note: In order not to depend on the database and on
        // the ORM, you might want to create mock users objects
        // (simulated users objects) and test features on these
        // objects instead...
        $user = \Model_User::find('first');

        // Testing that the profile context returns 4
```

```
        // attributes
        $profile = \Mapper_User::get('profile', $user);
        $this->assertCount(4, $profile);

        // Testing that the minimal context returns 1 attribute
        $minimal = \Mapper_User::get('minimal', $user);
        $this->assertCount(1, $minimal);

        // A lot more should be tested...
    }

    // This method is executed after all tests have been
    // executed
    static function tearDownAfterClass() {}
}
```

All methods beginning with `test` will be executed when running this test file. Read the comments in the preceding code and read the official documentation of PHPUnit for more information (`https://phpunit.de`).

When you are running test files, FuelPHP is in the test environment. Therefore, you have to configure the database access in the `APPPATH/config/test/db.php` file. It is recommended that you create a separate database for unit tests.

Now, run only your application tests by executing the following command line:

```
php oil test --group=App
```

The output will be something like this:

```
Tests Running...This may take a few moments.
..
Time: 22 ms, Memory: 18.50Mb
OK (2 tests, 3 assertions)
```

The tests have been correctly executed. However, as explained at the beginning of this section, we have written very superficial tests. If you want to have good test coverage of your application, you will need to write many more tests.

Possible improvements

First, you should protect all your forms from **Cross-Site Request Forgery** (**CSRF**) attacks as we did in *Chapter 3, Building a Blog Application*. As you are using Mustache templates, you will need to do things a little bit differently here (for instance, you will need to write your CSRF input in plain HTML). I recommend you read the official documentation at `http://fuelphp.com/docs/general/security.html#csrf`.

The documentation can be accessed on the FuelPHP website by navigating to **DOCS** | **FuelPHP** | **General** | **Security**.

Secondly, if you want to make your API easily available using JavaScript on an external website, you have to set the Access-Control-Allow-Origin header to `*`. This can be done in the `before` method inside the `Base` controller.

Next, we only used the `post/inside_list` partial in the JavaScript side of our application, but we could have done much more. For instance, since all the data is available, instead of loading the profile page HTML version when we click on a username, we could load the JSON data and use our partials to display the profile page.

Our microblog application is still very basic. However, we could manage subscriptions, notifications, mentions, and direct messages; allow the users to search for posts and other users; automatically transform URLs in posts; improve the user interface...

Summary

In this chapter, we built a basic microblogging application that supports several features such as user subscription, authentication, post creation, and profile pages. We have seen that an API can be implemented without any code duplication and much effort, if it is handled correctly. We have also used Mustache, a language-agnostic template engine, which allowed us to use the same views in the server (PHP) and client (JavaScript) sides. Finally, we have used unit tests to check whether the features of our application are behaving as expected.

In the next chapter, we will introduce you to Novius OS, a Content Management System based on the FuelPHP framework.

6
Building a Website Using Novius OS

In this chapter, we will introduce you to **Novius OS**, an open source **Content Management System** (or **CMS**) based on FuelPHP. Using Novius OS can greatly simplify the implementation and management of a website. Its back office includes important and user-friendly features such as web page, menu, template, applications, user, and rights management; it is currently available in six languages (English, French, Japanese, Russian, Spanish, and Interlingua). It is an excellent tool if you want to build a complex website easily manageable by non-programmer users.

By the end of this chapter, you will know:

- How to install and configure Novius OS
- Basic features of Novius OS and how to use them to create your website
- Novius OS filesystem hierarchy
- What is a Novius OS application, how to generate one, and what are its main components

About Novius OS

Novius OS is an open source CMS based on FuelPHP and powered by the jQuery UI and Wijmo libraries. It was officially launched in December 2011 by Novius, a small web agency based in Lyon, France. The core team that designed and implemented this project is comprised of one UX designer - Antoine Lefeuvre - and three engineers - Gilles Félix, Julian Espérat, and me. However, the software has also received numerous contributions from the open-source community.

In this chapter, we will assume that you use the Version 5.0.1 (Elche) of Novius OS (the current stable version at the time of writing). The official website of this CMS can be found at `http://www.novius-os.org/`.

Its official documentation is available at the following URLs:

- `http://docs.novius-os.org/en/elche/`
- `http://docs-api.novius-os.org/en/elche`

I included an introduction to Novius OS in this book as it is based on FuelPHP and I think some of you could find this system useful. Though, since I took part in the project, I am aware my opinion could be biased about it, and that is why this chapter is a rather short introduction about it.

Getting Novius OS

The requirements of Novius OS are similar to those of FuelPHP:

- PHP 5.3 or greater
- MySQL
- Apache with mod_rewrite enabled
- Windows (> Vista), Linux or Mac OS

Installation instructions can be found at the following URL:

`http://docs.novius-os.org/en/elche/install/install.html`

You are recommended to follow the instructions in the **Installation via Zip file** section (simplest and general solution). If you are developing on Linux or Mac OS, you might want to follow the instructions in the **Installation** section as it will download the latest fixes of this version.

You can also configure a virtual host as we did in the previous chapters for FuelPHP (refer to the **Advanced installation** section). However, we will assume that you only downloaded and unzipped Novius OS in the `novius-os` folder of your web server's root directory (`DOCUMENT_ROOT/novius-os`).

Configuring Novius OS

If you enter the URL `http://localhost/novius-os`, the Novius OS installation wizard will appear. Follow the directions; it will first check whether your server configuration is compatible with Novius OS, secondly ask for your database configuration (you will need to first create a database), then ask for some information to create the first user account (necessary to connect to the Novius OS' back office), and finally, ask you which languages you want your website to be available in.

You can now click on **Go to the back-office and sign-in**.

Exploring Novius OS

In this section, you will learn about the main Novius OS features by exploring the interface. This step is important if you have never used Novius OS earlier, because implementation details can't be understood if you don't know how to use the CMS.

The following sign-in webpage will be displayed:

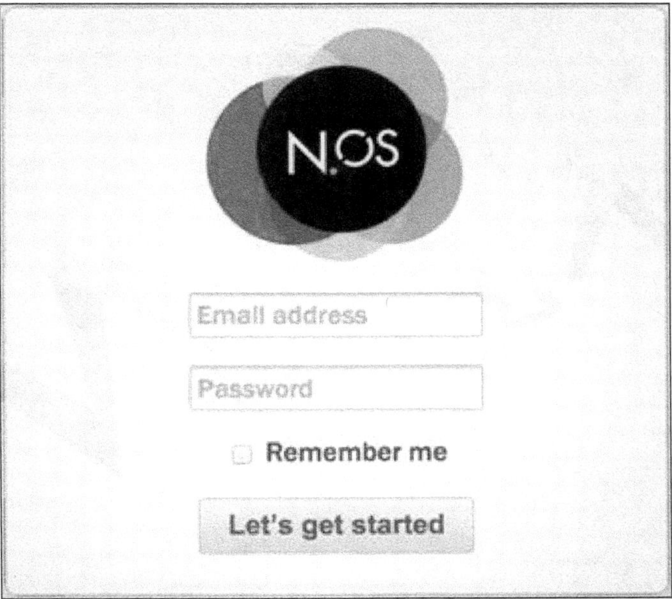

Enter the credentials you defined in the installation step.

The applications manager

Once connected, the applications manager will show up:

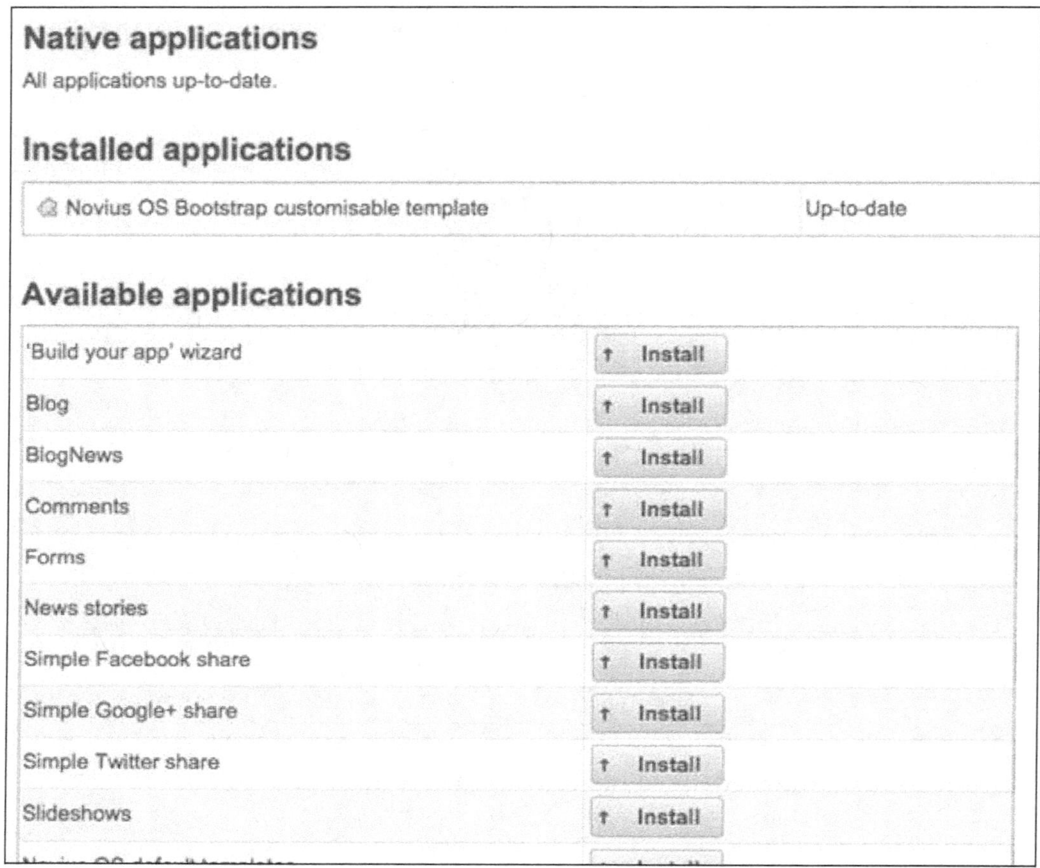

Applications allow you to add new features to Novius OS. For instance, the **Blog** application extends the Novius OS core functionalities to add a complete blog solution to your website. If you have already used another CMS, Novius OS's applications are synonymous with their modules or extensions. You are recommended to read the official documentation about applications and the application manager available at the following URLs:

- `http://docs.novius-os.org/en/elche/understand/applications.html`
- `http://docs.novius-os.org/en/elche/manage/install_app.html`

When you install Novius OS, several applications are already available. However, we will see later that it is possible to add other applications or create your own. Most Novius OS core features are implemented by native applications, which are applications directly included in the core. You can now understand that applications are a key feature of Novius OS and that they do most of the work.

Right now, most applications are only available but not installed. If you want to activate the features of an available application, you have to install it. Click on the **Install** button next to **Blog** in order to activate the blog's features. The following message will appear in the upper right corner of the screen:

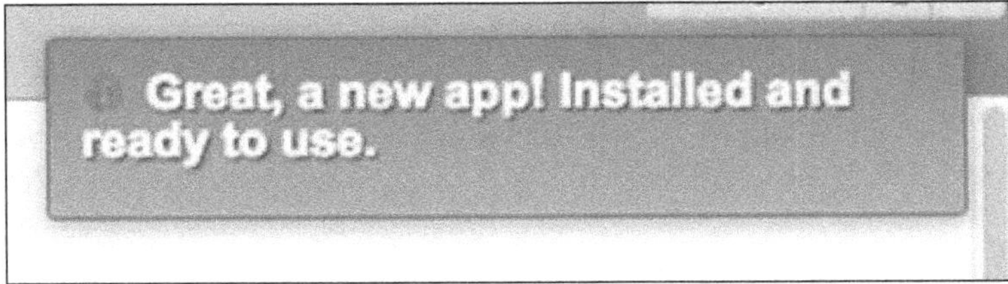

Under the **Installed application** section, the following three applications will now be displayed:

You can see that the **Blog** application was installed, but **BlogNews** and **Comments** were also installed along with it. This is because these applications are dependencies; the **Blog** application needs both of them. Novius OS allows applications to depend on each other and the system tries to manage any potential conflict. For instance, you can't uninstall the **BlogNews** application without uninstalling the **Blog** application first.

The Novius OS desktop

To leave the applications manager, click on the Novius OS icon in the upper left corner of the screen:

The Novius OS desktop will now be displayed:

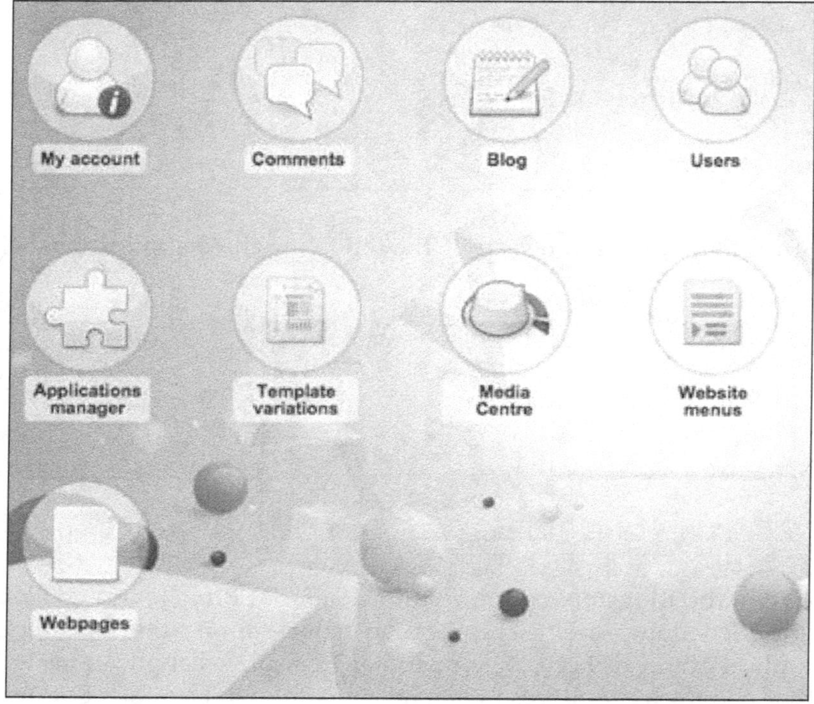

The desktop displays icons called *launchers* that can be clicked on; they generally allow you to access an application. For instance, if you click on **Applications manager**, you will return to the screen we saw earlier.

Novius OS' front and the default homepage

If you access your website home page (`http://localhost/novius-os`), you will only see the default Novius OS homepage, since we didn't define any content. Go back to the administration panel by requesting:

The Webpages application

Another important feature of Novius OS is the ability to manage your web pages. In order to do this, click on the **Webpages** launcher which will display the web pages administration panel. An empty table will appear, with a few buttons at the bottom. Click on the **Add a page** button to create your first page. The web page creation form will then appear:

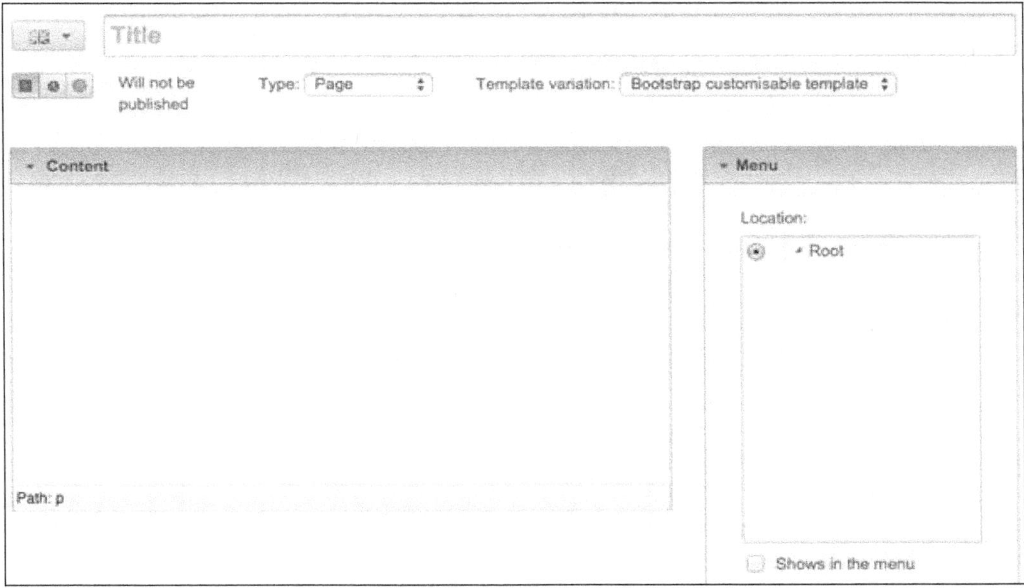

In this instance, the three fields you should change are the title, content, and publication setting.

The title field will define the metadata title of your web page . Generally, this title will also be displayed over the web page's content.

The content field will define the core content of your web page. It is a WYSIWYG field, so you can also format the text or add images, among other functions.

The publication setting allows you to define whether or not the content should be visible to visitors. It can be changed using the three small icons under the **Title** field:

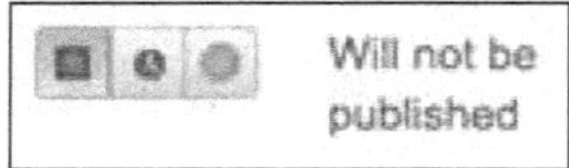

If the left button is set in an active state, as shown in the preceding screenshot, the web page won't be published; that is to say the web page will be invisible to visitors. The right button allows you to immediately publish the content (as soon as you click on the **Save/Add** button). The middle button allows you to schedule when your content should be published. Now click on the right button:

Click on the **Add** button to save the changes and create the new web page.

You probably noticed that new tabs appeared in the upper part of the screen since we clicked on the **Webpages** launcher:

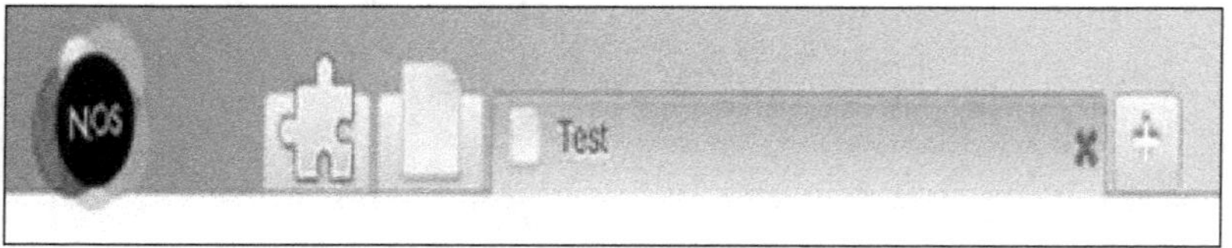

The Novius OS interface is designed around tabs. Just like browsers' tabs, Novius OS tabs allow you to open multiple administration pages. Though it can be destabilizing for new users, this tabs navigation system can be handy when you have to manage multiple elements at the same time.

The first tab contains the **Applications manager** application. As we won't need it anymore, click on it, and then click on the cross to close it.

Click on the new first tab (the one without any title), you will now be back at the web page administration panel. However, your newly created page will now be visible inside the table:

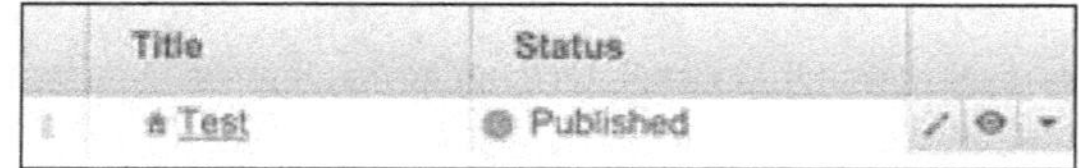

The house icon next to the web page title indicates that it is the home page. We did not specify it, but Novius OS automatically chooses the first created web page as the home page.

For each row in the table, you can see there are small buttons in the right corner. These buttons allow you to apply individual actions. In our instance, the first button allows you to edit the web page, the second to visualize it, and the third displays a drop-down that will show even more actions.

If you now request the home page (`http://localhost/novius-os`), you will see the following screen:

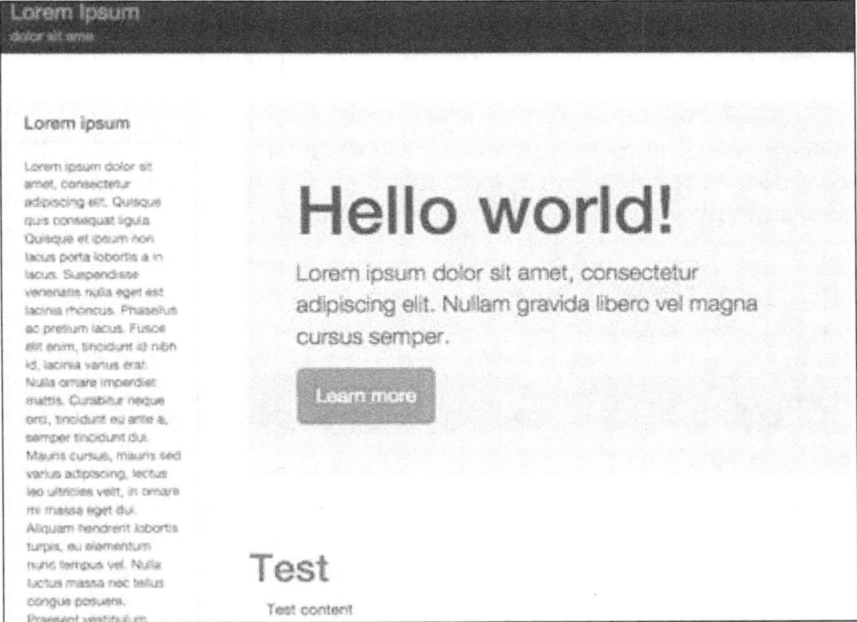

Our content is visible at the bottom, but there is a lot of sample content too, which we would naturally like to remove.

Novius OS templates

The content you define in a web page is displayed inside a template, in a similar way to the views that are displayed inside templates when using the **Template** controller in FuelPHP. If you go back to the web page edition form, you will notice that there is a field named **Template variations** with its value set to **Bootstrap customisable template**. Thus, to remove the sample content, we have to edit the **Bootstrap customisable template**.

In order to do this, go back to Novius OS desktop (by clicking on the **NOS** icon in the upper left corner of the screen), and then click on the **Template Variations** launcher.

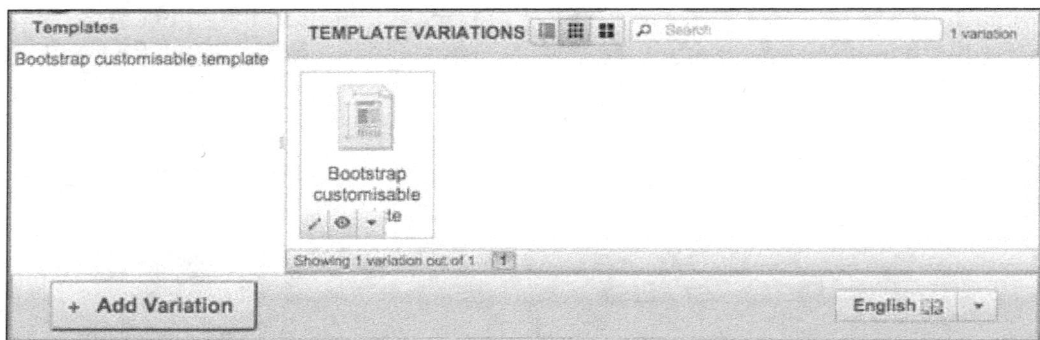

We will discuss this administration interface in the next section. First, click on the edit button (represented by a pencil icon) in the **Bootstrap customisable template** item. A new tab will open, as shown in the following screenshot:

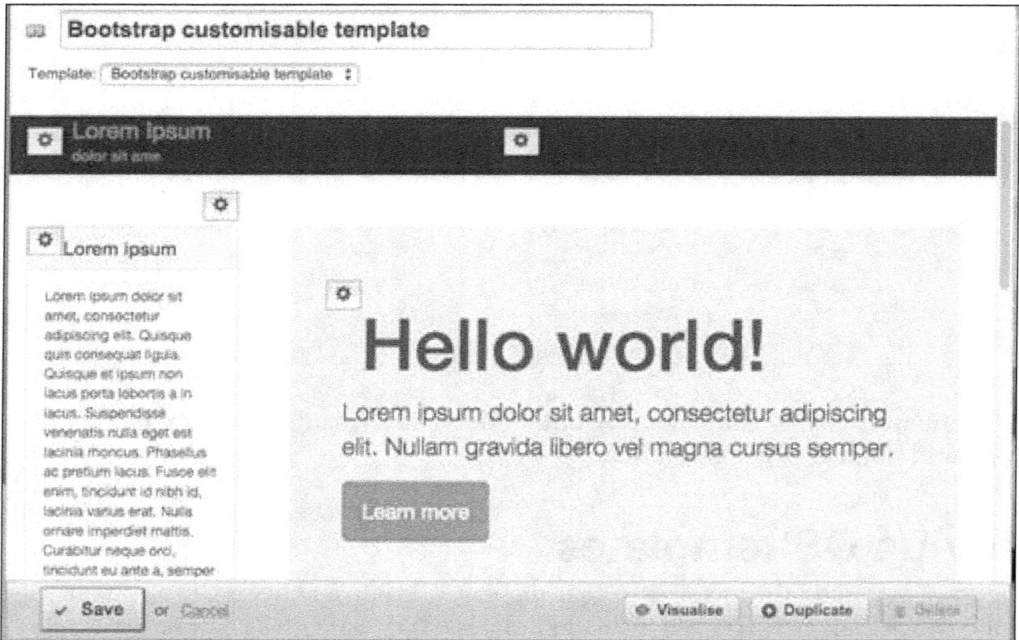

Each gear icon allows you to edit a specific part of the template. Feel free to adapt the template as you wish.

You can also add other template models by installing the **Novius OS default templates** application (this one is less configurable), external applications, or creating your own application.

You will notice that some template parts display the following menu field:

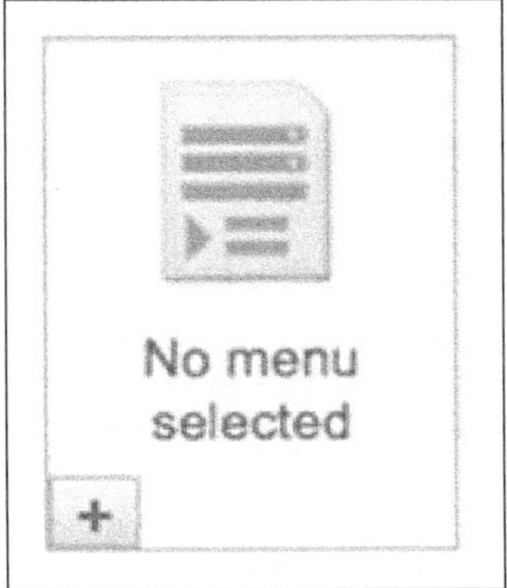

The menu field allows you to generate a menu on your website. By default, that is to say if no menu is selected, a default menu will be constructed from the web pages having the **Shows in the menu** configuration checked (you can change this configuration in the web page edition form). You can also create custom menus by clicking on the **Website menus** launcher on the administration desktop.

When you are finished changing the template, you will probably need to refresh the pages' cache. This can be done by clicking on the link **Renew pages' cache** inside the Webpages administration interface. In a general manner, if you see that your webpages don't change though you updated their content in the back office, it is a good idea to refresh this cache.

The App Desk

If you go back to the **Template variations** administration interface (you can do this using tabs or by clicking on the **NOS** icon and then clicking on the **Template variations** launcher), you will see that the administration panel is separated into three parts:

- The upper left part lists all original models of templates.

- The upper right part lists all the variations, that is to say the templates we adapted for our website.
- The bottom part contains the action buttons.

You can even change how the upper right part is displayed by clicking on the top buttons:

Here is how the administration panel is displayed when clicking on the list button:

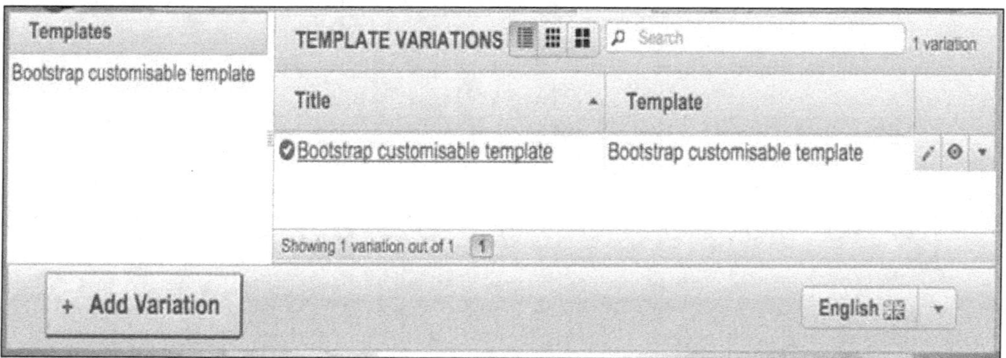

You can notice that the user interface is quite similar to the **Webpages** administration interface. Indeed, most applications of Novius OS will have a common user interface, as the core provides generic components that can be easily reused. The main administration interface, the one you are looking at right now, extends the **App Desk** component. With minimal configuration, you can display and manage your application's data in an organized and standardized way. For the sake of convenience, such administration interfaces are also called App Desk.

Here is the current standard layout of an App Desk:

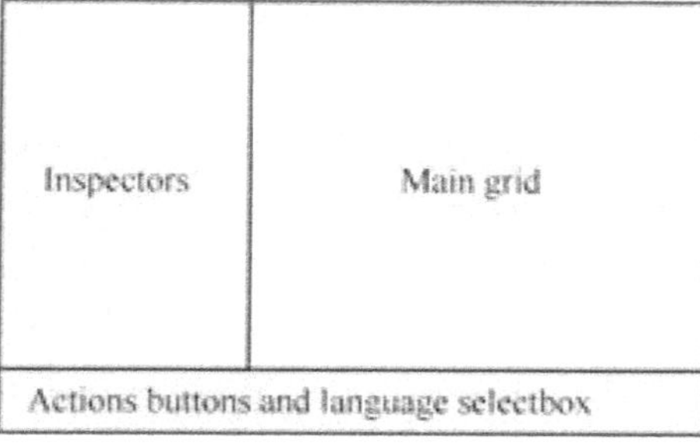

You can notice that there are 3 components, as follows:

- The main content is displayed in the main grid. As we saw earlier, it is generally possible to display the main grid in different ways (list, thumbnails, hierarchy, and so on).
- At the left, the inspectors display related content (categories for blog posts for example), and filters the content of the main grid (for example, it can filter the blog posts belonging to a specific category).
- At the bottom, buttons allow the user to execute general actions such as creating a new item or refreshing a cache. The language select box might also be displayed if the content depends on the language (for instance, a blog post will have different content in English, French, Spanish, and so on).

You are recommended to take a look at the official documentation about UI guidelines, available at `http://docs.novius-os.org/en/elche/understand/ergonomy.html`.

Inserting enhancers in your webpages

You might recall we installed the **Blog** application earlier. This application allows you to insert a complete blog solution in your website. Let's see how it is done in Novius OS.

First, go back to the **Webpages** administration tab and create a new page with its title set to **Blog**. Save and publish it. If you click on the **URL (page address)** tab inside the right menu (or accordion), you will see this:

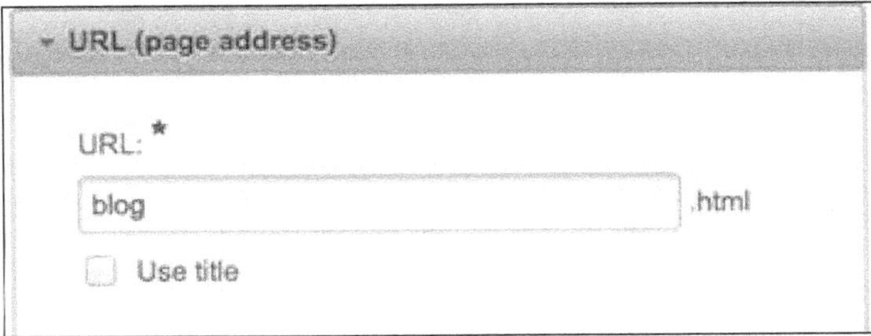

This field specifies the relative URL of the web page. In this instance, the web page you created can be accessed by entering the following URL:

```
http://localhost/novius-os/blog.html
```

The **Blog** application, as with most Novius OS applications that are displayed in the website frontend, can be inserted inside a web page's content. For doing this, click on the **Content** WYSIWYG input. You will see a toolbar appear on the top:

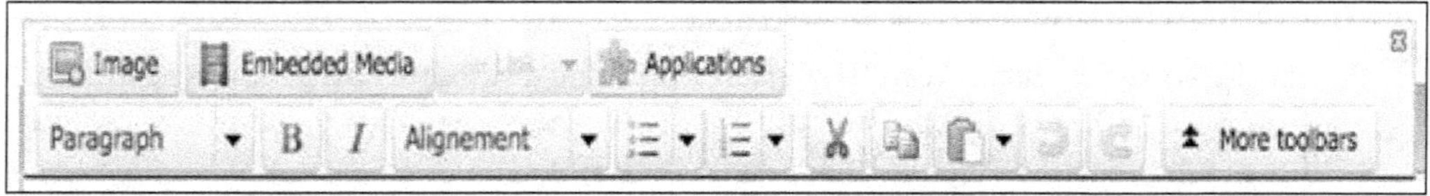

Click on the **Applications** button, and then on **Blog**:

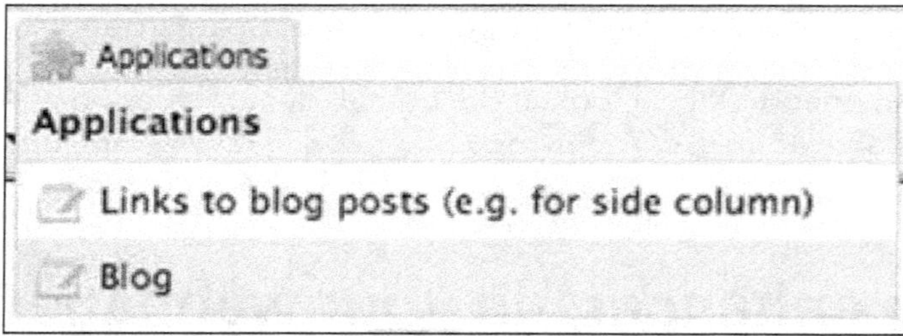

A configuration box will then appear; you don't have to change anything:

When you click on the **Insert** button, the following box will appear inside the WYSIWYG field:

This box indicates that the **Blog** application has been inserted into your web page. To use the correct term, you inserted the **Blog enhancer**. An enhancer is an application component that can be inserted in most WYSIWYG fields in order to allow the application to display content in the frontend. There can be several enhancers for a single application, as you saw earlier when clicking on the **Applications** button; you could choose between **Links to blog posts (e.g. for side column)** or **Blog**. Both of these enhancers belong to the **Blog** application, but they display the blog differently.

If you request the URL `http://localhost/novius-os/blog.html` again, you will not see any changes, and this is normal; you have to create blog posts first. In the Novius OS administration panel, go back to the desktop, click on the **Blog** launcher, and add several blog posts (don't forget to publish them).

If you request the blog web page again, you will see these posts:

You can view a specific blog post by clicking on its title. If you do, you will see a more complete view of the post, and the URL will look as follows:

```
http://localhost/novius-os/blog/POST_TITLE.html
```

As you can see, the **Blog enhancer** not only displays content, but also creates additional URLs. This is because it is an URL enhancer, a special type of enhancer that can respond to additional URLs. In concrete terms, if an URL enhancer is hosted on a webpage located at `http://localhost/novius-os/PAGE.html`, it can also respond to any URL similar to `http://localhost/novius-os/PAGE/ANY_STRING.html`.

Of course, the URL enhancer can respond differently to each URL, depending on its implementation and configuration.

The Novius OS file system hierarchy

Now that we have looked at the basics of Novius OS and its interface, let's dive into the directory in which we have installed Novius OS. At the time of writing, the current version of Novius OS (Elche) has the following directory hierarchy:

- `/local`: This folder contains all code, configuration, and applications that are specific to the website. It contains the following folders:
    - `/local/applications`: This folder contains all available non-core applications.
    - `/local/cache`: All files here allows Novius OS and its applications to cache data in order to improve the website's performance.
    - `/local/classes`: This includes classes used by the website that don't belong to the core or any application.
    - `/local/config`: This includes configuration files, including the FuelPHP main configuration file and the database configuration file.
    - `/local/data`: These are data files created by Novius OS and its applications.
    - `/local/metadata`: These are files created by Novius OS. Unlike in `/local/data`, files inside this folder are only changed when applications are installed, upgraded, or uninstalled.
    - `/local/views`: These are the views used by the website. It is possible to override applications views by creating files inside this folder.

- `/logs`: This contain the log files. It is similar to the logs folder of FuelPHP.
- `/novius-os`: This is the Novius OS core, you should not change anything inside it. Among other things, it contains FuelPHP core and packages.
- `/public`: This directory is accessible by external visitors. You can add publicly available files here (CSS, JS...).

Applications folder structure

Inside the `/local/applications` directory, each folder is an application. For your information, you should know that what Novius OS calls applications are, in fact, improved FuelPHP modules. If you look inside these folders, you will see the following structure:

- `/classes`: These are the classes used by the application.
    - `/classes/controller`: Application's controllers.
    - `/classes/menu`: Application's information about menus.
    - `/classes/model`: Application's models.
- `/config`: These are the application's configuration files. The following are the most important ones:
    - `/config/metadata.config.php`: This is the metadata configuration file. It contains all the key information about the application: name, icon, description, dependencies, launchers, enhancers, and so on.
    - `/config/permissions.config.php`: This allows the application to handle custom permissions.
- `/lang`: Application's translations files.
- `/migrations`: Application's migrations files.
- `/static`: This is the equivalent of the public folder but specific to the application. For instance, if the **Blog** application (located at `local/applications/noviusos_blog`) is installed, the `local/applications/noviusos_blog/static/img/blog-16.png` file can be accessed at `http://localhost/novius-os/static/apps/noviusos_blog/img/blog-16.png`.
- `/views`: Application's view files.

Files extensions

You might have noticed that some files have the following suffixes:

- Models' filenames end in `.model.php`
- Controllers' filenames end in `.ctrl.php`
- Configurations' filenames end in `.config.php`
- Views' filenames end in `.view.php`

This is a Novius OS convention to enhance the developer's experience. It was implemented because often developers named their files using the same filename (for instance, a `post.php` controller, a `post.php` view, and a `post.php` configuration file) and, if they opened them on multiple tabs on their IDE, most of the time they wouldn't know on which tab the file they were looking for was. This is an optional convention and it doesn't change the way files are executed.

Configurations and classes

Another important convention involves the configuration and class file's locations. As developers very often have to write a configuration for controllers and models, the configuration file paths are related to the class file paths. For instance, in an application, the `classes/controller/front.ctrl.php` controller can be configured using the `config/controller/front.config.php` configuration file. If the controller extends one of the default Novius OS controllers, the configuration file will will be automatically loaded.

In a general manner, the `config/FILE_PATH` configuration file will be associated with the `classes/FILE_PATH` class file. This way, when you want to understand an application someone else implemented, you can easily know to which class each configuration file is associated with.

Creating an application

The only way to understand how Novius OS works further is to create an application. First, we will generate one application using the Novius OS **'Build you app'** wizard, which tries to fulfill the same objective as the `oil generate` utility, except it generates Novius OS applications instead of FuelPHP scaffolds. Then, we will take a look at most files that were generated and see what happens when we tweak them.

Installing the 'Build your app' wizard

The application is available but needs to be installed. To do this, go to the Novius OS desktop, click on the **Applications manager** launcher and, under **Available** applications, click on the **Install** button next to **'Build your app' wizard**.

Generating the application

Go back to the Novius OS desktop and click on the **'Build your app' wizard** launcher. A form will appear. As in *Chapter 1, Building Your First FuelPHP Application*, we will generate an application that will manage monkeys in our zoo.

First, under **About the application**, set the **Application name** field's value to **My first application**. The **Application** folder and **Application namespace** fields should be automatically completed but you can always change them if you want.

Next, under **Model**, set the **Name** field to `Monkey`, as we want to generate a `Monkey` model. The **Table name** and **Column prefix** fields should be automatically completed.

As we want to publish the application's content, check the **URL enhancer** checkbox. We also want to choose precisely which monkey we want to display on our website, as some might be in the zoo temporarily, so check the **Publishable behavior** checkbox. Finally, we want to know which user entered the monkey into the application, so check the **Author behavior** checkbox.

The form will now look as follows:

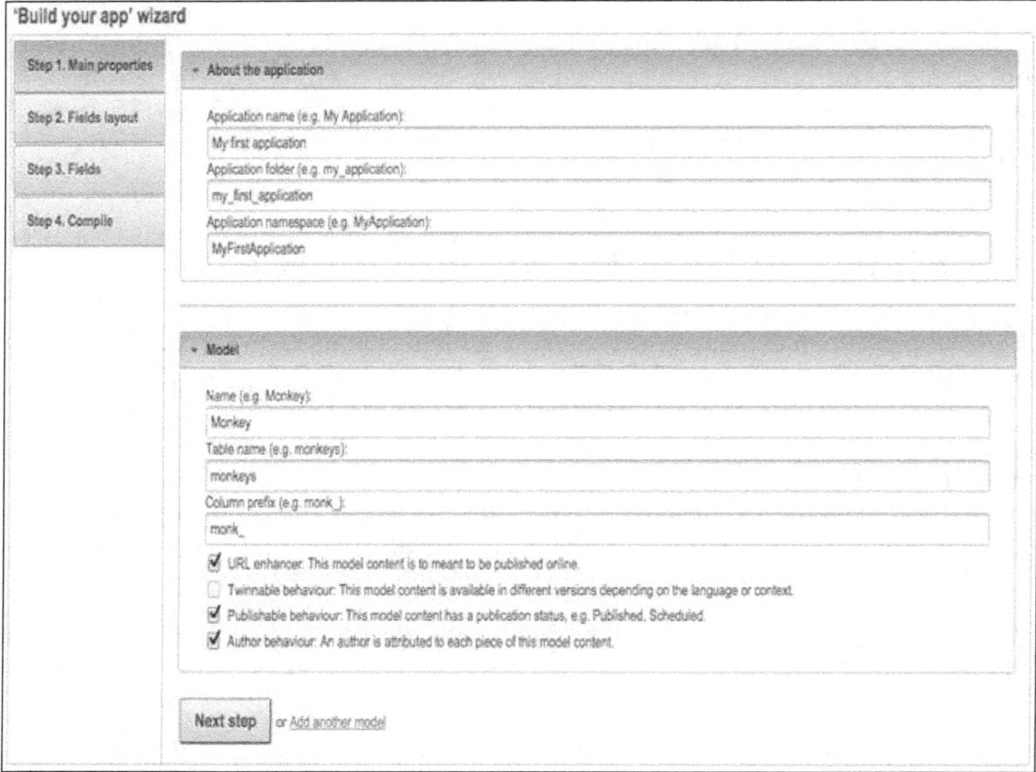

You can now click on **Next step**.

Here, we will define the layout of the administration form (the one we will use when creating and editing monkeys). The layout is defined by **Fields groups**, which can be split into two types:

- **Main column fields groups**: These contain the most important information (or the information that requires the most space) of your model, and thus they will always be visible and take most of the form area. Generally, these fields groups will contain WYSIWYG editors or very important fields.
- **Side column fields groups**: These contain secondary information that doesn't need a lot of space. They will appear in the menu (or accordion) on the right part of the screen.

The first main column field group named `Properties` is created by default. Create a new field group by clicking on **Add another fields group** next to the **Next Step** button. Set its **Title** field to `Additional informations` and its type to `Side column`. The form should now look as follows:

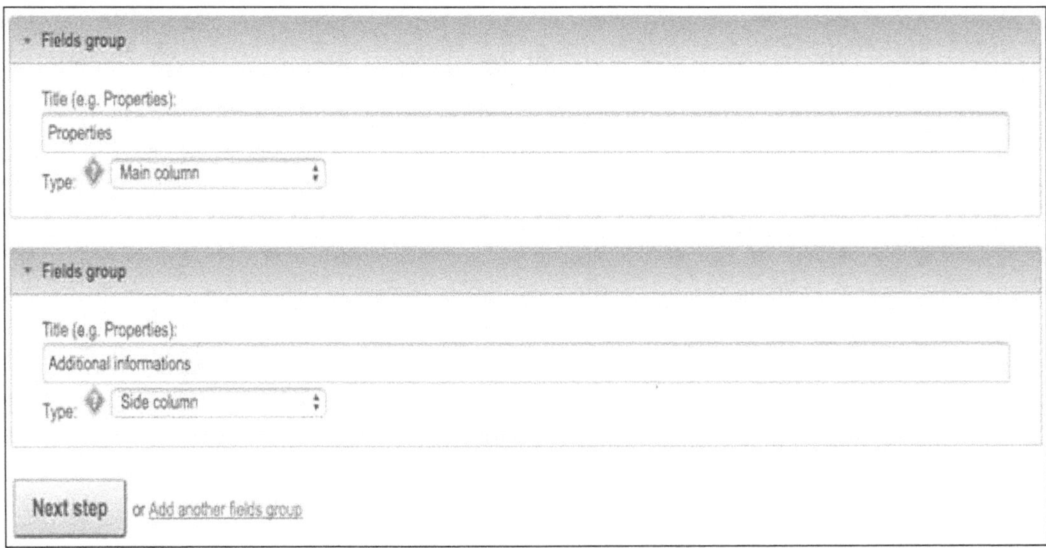

You can now click on **Next step**.

We will now define our model fields and properties. For the first field, define its **Label** attribute as `Name`, the **column name** attribute should be autocompleted, then check the **Is the form title** checkbox (as this field will be used as a title).

Click on **Add another field**. For the new field, define the **Label** attribute to `Still here`, select **Checkbox** in the **Type** select box, check the **Shows in the App Desk** checkbox, and then select **Additional informations (Side column)** in the **Fields** group select box.

Click on **Add another field**. For the new field, define the **Label** attribute as `Height`, check **Shows in the App Desk** checkbox, and then select **Additional informations (Side column)** in the **Fields** group select box.

Click on **Add another field**. For the new field, define the **Label** attribute as `Description` and then select **WYSIWYG text editor** in the **Type** select box.

The end of the form should look as follows:

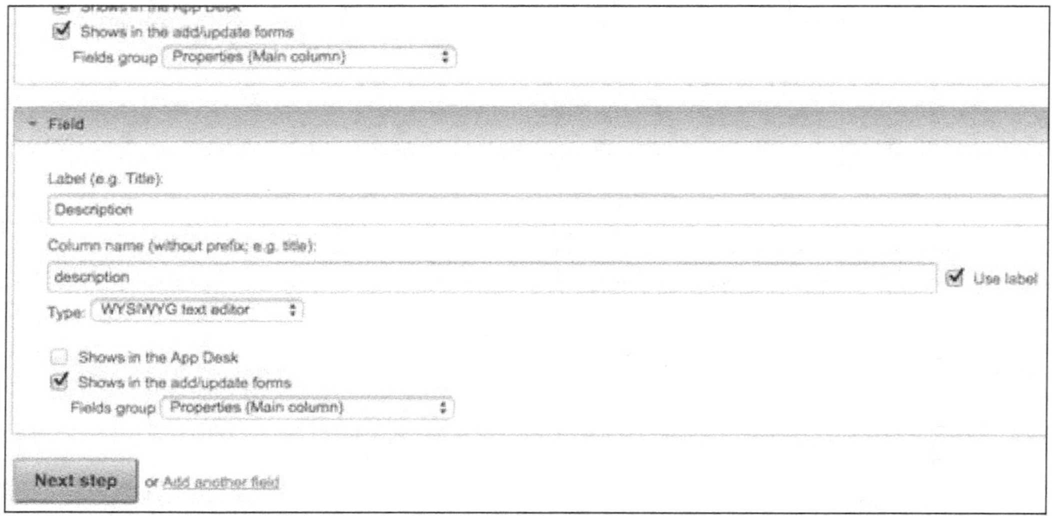

You can now click on **Next step**. The following dialog box will appear:

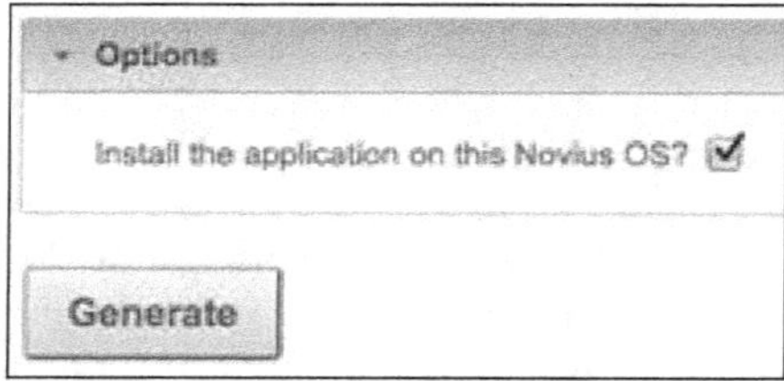

Since we want to install this application, don't change anything.

Click on the **Generate** button. You will see a confirmation message appear with various links to the documentation to help you improve your generated application. You are recommended to take a look at this documentation.

Testing your generated application

Go back to the Novius OS desktop and click on the **Monkey** launcher. You will see an empty **App Desk** appear. Click on the **Add Monkey** button, and the creation form will appear as you configured it in the **'Build your app' wizard** form. Create as many monkeys as you want and you will see the **App Desk** progressively fill up.

Since we checked the **URL enhancer** checkbox, our content is displayable on a web page. Go back to Novius OS desktop, click on the **Webpages** launcher, and then on the **Add a page** button. Set the web page's title to `Monkey`, set its publication status to **Published**. Next, in order to add our application's URL enhancer, click on the **Content** WYSIWYG. Next, click on **Applications**, and then click on **My first application Monkey**. Finally, save the web page by clicking on the **Add** button.

Now, if you check the URL `http://localhost/novius-os/monkey.html`, you will see your list of monkeys:

Monkey

- My first monkey
- My second monkey

If you click on an item of the list, a more detailed view will appear:

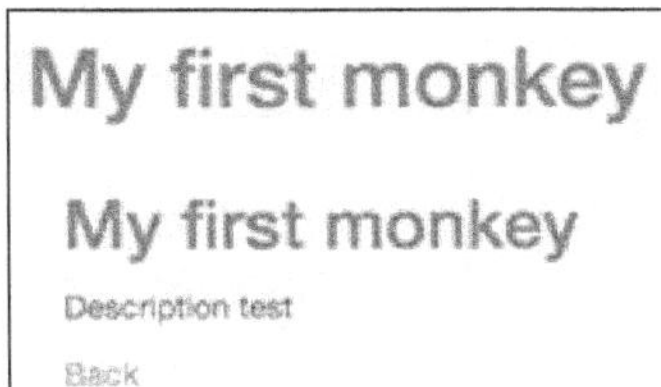

The detailed view's URL in this case will be as follows:

```
http://localhost/novius-os/monkey/my-first-monkey.html
```

As you can see, by using the **'Build your app' wizard** option and by filling very few inputs, we created a complete application scaffold. As with the `oil generate` utility, you should use the wizard every time you want to implement an application because it will speed up your development process and you will start on good foundations.

Application basics

We will use this generated application to describe how an application works in Novius OS. We won't go too much into detail, but it should be enough for you to get started and know where to look for more information.

The application we generated can be found at the `local/applications/my_first_application` directory. All the files we will look into are located inside the folder.

The metadata configuration file

Where is defined the application's name, its dependencies, icons, launchers, enhancers?

All this basic information is contained inside `config/metadata.config.php`. This is the only file required to create an application. If you open this configuration file, the application's name is defined by the `name` key, its namespace by the `namespace` key, its launchers by the `launchers` key. It is pretty straightforward, and you can read about it in the official documentation available at `http://docs-api.novius-os.org/en/elche/php/configuration/application/metadata.html`.

The migration files

The migration files are located inside the `migrations` folder, and are executed when the application is installed. They can be implemented as normal FuelPHP migration files but, if you open `migrations/001_install.php`, you will see that it is empty:

```
<?php
namespace MyFirstApplication\Migrations;

class Install extends \Nos\Migration
{
}
```

This is because the `migration` file extends `\Nos\Migration`. By default, the `up` method will try to execute a SQL file with a similar filename to the `migration` file, in our case `migrations/001_install.sql`. If you open this SQL file, you will see that it simply creates the `monkeys` table.

The App desk

Your application's App Desk is loaded from the following URL (you can check using your browser's developer tools if you want to):

```
http://localhost/novius-os/admin/my_first_application/monkey/appdesk
```

In a general manner, when you enter `http://WEBSITE/admin/APPLICATION_FOLDER/CONTROLLER_PATH(/ACTION)`, the `ACTION` action of the controller located at `local/applications/APPLICATION_FOLDER/classes/controller/admin/CONTROLLER_PATH` will be executed.

Thus, in our case, the URL executes the `index` action (because as you may recall, when no action is defined in the URL, FuelPHP executes the `index` action) of the `controller/admin/monkey/appdesk.ctrl.php` controller inside the `my_first_application` application. Let's open this controller:

```
<?php
namespace MyFirstApplication;

class Controller_Admin_Monkey_Appdesk extends \Nos\Controller_Admin_
Appdesk
{
}
```

Once again, you can see an empty class. All the actions are defined inside the `\Nos\Controller_Admin_Appdesk` class that is extended by our controller. Though, the returned listing is not automatically generated by some sort of magic process, it is generated from configuration files.

As you might recall, we wrote earlier that configuration file paths are related to the class file paths. Thus, we can find our controller's configuration file at `config/controller/admin/monkey/appdesk.config.php`. If you open this file, you will see the following code snippet (comments have been stripped):

```
<?php
return array(
    'model' => 'MyFirstApplication\Model_Monkey',
    'search_text' => 'monk_name',
);
```

It defines the model that must be displayed by the **App Desk** and which column to scan when writing something in the **Search** bar. You can define more keys, as inspectors or queries. You are recommended to read the official documentation to learn more about this configuration file:

`http://docs-api.novius-os.org/en/elche/php/configuration/application/appdesk.html`

The configuration defined here is a start, but certainly not sufficient to display the whole **App Desk**. Most of the necessary information is defined inside the `config/common/monkey.config.php` configuration file (comments have been stripped):

```
<?php
return array(
    'controller' => 'monkey/crud',
    'data_mapping' => array(
```

```
            'monk_name' => array(
                'title' => __('Name'),
            ),
            'monk_still_here' => array(
                'title' => __('Still here'),
                'value' => function($item) {
                    return $item->monk_still_here ? __('Yes') :
                                   __('No');
                },
            ),
            'monk_height' => array(
                'title' => __('Height'),
            ),
            'publication_status' => true,
        ),
    );
```

As you can see, displayed columns are defined inside the `data_mapping` key. Each column's title is defined by the `title` key, except for `publication_status`, which is a particular case. The row values are either determined from the key or from the `value` callback. In concrete terms, each row of the App Desk will display the following properties:

- Under the **Name** column, the `monk_name` property
- Under the **Still here** column, **Yes** or **No** depending on the `monk_still_here` property
- Under the **Height** column, the `monk_height` property

In order to train yourself, try to change a column title or add a `value` callback.

We are just scratching the surface here, it is recommended that you read the official documentation at `http://docs-api.novius-os.org/en/elche/php/configuration/application/common.html`.

The edition and creation forms

If you create or edit a monkey, you will see that Novius OS will request the following URL:

`http://localhost/novius-os/admin/my_first_application/monkey/crud/insert_update(/ID)`

Therefore, we can deduce that the `insert_update` action of the `classes/controller/admin/monkey/crud.ctrl.php` controller is called. If you open the controller, you will see, you guessed it, an empty class. Again, everything is defined inside the extended `\Nos\Controller_Admin_Crud` controller.

If you read the associated `config/controller/admin/monkey/crud.config.php` configuration file, you will see that it defines the layout and fields of the edition and creation forms. All the fields are defined inside the `fields` key.

In order to train yourself, you can change some field labels by editing their `label` key.

Again, we are just scratching the surface. It is recommended that you read the official documentation at `http://docs-api.novius-os.org/en/elche/php/configuration/application/crud.html`.

The front controller

Now that we have seen how things work in the back office, we have to see how our URL enhancer works.

As you might recall, enhancers are declared inside the `config/metadata.config.php` configuration file:

```
'enhancers' => array(
    'my_first_application_monkey' => array(
        'title' => 'My first application Monkey',
        'desc'  => '',
        'urlEnhancer' => 'my_first_application/front/monkey/main',
    ),
),
```

Once again, it is recommended that you read the official documentation about metadata. The interesting key here is `urlEnhancer`; if you insert an enhancer into a web page, each time the web page will be displayed, Novius OS will trigger an internal HMVC request to `urlEnhancer` and display the returned content. In our case, when you display the `http://localhost/novius-os/monkey.html` web page (and the monkey enhancer inside it), Novius OS will internally request `my_first_application/front/monkey/main` and display the returned content.

As you might have guessed, it calls the `main` action of the `Front_Monkey` controller. Open `classes/controller/front/monkey.ctrl.php`, and take a look at its `action_main` method. You will see that the method returns either a single monkey view or a listing, depending on the `$enhancer_url` variable. This variable is defined at the beginning of the action:

```
$enhancer_url = $this->main_controller->getEnhancerUrl();
```

Let's illustrate what the `$this->main_controller->getEnhancerUrl()` method returns in our example:

- If you request `http://localhost/novius-os/monkey.html`, it will return an empty string
- If you request `http://localhost/novius-os/monkey/first.html`, it will return `first`
- If you request `http://localhost/novius-os/monkey/one/two.html`, it will return `one/two`

You got it; it allows the controller to know which URL relative to the web page URL is being requested when displaying the enhancer. It now makes sense; if you request the `monkey.html` root web page, the action will return the listing, otherwise it will try to find a monkey with a similar URL.

If you take a look at the `display_list_monkey` and `display_monkey` methods, you will hopefully not feel lost, as they contain only FuelPHP code (`ORM`, `View::forge`, and so on). You can see that they display the `front/monkey_list` and `front/monkey_item` views, respectively, located at `views/front/monkey_list.view.php` and `views/front/monkey_item.view.php`. In order to train yourself, you can try to tweak them a little bit.

If you edit your views, refresh the web page and nothing happens, you might need to refresh the Novius OS web page cache. To do this, go back to the back office of Novius OS, open the Webpages App Desk, and click on **Renew pages' cache** next to the **Add a page** button.

The `getUrlEnhanced` method inside the Front_Monkey controller allows Novius OS to map monkey instances to URL.

Again, we are just scratching the surface here. It is recommended that you read the official documentation at `http://docs.novius-os.org/en/latest/app_create/enhancer.html`.

More about Novius OS

We didn't tackle a lot of very important features such as application extensions, behaviors, the twinnable behavior, data sharers, and permissions, but it would require writing another book entirely about Novius OS. It is again recommended that you read the official documentation to learn more about these features:

- `http://www.novius-os.org/`
- `http://docs.novius-os.org/en/elche/`
- `http://docs-api.novius-os.org/en/elche/`

If you have any question or encounter issues, you can also seek help in the community forum at:

`http://forums.novius-os.org/en/`

Summary

You should now have an idea of what you can do using Novius OS. Please note that this was just a small introduction: you should read the documentation in order to have a better understanding of this promising CMS.

During this journey, by implementing various projects, we illustrated how we can use the main FuelPHP features to build robust, complex and yet efficient applications.

Most of all, I hope you enjoyed reading this book and learned some valuable skills.

Don't hesitate to send me an e-mail or tweet me if you need help on anything from the book or the FuelPHP framework.

Thank you very much for your interest.

Index

A

I

K

L

M

N

Q

R

S

Thank you for buying
FuelPHP Application Development Blueprints

About Packt Publishing

Packt, pronounced 'packed', published its first book, *Mastering phpMyAdmin for Effective MySQL Management*, in April 2004, and subsequently continued to specialize in publishing highly focused books on specific technologies and solutions.

Our books and publications share the experiences of your fellow IT professionals in adapting and customizing today's systems, applications, and frameworks. Our solution-based books give you the knowledge and power to customize the software and technologies you're using to get the job done. Packt books are more specific and less general than the IT books you have seen in the past. Our unique business model allows us to bring you more focused information, giving you more of what you need to know, and less of what you don't.

Packt is a modern yet unique publishing company that focuses on producing quality, cutting-edge books for communities of developers, administrators, and newbies alike. For more information, please visit our website at `www.packtpub.com`.

About Packt Open Source

In 2010, Packt launched two new brands, Packt Open Source and Packt Enterprise, in order to continue its focus on specialization. This book is part of the Packt Open Source brand, home to books published on software built around open source licenses, and offering information to anybody from advanced developers to budding web designers. The Open Source brand also runs Packt's Open Source Royalty Scheme, by which Packt gives a royalty to each open source project about whose software a book is sold.

Writing for Packt

We welcome all inquiries from people who are interested in authoring. Book proposals should be sent to `author@packtpub.com`. If your book idea is still at an early stage and you would like to discuss it first before writing a formal book proposal, then please contact us; one of our commissioning editors will get in touch with you.

We're not just looking for published authors; if you have strong technical skills but no writing experience, our experienced editors can help you develop a writing career, or simply get some additional reward for your expertise.

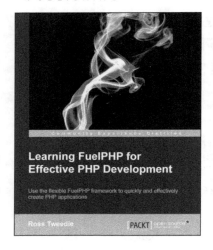

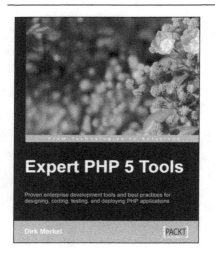

Object-Oriented Programming with PHP5

ISBN: 978-1-84719-256-1 Paperback: 272 pages

Learn to leverage PHP5's OOP features to write manageable applications with ease

1. General OOP concepts explained.
2. Implement Design Patterns in your applications and solve common OOP Problems.
3. Take full advantage of native built-in objects
4. Test your code by writing unit tests with PHPUnit.

PHP Ajax Cookbook

ISBN: 978-1-84951-308-1 Paperback: 340 pages

Over 60 simple but incredibly effective recipes to Ajaxify PHP websites

1. Learn how to develop and deploy iPhone web and native apps.
2. Optimize the performance of Ajax applications.
3. Build dynamic websites with faster response from the server using the asynchronous call feature of PHP Ajax.
4. Using Ajax allows quick and efficient access of data from the server, thus precluding a total web page refresh.

www.ingramcontent.com/pod-product-compliance
Lightning Source LLC
La Vergne TN
LVHW081337050326
832903LV00024B/1189